Management Tecl
and Quantitative Methods

Management Techniques and Quantitative Methods

Robert Ball MA, MSc, PhD

Heinemann: London

William Heinemann Ltd
10 Upper Grosvenor Street, London W1X 9PA

LONDON MELBOURNE TORONTO
JOHANNESBURG AUCKLAND

First published 1984
© R Ball 1984
Reprinted 1985

0 434 90083 4

Printed in England by
Redwood Burn Ltd, Trowbridge

Contents

Preface

The aim of this book is to provide students with a basic understanding of quantitative methods and management science. It assumes that the reader possesses basic numeracy rather than sophisticated mathematical skills.

The emphasis of the book is on the practical applications of the techniques described. There is, however, sufficient treatment of the underlying concepts and theory to make the book readily intelligible. A number of the practical applications described are drawn from the author's own industrial and consultancy experience. There is also due emphasis on problem formulation, and student exercises are introduced at regular intervals throughout the text.

The coverage of the text will meet the needs of the students who are taking degrees in Management Studies or in Business Studies who need introductory courses in quantitative methods. It may also be relevant as an introductory text for students pursuing specialist courses in Management Science or Operational Research.

Students on postgraduate management courses such as the MBA should also find the book valuable.

ROBERT BALL

STIRLING

1

The Quantitative Approach to Management

1.1 Management

From primitive times men have sought to enhance their welfare through co-operation. Over time *organizations* evolved through which such co-operation could be channelled to achieve mutually agreed objectives. *Management* can be regarded as the control of the activities which are undertaken to achieve the objectives of the organization. It thus includes such activities as taking decisions about the acquisition or allocation of resources within an organization, control of the organizational structure, together with leadership and motivation. Management is intimately related to *decision-making*.

It thus follows that all organizations, whether economic, political, religious or sporting, will require effective management if they are to operate efficiently. The task of the manager may become increasingly difficult as organizations become more complex. For example, the managerial task involved in the completion of an oil platform project, which includes co-ordinating the efforts of thousands of people working for many organizations, may be almost as complex as the high technology involved in the project itself.

1.2 The Quantitative Approach to Management

The quantitative approach to management decision-making emphasizes the use of quantitative information and objectively measured criteria. It also recognizes that certain categories of management problems may be represented by a series of mathematical relationships (mathematical models).

Although an approach to scientific management was made during the late nineteenth and early twentieth centuries, it was not until World War II that consistent efforts were made to apply quantitative methods to management problems. Among the problems tackled was the determination of the most effective depth for the detonation of depth charges, determination of optimum convoy sizes and location of the most vulnerable spots in enemy bombers. Such work was called *Operational Research*. Later on, the term *Management Science* came to be applied to more or less the same activities. After the war, this approach was used extensively to handle a range of industrial problems, again with a fair degree of success.

The quantitative approach to management is not necessarily in conflict with the intuitive or creative approach to management. Management Science methods can be used to produce routine answers (so called programmed decisions) to certain standard types of recurring problems. Such a problem might be deciding the size of batch of particular components that should be reordered. The availability of such routine answers will enable the manager to spend more of his available time concentrating on less structured and more strategic problems. In other situations, where a manager is attempting to decide which of a number of alternative courses of action to adopt, the quantitative approach may enable the consequence of each decision to be fully evaluated and may, on occasion, suggest further alternatives to be explored.

This approach can also be useful for analysing more strategic and less well defined problems. The quantitative approach does not, of course, lessen the need for good industrial and human relations in an organization.

1.3 The Elements of the Quantitative Approach to Management

The elements of the quantitative approach to management can be considered as the following: (1) the Systems approach; (2) the use of scientific method; (3) interdisciplinary approach; (4) the use of models.

1.3.1 The Systems Approach

The systems approach recognizes that a decision made in one section of a particular organization may have important consequences not only for the operation of that section, but the operation of other sections as well. Thus, problems should be considered from the point of view of the systems involved and their interaction with each other. A *system* can be defined as a set of interdependent and interactive parts designed to achieve a set of goals or objectives. Thus, we can conceive of transport systems, computer systems, financial systems and so on. A systems boundary is drawn to clearly designate the boundaries of the system from the rest of the Universe. Further details of the philosophy of the systems approach can be found in reference [1].

Let's take a practical example of the use of systems thinking in management. The management of a railway network who were using systems thinking would not make decisions on the viability of a branch line purely on the basis of the revenues generated and costs incurred on that particular stretch of line. It might be that, if considered in these terms, the branch line would be a heavy loss-maker. Nevertheless, it could also be the case that the branch line acted as an important 'feeder' for the rest of the railway network in that many passengers who used this branch line continued to make lengthy and profitable journeys in other parts of the railway system. Thus, when considered from the point of view of the *railway system as a whole,* the branch line could well be a significant profit maker.

If the Government or a local authority were considering subsidizing the branch line they might be concerned about the linkage between the line and the rest of the transport system (e.g. bus–rail interconnections), relationship to the economic system (e.g. employees getting to work, movement of goods) and to the social system (facilities for making leisure and social trips).

To take a further example; the Central Electricity Generating Board evaluates the economics of a new power station in terms of the contribution it makes to the grid system as a whole. A new power station may enable older and very inefficient stations to be used at times of peak demand rather than be used practically continuously (i.e. part of the 'base-load'). In some circumstances this could lead to substantial savings for the system as a whole.

Likewise, a company who were transporting goods from a national network of depots to customers situated all over Britain, would be unwise to optimize transport over, say, Oxfordshire without considering the interactions with the rest of their transport system. Such a procedure is known as *sub-optimization*.

In real life we will, on occasion, need to define the system boundary rather tightly and run the risk of sub-optimization in order to obtain a manageable problem. For example, we may attempt to improve the operation of a stock control system in isolation when we could widen the system boundary to incorporate consideration of the mix of products produced by the company, or still further, to include the company's entire corporate strategy. Nevertheless, the interaction of the operation of the stock control system with these other factors may be slight; thus improving this system in isolation may be a reasonable course of action.

1.3.2   The Scientific Method

The first attempts to follow systematically a scientific approach to management was made by the School of Scientific Management associated with Taylor, Gilbreth, Gantt and others in the late nineteenth and early twentieth century. The use of scientific method involves adopting a formalized reasoning process. The problem area under analysis is defined and some statement which can be subjected to verification is made about the phenomenon in question (this 'statement' is known as a 'hypothesis'). An experiment is then carried out and observations are made. These observations are then used to decide whether the hypothesis should be accepted or rejected.

If this seems a little esoteric, let's take a practical example. Suppose a supplier of electric light bulbs sells large batches to customers and guarantees that not more than 1% of the batch is defective. A customer, on receiving such a batch, might therefore start with the hypothesis that the batch is acceptable (i.e. there are in fact less than 1% defective). He may then carry out an experiment, testing say a selection of ten bulbs taken from the batch at random. The decision as to whether to accept or reject the hypothesis is based on the observation of the number of defectives found in this small selection.

1.3.3 The Interdisciplinary Approach

The entire field of knowledge has, partly for convenience, been broken up into a number of academic disciplines, mathematics, engineering, physics, economics, etc. This approach has been enormously successful in allowing huge advances to be made in each discipline. It could, however, be a mistake to expect real problems to obligingly restrict themselves to our, somewhat arbitrary, discipline boundaries. Also an analytical approach which has been useful in handling problems in biological or physical science might on occasion be valuable in handling a managerial problem (perhaps looking at movement of people rather than molecules). A team of workers with different discipline backgrounds may be able to give an appropriate interdisciplinary approach.

1.3.4 The Use of Models

A model is a simplified representation or abstraction of some aspect of reality. It is usually simplified because reality is too complex to copy exactly and because, for practical purposes, some of the complexities can be ignored. Models may be *physical, analogue* or *mathematical.*

(i) Physical models
Physical models provide a physical representation of the subject under investigation. For example, stresses experienced by the air frame of an aircraft may be investigated by experimenting with a smaller-scale physical model in a wind-tunnel.

(ii) Analogue models
An analogue model attempts to represent the system under consideration by associating it with a physical quantity. For example, the flow of water through a system could be reproduced by an electrical voltage.

(iii) Mathematical models
A mathematical model represents those aspects of a system we are studying by a series of mathematical relationships. This model may then be used to investigate the optimum way to operate the system

or simply to try to understand how the system will operate under certain conditions.

Suppose a car hire company fixes its charges as a flat charge of £10 plus 2p per mile travelled; then the relationship between the cost of the car hire (*F* pounds) and distance travelled (*D* miles) is given by the mathematical model:

$$F = 10 + 0.02D$$

This model can then be used to predict the cost of a particular journey.

Obviously, this is a very simple model but in the rest of this book and, indeed, later in this chapter we shall be introducing some considerably more complex mathematical models.

1.4 The Role of Computer Systems

The development of computer systems has played a crucial role in widening the scope and availability of management science techniques and quantitative methods in general. There are many managerial problems whose formulation and solution are, in principle, relatively straightforward, but which involve such extensive computational work that the task of tackling them by manual means is quite impractical.

In addition there are many categories of problem (e.g. blending problems, scheduling problems) where the adopted course of action needs to be re-evaluated on a regular or even daily basis.

1.4.1 Brief History of Computer Development

Many of the basic principles of the modern computer were established by Charles Babbage, early in the nineteenth century. He never managed to construct a working protype, however, mainly because of the limited state of technology at that time.

It was not until the 1940s that the first computers were constructed. They were based on electronic valve technology and were physically enormous. In addition, in order to change the sequence of tasks carried out by the machine, physical interconnection betweeen different components had to be altered.

The next significant development was that of the stored

program. A stored program enables the function of the computer to be changed without having to physically rewire connections. Even so, the task of programming the computer was a difficult mathematical task. This task was in time greatly simplified by the development of so-called 'high level' programming language. A *compiler* automatically translated a program written in the simplified high level language into machine code.

The best-known languages were FORTRAN, ALGOL and BASIC, so-called scientific languages designed for handling problems with complex calculations, but relatively limited amounts of data, and COBOL, a commercial language, best suited to business problems with limited computations, but large volumes of data. A number of other languages are available although sometimes these are limited to particular machines.

Significant developments in hardware were then made based on, first, the technology of the transistor and, then, that of the microchip. This has resulted in computers of much smaller physical size and greatly enhanced computing power.

1.4.2 More Recent Developments

There have also been developments in *remote, interactive* computing. This has meant that a number of users may have access to a machine simultaneously through terminals. The terminals are connected by telephone links and can be many miles away from the computer. An equally important development is that of mini- and micro-computers. These are smaller, less powerful and much less expensive machines. Their development has meant that many more organizations can now afford their own facilities. Although these machines are smaller and less powerful, they still have computing power comparable with most of the commercial computers in the early 1960s.

1.4.3 Program Packages

In spite of the development of high level programming language, the development, implementation and maintenance of a computer program is an expensive and difficult task. There are, however, many standard problems which are met on many different occasions and by many different organizations. Standard programs called 'program packages' or 'canned software' are written to meet these contingencies. In order to use such a program the user has only to supply data in some prescribed format. Such packages may be supplied free with the computer or they may be purchased from a software house. Packages are, of course, available for mini- and micro-computers as well, and a number of examples of the use of such packages will be presented throughout this book. It is, however, essential to ensure that the proposed package actually does cope adequately with the problem being considered.

1.5 An Example of the Use of Quantative Techniques — Break-Even Analysis

Break-even analysis can be used to study the inter-relationships between cost, volume of output, revenue and profit for a single product or set of products. The *break-even point,* is defined as that level of output of the product at which total revenues equal total costs. Thus, operation at below the break-even point involves running at a loss; operation above the break-even point enables a profit to be obtained. We shall first of all define two classes of cost.

(i) Fixed costs
Fixed costs remain constant regardless of sales volume or production level, e.g., rent or rates for property, interest on loans that have been incurred to purchase capital equipment.

(ii) Variable costs
These costs vary directly with level of production and include such costs as materials or direct labour. Thus, say, doubling the level of production will double the variable cost.

Taking a practical example: Suppose producing a newspaper involves fixed costs of £10,000, that the cost of production for each unit is 5p and that revenue of 15p is obtained for each copy sold. Let us then proceed to obtain the break-even quantity.

We can construct mathematical models for revenue and cost.

Let R represent total revenue generated,
    p represent price sold,
and N represent no. sold.

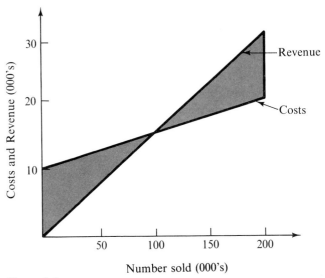

Figure 1.1

Hence our model for revenue $(R) = p \times N$
(i.e. price × no. sold).

Let C represent total cost,
  Q, fixed costs,
  c, variable cost per unit.

Hence our model for cost $(C) = Q + c \times N$
(i.e. fixed cost + no. sold × variable cost).

Now the break-even point is reached when revenue = total cost,
  i.e. $p \times N = Q + c \times N$
  Thus $(p - c) \times N = Q$
      or $N = Q/(p - c)$

Applying this model to the newspaper situation we find that, when
$Q = 10,000$, $p = 0.15$, $c = 0.05$

  $N = 10,000/(0.15 - 0.05) = 100,000$ copies

Exercise 1.1

Find out how the break-even point is affected

(a) If the cost of production rises to 6p per copy
(b) The selling price rises to 16p per copy

1.6 Implementation

The process of putting a recommended solution of a problem to use is called implementation. Clearly, any amount of effort or sophisticated model building that has been exerted on the problem will be in vain if the results are not eventually used in some way. A number of workers have identified problems which in some cases have led to non-implementation of results. One of the most important is poor communication between manager and analyst. Failure to take account of political factors or the personality of managers has sometimes led to rejection of the quantitative approach. Analysts have also been criticized for not having sufficient persistence or social skills to get their output used.

It is also, however, the responsibility of management to ensure that the analyst's work is effectively used. Thus, it is helpful for projects to have the support of senior management from the outset. Such managers can ensure that the project is consonant with the strategic aims of the organization. Early involvement of line management is also important. These managers should have comprehensive understanding of the operation and limitations of the existing system. They are also likely to be crucially involved in the implementation of subsequent changes and any lack of support on their part may well frustrate the success of the project.

2

Descriptive Statistics

2.1 Introduction to Statistics

There are, perhaps, two extreme views amongst those held by the general public on the subject of statistics and statistical methods. At one extreme might be the view that statistical methods can provide some kind of absolute truth in the manner of Pythagoras' theorem. On the other hand there is the notion that 'statistics can prove anything' and that most statisticians are either liars or charlatans. Perhaps Disraeli's famous dictum on the subject of 'lies, damned lies and statistics' best sums up the feeling of this school of thought.

All of us are, of course, familiar with vested interests presenting statistical information in a downright fraudulent manner. Amongst these are claims by double glazing manufacturers that installation of their products will result in a reduction in heating bills of up to 30% (it would in fact be necessary to live in a greenhouse to secure savings of this order of magnitude!) Huff's book on *How to Lie with Statistics*[1] presents many examples of how statistics can be used to mislead. Nevertheless, managers find that statistical information, if objectively presented and analysed, is an essential tool in enabling them to understand what has been happening to their organization in the past and to plan for the future. As we shall see, relevant statistical information is invaluable when trying to make decisions in an uncertain environment.

It does not follow from this, however, that providing everyone is entirely honest and objective in their statistical analysis then their interpretation will be the same. In many instances, there can be legitimate grounds for debate over the implications of a particular piece of statistical work. We are familiar with the work of economic forecasters who come to very different conclusions about the likely future development of the economy even though more or less the same basic statistical information is available to all. Again, if a particular statistical relationship can be derived between two quantities, there can be arguments about whether it is a cause-and-effect relationship (even if a convincing statistical relationship between the money supply and rate of inflation could be demonstrated there could still be doubt about whether an increase in one caused an increase in the other, or both were caused by an increase in some third factor.)

Statistical methods can be sub-divided into two branches called *descriptive* statistics and *statistical inference*. *Descriptive statistics* means the collection, summarization and presentation of statistical information. The Census is a well-known piece of descriptive statistics. The Domesday Book, dating from around 1086, which provided a record of the ownership, extent and value of the lands in England, is a very early development in descriptive statistics. On the other hand, should we wish to draw conclusions or judgements from statistical information we are into the field of *statistical inference*. (Progress in this area developed originally from analysis of games of chance.) An example of the use of statistical inference might be a manager who was interested in using statistical analysis to try to ascertain whether there was a relationship between sales in a particular part of the country and a recent promotional campaign. The use of statistical information in quality control to try to identify when a machine is out of order is another example of statistical inference.

This chapter will be devoted to the subject of descriptive statistics, while in the next three we shall handle statistical inference including the subject of forecasting.

2.2   Statistics represented pictorially

2.2.1   Organizing and Summarizing Data to Convey Meaning: Tables and Graphs

(i) Frequency distribution
Supposing that we have obtained the following information on

monthly sales of a number of car salesmen. (In £000s.)

75.1, 100.3, 62.6, 79.8, 85.0, 97.4, 50.5, 104.8, 61.9, 68.2,
72.5, 89.4, 92.6, 64.5, 46.3, 77.3, 34.2, 92.0, 84.9, 66.1.

This data is called *raw data* which means that it has not been processed by any statistical procedure. We may however want to try and present the above information in a coherent and organized form. One way of doing this would be to construct what is known as a *frequency distribution*. Although this will result in some loss of detail, new insights into the pattern of the data may be achieved. We construct a frequency distribution in the following way:

(a) We divide the scale from which the data comes into equal intervals (called *class intervals*). In the above example it might be appropriate to take five class intervals of 20, i.e. 20.0—39.9, 40.0—59.9, 60.0—79.9, 80.0—99.9 and 100.0—119.9.
(b) Calculate the frequency of occurrence of data in each class interval (*class frequency*).

If this is done it gives the following table (Table 2.1).

Table 2.1

Class interval	Class frequency
20.0— 39.9	1
40.0— 59.9	2
60.0— 79.9	9
80.0— 99.9	6
100.0—119.9	2

This frequency distribution shows the basic pattern of salesmen's performance in a comparatively clear way, i.e. most salesmen sell between 60.0—79.9 and 80.0—99.9 thousand with a few falling into the outlying intervals.

(ii) Frequency polygon
We may also decide that we wish to represent the frequency distribution graphically. One method of doing this is to construct the *frequency polygon*.

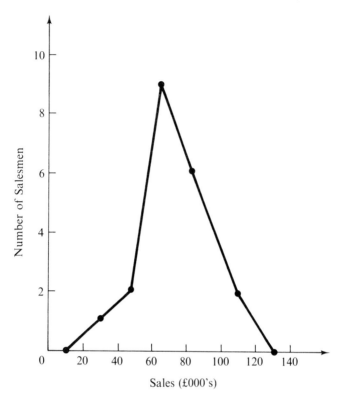

Figure 2.1   Frequency polygon

The class intervals are marked on the horizontal axis and the corresponding frequency values on the vertical axis (see Figure 2.1). The class frequencies are marked with a dot at the midpoint of the corresponding class intervals and successive dots are joined with a straight line.

(iii)   Histogram
Use of a *histogram* involves representing the frequency distribution by a number of rectangles. The width of the rectangles is drawn to be proportional to the size of the corresponding class interval. Height of rectangles should then be chosen so that the area of each rectangle is proportional to the class frequency of that interval.

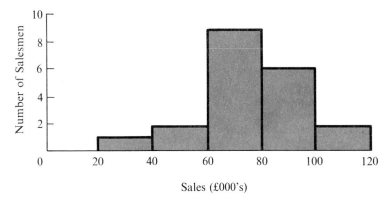

Figure 2.2   Histogram (Car salesmen)

This means that if all class intervals are the same width then the heights of rectangles will be proportional to the class frequency. The histogram for the car salesmen example is shown in Figure 2.2.

Exercise 2.1

The following table gives the weights of 40 pieces of equipment recorded correct to the nearest pound:

138, 164, 150, 132, 144, 125, 149, 157, 146, 158,
140, 147, 136, 148, 152, 144, 168, 126, 138, 176,
163, 119, 154, 165, 146, 173, 142, 147, 135, 153,
140, 135, 161, 145, 135, 142, 150, 156, 145, 128.

Construct an appropriate frequency distribution, frequency polygon and histogram to illustrate this data.

2.2.2 Cumulative frequency distribution

A cumulative frequency distribution enables us to see how many of our observations lie above or below certain values. For example, if we wished to know how many salesmen had sold less than £60,000 of goods we should construct a table of cumulative frequencies.

The cumulative frequency distribution can be constructed by calculating the number of observations up to a particular class interval. Taking the car salesman example we then obtain Table 2.2

below. We have also calculated the *cumulative relative frequency* which corresponds to the *proportion* of the total number of observations up to that particular interval.

Table 2.2

	Cumulative Frequency	Cumulative Relative Frequency
less than 40.0	1	0.05
less than 60.0	3	0.15
less than 80.0	12	0.60
less than 100.0	18	0.90
less than 120.0	20	1.00

If we wish to represent the data pictorially we can plot a graph of the cumulative frequency distribution as shown in Figure 2.3:

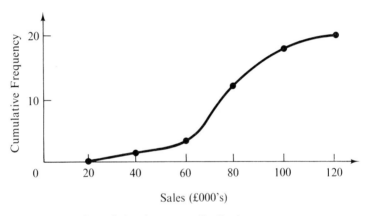

Figure 2.3   Cumulative frequency distribution

The curve in Figure 2.3 has the 'S' shape which is typical of cumulative frequency distributions.

Exercise 2.2
Construct and plot the graph of the cumulative frequency distribution for the data shown in Exercise 2.1.

2.3   Other Diagrammatic Ways of Presenting Data

A number of other forms of data presentation are used in certain circumstances.

(i)   The Pie Chart
This is a particularly useful way of presenting information when we are trying to highlight shares of a quantity (e.g. market shares, shares of a vote, breakdown of a budget). For example, suppose a company have divided the U.K. up into five sales areas and the percentage of its sales in each area is as given below:

Area	Percentage of sales (%)
1. London and S.E. England	30
2. Midlands	10
3. Eastern England	20
4. Wales and West	25
5. Scotland	15
	100

We can represent this situation pictorially by constructing the areas of the pie to correspond to percentage of sales as shown in Figure 2.4.

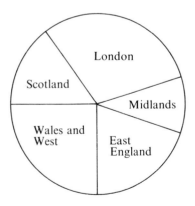

Figure 2.4   *Pie chart*

It is, of course, possible to ensure that the appropriate areas are designated by dividing the 360° angle at the centre of the circle into appropriate sections corresponding to percentage shares, i.e. London and S.E. (30%) 108°; Midlands (10%) 36°; East England (20%) 72°; Wales and West (25%) 90°; Scotland (15%) 54°.

(ii)   The Pictogram

A pictogram represents the quantity we are trying to illustrate by repetition of a number of identical simplified symbolic diagrams. For example, given the following table of figures for the world's major oil consumers, we can represent this by repetition of a number of small barrels of oil symbols as below. Note each ⊟ symbol represents 100 million tonnes.

Oil Consumption 1977 (hundred million tonnes)

U.S.A.	8
Western Europe	7
U.S.S.R. etc.	4
Japan	3
Rest of World	5

U.S.A.	⊟ ⊟ ⊟ ⊟ ⊟ ⊟ ⊟ ⊟
Western Europe	⊟ ⊟ ⊟ ⊟ ⊟ ⊟ ⊟
U.S.S.R. etc.	⊟ ⊟ ⊟ ⊟
Japan	⊟ ⊟ ⊟
Rest of World	⊟ ⊟ ⊟ ⊟ ⊟

Exercise 2.3

The sources of U.K. primary energy (1976) are as follows:

Coal	120.1	mtce*
Natural Gas	57.9	mtce
Oil	149.4	mtce
Nuclear and hydro	14.6	mtce
	342.0	

Construct a pie chart to illustrate division of energy supply amongst the various primary fuels.

*mtce = million tonnes of coal equivalent

Exercise 2.4

Examine newspapers and magazines for two or three examples where data has been represented in pictorial form. Discuss how this has been done and whether you feel that the information has been presented in a fair and objective manner.

2.4 Summary Measures: Measures of Central Tendency (Averages)

The use of frequency distributions which was described in the previous section enables us to detect trends and patterns in the data. Sometimes, however, we wish to derive more exact measures to summarize the data. One such measure is that of the average or central tendency of the data. There are a number of different kinds of average which are used.

2.4.1 Arithmetic Mean

The arithmetic mean is the quantity usually referred to when the term 'average' is used.

If we have a set of N data items $x_1, x_2, x_3 \ldots x_N$ then the arithmetic mean $\bar{x}$ is defined by:

$$\bar{x} = \frac{x_1 + x_2 \ldots + x_i + \ldots + x_N}{N} = \frac{\sum_{i=1}^{N} x_i}{N}$$

For example, suppose the workers in a particular section of a factory have the following annual wages: £4,000, £6,500, £4,000, £5,000, £6,500, £7,000, £6,000, £5,000, £8,000, £6,000. The mean wage is given by:

$x = $ (£4,000 + £6,500 + £4,000 + £5,500 + £6,500 + £7,000 + £6,000 + £5,000 + £8,000 + £6,000)/10,

i.e. mean wage = £5,850.

2.4.2 Grouped Data

Sometimes we may encounter *grouped data* (i.e. where some

observations occur more than once). This would be particularly the case if we were trying to calculate the arithmetic mean using the data from a frequency distribution.

If observation x_1 occurs f_1 times, x_2 occurs f_2 times, ... x_i occurs f_i times and x_n, f_n times then the mean is

$$\frac{f_1 x_1 + f_2 x_2 \ldots + f_i x_i + \ldots f_n x_n}{f_1 + f_2 \ldots + f_n}$$

$$= \frac{\sum\limits_{i=1}^{n} f_i x_i}{\sum\limits_{i=1}^{n} f_i}.$$

If we attempt to calculate average sales from the frequency distribution derived from the car salesmen's example, we are faced with a set of grouped data (taking each value as the mid-point of the corresponding class interval).

Class Interval	Mid-point of Class Interval (x) (000s)	Class frequency (f)	$f \times x$
20.0 — 39.9	30.0	1	30.0
40.0 — 59.9	50.0	2	100.0
60.0 — 79.9	70.0	9	630.0
80.0 — 99.9	90.0	6	540.0
100.0 — 119.9	110.0	2	220.0
		20	1,520.0

Hence the mean $= \dfrac{1,520.0}{20} = 76.0$ (thousand).

If we go back to the original raw data and calculate the mean we get $\bar{x} = 75.27$ (thousand). Thus, the use of grouped data has, not surprisingly, entailed introducing a small error.

2.4.3   The Weighted Mean

The weighted mean enables us to calculate an average that takes into account the importance of each value to the overall total. This is a concept that we shall make use of in the subsequent section on index numbers.

The data is handled in a very similar way to that of the previous section; if w_i is the weight given to the ith observation x_i, then the weighted mean:

$$\bar{x} = \frac{\sum\limits_{i=1}^{n} w_i x_i}{\sum\limits_{i=1}^{n} w_i}$$

For instance, supposing we know that a company workforce is composed of 3 grades of worker and that 45% of workers are in grade 1 with a wage of £6,500. Suppose a further 30% are in grade 2 with a wage of £8,000 and the remaining 25% are in grade 3 with wages of £9,000.

In order to calculate the weighted mean it is important that each factor is multiplied by its appropriate weight. Since 45% of workers are in grade 1, 30% in grade 2 and 25% in grade 3, appropriate weights would be 0.45, 0.30 and 0.25.

Then the weighted mean becomes

$$\frac{0.45 \times 6,500 + 0.30 \times 8,000 + 0.25 \times 9,000}{0.45 + 0.30 + 0.25}$$
$$= 2,925 + 2,400 + 2,250$$
$$= £7,575$$

2.4.4 Use of the Mean

The mean is readily understood and is very widely used in statistical analysis. One reservation about the mean is that the presence of extreme values can lead to a mean value that gives a rather distorted impression of central tendency. For example, if the wages of ten employees were £4,000, £6,500, £4,000, £5,500, £6,500, £7,000, £6,500, £5,000, £8,000, and £50,000 (this time we have included the managing director), we now get a mean of £10,300.

The £50,000 figure has distorted the mean to such an extent that the mean figure of £10,300 could be said to be not really representative of the data as a whole.

2.4.5   The Median

The median is a single value drawn from the data to represent its central point. In order to find the median of a data set the data is arranged in ascending or descending order. If the data set contains an odd number of items then the middle item of the array is the median. Should there be an even number of data items then the median is the arithmetic mean of the two middle items. Thus half the data items should be above the median and half below it. For instance, if the ages of a group of eleven workers are 28, 49, 32, 61, 43, 57, 50, 44, 42, 58, 40, we would first of all arrange them in ascending order: 28, 32, 40, 42, 43, 44, 49, 50, 57, 58, 61.

Since 44 is the sixth data item and thus the middle one, it is therefore the median value.

2.4.6   Use of the Median

Unlike the mean, the median is not unduly affected by extreme values. In the example in Section 2.4.4 the median value would be £6,500 compared to a mean of £10,300. Another situation where the median is invaluable is where data takes the form of qualitative descriptions. For example, a wine merchant could grade his wines in order of quality and hence identify the grade of median quality.

2.4.7   The mode

The mode of a particular data set is simply that value which occurs most often in a data set. Thus if a shoe shop has the following sales of women's shoes:

Size	3	4	5	6	7	8	9	10
No. of sales	24	216	342	419	209	139	62	21

We can then say that size six is the *modal* size since this is the size that is purchased most often.

Sometimes, however, the data set only contains a small number of data items that are repeated. In this case, chance may determine which item becomes the mode or there may even be no values which are repeated. This is the case for the monthly sales of the car salesmen in Section 2.2.1. If, however, we grouped the data into a frequency distribution we can select the class with the most observations and this is then designated the *modal class*. In the car salesmen example, examination of the frequency distribution given in Table 2.1 indicates that the class interval 60.0—79.9 (£000s) is the modal class.

Exercise 2.5

Find the mean, median and mode of the data set presented in Exercise 2.1.

2.5 Variability in Data Sets

In the preceding section we have dealt with finding the central tendency of a set of data. In addition to this, however, in most cases we shall also be interested in the variability or spread of the data. For instance, if a sales manager knows that his mean monthly sales in a particular area are valued at £50,000 he will also be interested in knowing whether this is a relatively stable figure or whether there are wide fluctuations about this amount.

Again, a production process producing ball-bearings could produce output whose mean weight conformed very closely to target, but whose variation was such that it was useless for fulfilling its required purpose.

2.5.1 The Range

The range is the simplest measure of variability and is simply the difference between the largest and smallest values in the data set.

If we take the ages of the group of eleven workers discussed in Section 2.4.5 (i.e. 28, 49, 32, 61, 43, 57, 50, 44, 42, 58 and 40) we find that the youngest is 28 and the oldest 61 hence the range is 33 years.

The great advantage of the range is its simplicity and ease of calculation. For this reason it is commonly used in much quality control work. Obviously its major drawback is that, since it uses only two values from the data set, it can be drastically influenced by a single, perhaps spurious, extreme value. It is also highly dependent on the number of items contained in the data set. The more observations present, the greater the chances of extreme values occurring and the greater the likelihood of a wide range of values being observed.

2.5.2   Mean Deviaiton

Unlike the range this measure of variability takes all data items into account.

To compute the mean deviation we find the *absolute value* of the difference between each item in the data set and the mean. (Absolute value means ignoring the sign thereby taking each to be positive). Thus, if we have N data items $x_1, x_2, \ldots x_N$ and the mean of the data set is $\bar{x}$:

$$\text{Mean deviation} = \frac{\sum\limits_{i=1}^{N} |x_i - \bar{x}|}{N}.$$

Let us take the example from the last section, i.e. data set 28, 49, 32, 61, 43, 57, 50, 44, 42, 58 and 40. We observe that the mean is 45.8.

To calculate the mean deviation we proceed as follows:

Data Point	Deviation $(x_i - \bar{x})$	Absolute Deviation $|x_i - \bar{x}|$
28	− 17.8	17.8
49	3.2	3.2
32	− 13.8	13.8
61	15.2	15.2
43	− 2.8	2.8
57	11.2	11.2
50	4.2	4.2
44	− 1.8	1.8
42	− 3.8	3.8
58	12.2	12.2
40	− 5.8	5.8
		91.8

Hence, mean deviation $= \dfrac{91.8}{11} = 8.35$.

The mean deviation is a better measure of dispersion than the range because it takes all observations into account and affords them all equal weight. It is rarely used in practice because for technical reasons the standard deviation is much more useful.

2.5.3 Standard Deviation

Standard deviation is the measure of variation which is most commonly used in practice. This measure is based on the sum of the squares of the differences between the data items and the arithmetic mean. If the N data items are $x_1, x_2, x_3, \ldots x_i \ldots x_N$, then the standard deviation is defined as:

$$\text{Standard deviation} = \sqrt{\left(\frac{\sum\limits_{i=1}^{N} (x_i - \bar{x})^2}{N - 1} \right)}.$$

The *variance* of a data set is simply the square of the standard deviation.

If we have grouped data (i.e. x_1 occurs f_1 times, $x_i f_i$ times and x_n occurs f_n times and there are N data items altogether) then the standard deviation is given by:

$$\frac{\sum\limits_{i=1}^{n} f_i (x_i - \bar{x})^2}{\sum\limits_{i=1}^{n} f_i - 1}.$$

Note that, of course $\sum\limits_{i=1}^{n} f_i = N$.

Manual calculation of standard deviation is somewhat tedious although many modern pocket electronic calculators have specific functions for calculating standard deviations. However, in order to make manual calculation a little easier it is possible to simplify the above equation and we get:

For the ungrouped data

$$\sqrt{\left(\frac{\sum_{i=1}^{N} x_i^{2} - \left(\sum_{i=1}^{N} x_i\right)^{2} / N}{N - 1}\right)}.$$

For the grouped data:

$$\sqrt{\left(\frac{\sum_{i=1}^{n} f_i x_i^{2} - \left(\sum_{i=1}^{n} f_i x_i\right)^{2} / N}{N - 1}\right)}.$$

To demonstrate how this can be used in practice we will now calculate the standard deviation of the data set in the previous section.

Data point (x_i)	x_i^2	
28	784	
49	2,401	
32	1,024	$\sum_{i=1}^{N} x_i^2 = 24{,}192$
61	3,721	
43	1,849	
57	3,249	
50	2,500	$\sum_{i=1}^{N} x_i = 504$
44	1,936	
42	1,764	
58	3,364	
40	1,600	
504	24,192	

$$\text{Standard deviation} = \sqrt{\frac{24{,}192 - (504)^2/11}{10}}$$

$$= \sqrt{\frac{24,192 - 23,092}{10}} \qquad = \sqrt{\frac{1,100}{10}} = \sqrt{110} = 10.49$$

The standard deviation does take into account all of the information available, however, and it is not easy to visualize its relationship with the original data set. Nevertheless it is of great importance in statistical theory and, because of this, it is easily the most widely used measure of variation.

Exercise 2.6

Calculate range, mean deviation, variance and standard deviation for the data on workers' wage rates introduced in Section 2.4.1.

2.6 Index Numbers

2.6.1 Introduction

An index number is a statistical measure of how much a variable is changing over time. Index numbers are particularly important for assessing the performance of the economy over a period of time. We may, for instance, be interested in how retail prices, values of shares, and the level of industrial output are varying over time. Thus, the *retail price index* measures variations in retail prices over time. The *Financial Times Share price index* measures the change in share prices and the *index of industrial production* the change in volume of industrial production over a particular time period.

The principal types of index are price indices, quantity indices, and value indices. The retail price index and FT share index are price indices whilst the index of production is a quantity index.

It is a general convention to express the current level of an index in relation to a base period in which the index has arbitrarily been given the value of 100.

2.6.2 Index Numbers: General Principles

Consider a subsistence economy where the only food of significance was rice. Suppose the price of rice in 1980—1982 was as follows:

Cost in 1980 (base year) = 16p per lb
1981   = 20p per lb
1982   = 12p per lb

Suppose we make 1980 the base year (value 100). Then if we define the price index by:

$$\frac{p_c}{p_b} \times 100$$

where p_c is price in current year,
p_b is price in base year.

In 1981, price index $= \dfrac{20}{16} \times 100 = \underline{125}$

and in 1982, price index $= \dfrac{12}{16} \times 100 = \underline{\ 75}$

Let us take a more advanced economy (e.g. Scotland) and assume that the diet consists of five staple items: haggis, porridge oats, oatcakes, fish suppers and whisky. Suppose we want to derive a food price index for 1980 using 1975 as a base year given the following information:

Item	Unit	1975 Price (p_b)	1980 Price (p_c)
Haggis	1 lb	40	50
Porridge	½ lb	15	30
Oatcakes	1 lb	20	32
Fish supper	one	32	56
Whisky	one measure	28	42

Now we are dealing with more than a single food item and we therefore need to construct a composite food price index.

The simplest index to construct would be an *unweighted aggregates* index.

This can be defined as $\dfrac{\sum p_c}{\sum p_b} \times 100$

For the example above we get:

$$\text{Price index} = \frac{50 + 30 + 32 + 56 + 42}{40 + 15 + 20 + 32 + 28} \times 100$$

$$= \frac{210}{135} \times 100 = 156$$

This index is, however, unweighted. In most situations, though, we would want to give different items which are incorporated into the index different weights. Thus if, say, both bread and caviar were included in an index of food prices we would want to give bread a considerably higher weighting than caviar. This is because bread is a much more important constituent in the diet of the average family than caviar; thus, a rise in the price of bread is much more significant than a rise in the price of caviar and the index should accordingly reflect this.

2.6.3   Problems of Weighting

We have established the importance of choosing appropriate weights. However, the period on which to base the weighting is still an unresolved question. We will consider two approaches to this problem.

(i)   Laspeyre's method (Base period)
This index is based on quantities consumed during the base period (q_b). It is a very convenient method since it requires quantity measures for one period only.

$$\text{Then Laspeyre's aggregates index} = \frac{\sum p_c q_b}{\sum p_b q_b} \times 100.$$

Suppose in the previous example that in 1975 the proportion of expenditure on food items by the average family was: Haggis, 0.10; porridge, 0.20; oatcakes, 0.20; fish supper, 0.30; and whisky, 0.20. If we take these as base weights then the Laspeyre's price index is as below:

Item	p_b	p_c	q_b	$p_c q_b$	$p_b q_b$
Haggis	40	50	0.10	5.0	4.0
Porridge	15	30	0.20	6.0	3.0
Oatcakes	20	32	0.20	6.4	4.0
Fish supper	32	56	0.30	16.8	9.6
Whisky	28	42	0.20	8.4	5.6
				42.6	26.2

$$\text{Hence Laspeyre's index} = \frac{42.6}{26.2} \times 100$$

$$= 162.6$$

(ii)   Current weights (Paasche)
The difference between this and the previous index is that this index uses *current* period weighting rather than *base* period weighting.

$$\text{The index is defined as} \quad \frac{\Sigma p_c q_c}{\Sigma p_b q_c} \times 100,$$

where q_c are current year weights.

If we use this method of weighting, however, we do get involved in recalculating quantity values each year.

Suppose that in 1980 the proportion of income spent on food items by the average family is as follows:
Haggis, 0.20, porridge, 0.10, oatcakes, 0.20, fish supper, 0.25, and whisky, 0.25.

If these are the current weights then the Paasche price index is:

Item	p_b	p_c	q_c	$p_c q_c$	$p_b q_c$
Haggis	40	50	0.20	10.0	8.0
Porridge	15	30	0.10	3.0	1.5
Oatcakes	20	32	0.20	6.4	4.0
Fish supper	32	56	0.25	14.0	8.0
Whisky	28	42	0.25	10.5	7.0
				43.9	28.5

$$\therefore \text{ Paasche index} = \frac{43.9}{28.5} \times 100 = 154$$

It will be noted that the Paasche index shows a lower rise in prices than the Laspeyre's index. This is because changes in consumption patterns will tend to result in families consuming relatively more of food items whose price rises have been less than average and vice versa.

2.6.4 Quantity Indices

Should we be interested in measuring changes in quantities rather than prices, we can design quantity index numbers in a very similar manner to the above.

$$\text{Base weighted quantity index} = \frac{\sum p_b \, q_c}{\sum p_b \, q_b} \times 100.$$

$$\text{Current weighted quantity index} = \frac{\sum p_c \, q_c}{\sum p_c \, q_b} \times 100.$$

2.6.5 Problems in Constructing and Interpreting Index Numbers

(i)   Selecting base period
It is important that the 'base period' should be 'normal'. Thus, if one was trying to construct an index of industrial production one would try to avoid using 1973 because this was the year of the 'three day week'.

(ii)   Selection of items to be included in index
If we are constructing a retail price index it is quite obviously impossible to include all the thousands of products that are available for sale. Nevertheless a wide enough range of items must be chosen to make the index representative.

(iii)   Selecting appropriate weights
We have discussed some of these problems in the previous section.

(iv)   Quality changes
It is difficult to take quality changes into account particularly as the basic item may no longer be available (e.g. basic Mini).

(v) Interpretation of index

There is a danger of misapplying an index. For example, the retail price index has been derived on the basis of the consumption pattern of typical families. There is a danger in attempting to use such an index to assess changes in the standards of living of unrepresentative groups such as old-age pensioners. Old-age pensioners spend a higher proportion of their income than the average family on food and heat, thus a rise in price in these items will have a disproportionate effect on their standard of living. This will not be reflected in the weighting given to these items in the retail price index. For this reason special indices for groups such as OAPs are constructed.

Exercise 2.7

The following table gives prices of three metals and the amounts used in industry for 1980 and 1982. Calculate a base and current weighted metal price index taking 1980 as a base year.

Metal	Consumption tonne(s)		Price (£100 per tonne(s))	
	1980	1982	1980	1982
Alphanum	1,200	1,600	5	6
Betacom	800	1,500	7	6
Gammanick	2,000	800	5	9

Exercise 2.8

Try to find out as much as you can about the retail price index. How is this index constructed, how are its weightings arrived at? What is the base year? What items are included?

Exercise 2.9

The Minister of Education has decided to link student grants to a student cost of living index. Explain why the retail price index is inappropriate for this purpose. Discuss how you might approach the problem of constructing such an index. What items would you include and how would you weight them?

2.7 Social Indicators

2.7.1 Introduction

There are many social situations in which we may wish to indicate priorities for the allocation of scarce resources. For example, the Government may wish to designate particular deprived areas as areas of multiple deprivation so that it can concentrate additional resources for education, housing and environmental improvement on the most needy areas. Amongst Local Authorities' responsibilities are the tasks of allocating Local Authority Housing to those on the housing waiting list, and allocating a limited Education Capital Budget amongst competing claimants.

There are no clear quantitative criteria on which such decisions can be based and in any event decisions must be subjective in representing the political priorities of elected members. Nevertheless a procedure where, for instance, elected members discuss the merits of each individual application on the housing list may be undesirable.

It is likely that such a system, as well as being unwieldly and time-consuming, could result in inconsistency in applying priorities and there is always the danger of accusations of bias, parochialism or nepotism.

Thus, one approach to this sort of problem has been the development of appropriate indicators. This involves decision-makers expressing their priorities in quantitative form. If this is done, officials can then apply these priorities administratively. Such a quantitative measure is called a *social indicator*.

2.7.2 Social Indicators (Example)—A Points Scheme for Assessing Priorities of Housing Need

The scheme described below is a fairly typical index of housing need. The local authority's area is divided up into a number of separate housing allocation areas. The index is compiled on the basis of the following seven factors:

A number of points (depending on family circumstances) are allocated under each factor. Families with the largest aggregate points score receive priority for housing allocations.

(i)   Waiting
For each year the eldest member of the household is above sixty
–1 point.

(ii)   Residence
(a) For each five years' residence in the local authority's area—*1 point* (up to a maximum of *2 points*).
(b) *Residence in housing allocation area*
      For each years' residence in first choice housing allocation area—*1 point* (up to a maximum of *5 points*)

(iii)   Tenure
For no security of tenure (i.e. tenants living in tied cottages, people living as sub-tenants (lodgers) in other peoples' houses, caravan dwellers, etc.—*5 points.*

(iv)   Overcrowding
(a) For each person living in a property above the correct notional capacity as determined by the environmental health officer—*2 points.*

(b) *Medical overcrowding*
      For each unit of medical overcrowding — *2 points.* (Note: certain types of medical condition result in the notional capacity of the property being reduced.)

(v)   Condition of property
(a) For conditions below satisfactory standard as assessed by the environmental health officer (such factors as outside toilet, lack of bathroom, fabric of building, would be taken into account) — *up to 12 points*
(b) For caravan dwellers and dwellers in multiple occupancy (i.e. a single accommodation unit occupied by more than one household) — *2 points*

(vi)   Medical
For medical conditions as assessed by the local health board — *up to 10 points.*

(vii) Age

For each year the eldest member of the household is above sixty
–*1 point.*

   For example, consider an elderly couple aged 63 and 60 who have
been on the housing waiting list for 1½ years. They live in a two-
bedroom tied cottage with no bathroom and an outside toilet. They
have been resident in the district and first choice housing allocation
area for seven years. The wife has a mild arthritic condition. Under
the above system the points allocation for the above couple might
be as follows:

(i)	*Waiting*—1½ years:	1 point
(ii)	*Residence* (a) 7 yr in district	1
	(b) 7 yr in housing allocation area	5 (max)
(iii)	*Tenure*—Tied cottage, thus no tenure	5
(iv)	*Overcrowding*—no overcrowding	0
(v)	*Condition*—Poor: no bathroom, outside toilet; say 8 pts out of 12	8
(vi)	*Medical*—mild arthritic condition (say 4 pts out of 10)	4
(vii)	*Age*—eldest person is 63	3
	TOTAL POINTS SCORE	27

Exercise 2.10

Produce an index of housing need that reflects your own priorities.
Use (a) your scheme, (b) the scheme described in the example, to
establish priorities for housing need for the following three
families; you will have to use your judgement to allocate points for
housing conditions and medical conditions. (Note: 2 apartment
means living room plus 1 bedroom, 3 apartment means living room
plus 2 bedrooms etc.) (c) Are you happy for these cases to be dealt
with administratively without reference back to any elected
members?

(1)   Widower with four children: 10, 11, 13, 16 (two boys and two
      girls). Works as part-time security guard with total income of
      £3,500 per year. At present, living in own 3 apartment flat
      (i.e. living room and two bedrooms). Flat has no running hot
      water and outside toilet. No medical problems. Lived in

district and housing allocation area for five years and has been on housing list for the entire time.

(2)   Family of two parents, two children aged 3 and 1 and invalid grandfather. Family income totals £5,000 per year.

At present living in privately rented 2 apartment flat with no bathroom and shared toilet facilities. Resident in district for ten years and on council waiting list for four years. Has lived in the housing allocation area for two years. Grandfather is visited weekly by health visitors for miscellaneous health problems.

(3)   Family of two parents and two young children (aged 5, 7) illegally rehoused in old, empty, condemned (3 apartment) Council property by squatters' organization. All facilities with exception of running water have been removed. Father is unemployed and on waiting list only six months. Has lived in district and housing allocation area for 18 months. No health problems.

Exercise 2.11

Suggest how you might approach the problem of identifying areas of multiple deprivation. What factors would you take into account in your index? Suggest how you might quantify these factors.

3
Statistical Methods I

3.1 Statistical Inference

In the previous chapter we dealt with the subject of *descriptive statistics*. As we have seen, the use of these methods enables us to present available statistical information in more meaningful and useful ways.

Often we want to use statistical information to derive conclusions or make judgements. This part of the subject, as we observed in the last chapter, is called *statistical inference*.

3.2 Scope of Coverage of Statistical Methods

This chapter will be mainly concerned with probability concepts and probability distributions. Even though they may not have had any formal training in statistics most of our readers will have some intuitive grasp of probability, gained through every-day life. Chapter 4 deals mainly with handling sample information and hypothesis testing. Finally, Chapter 5 outlines the use of statistical methods in forecasting.

3.3 Probability Theory

3.3.1 Introduction

This is a well established branch of statistical knowledge and originally dates from analysis of games of chance.

3.3.2   Sample Space

Before we proceed to judge what is probable in any situation we have to attempt to identify what is possible. The use of *sample space* helps us in this respect. An activity that can result in a number of possible outcomes is called an *experiment*. Sample space is the set of all possible outcomes of such an experiment.

For example, suppose we decide to launch a new type of solid state electronic device, and suppose that the outcome of this launching can be categorized as high sales, moderate sales or low sales. These three outcomes can be represented by three points in the sample space as given below:

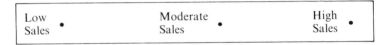

| Low Sales • | Moderate Sales • | High Sales • |

Figure 3.1

3.3.3   Events

The outcome of an experiment and the points in the sample space corresponding to such outcomes are called events. For example, suppose two different solid state devices A and B are marketed and, as before, each device can have high, moderate or low sales. The sample space for this experiment can be represented by the nine points shown in Figure 3.2.

Supposing we represent low, medium and high sales by points 0, 1,2 on axes of sample space as shown in the diagram. Then point (2,1), for example, corresponds to high sales of product B and medium sales of product A.

The event that product A has low sales (say, event X) corresponds to the three points in sample space (0,0), (1,0), and (2,0). Points (1,2) and (2,1) correspond to the event that one product has moderate sales and the other product has high sales (event W). Sample points (0,0) (0,1) and (0,2) correspond to the event that product B has low sales (event V).

Suppose we wish to consider the event that at least one product has low sales. Sample points (0,2), (0,1), (0,0), (1,0) and (2,0) constitute this event. These points, however, are all the sample

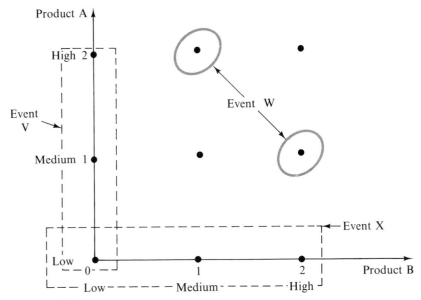

Figure 3.2

points contained in events V and X. This can be written as $X \cup V$, the *union* of events X and V.

Thus the *union* of two events is that event which consists of all the sample points corresponding to either of the two events.

Supposing we are interested in the event that both products have low sales. This event will correspond to sample points which occur both in event V and in event X. The only sample point to appear in both event V and event X is the sample point (0,0). This event is the *intersection* of events X and V and can be written $V \cap X$.

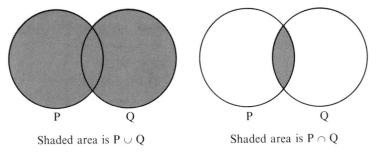

Shaded area is $P \cup Q$ Shaded area is $P \cap Q$

Figure 3.3

Thus the *intersection* of two events is the event which consists of all the points in sample space which the two events have in common.

More generally, consider events P and Q represented by corresponding sample spaces. Then the shaded areas in Figure 3.3 give the union and intersection of the two events.

Exercise 3.1

Construct a sample space for two tosses of a coin. Which points correspond to the events, (i) at least one head occurs, (ii) both tosses results in heads?

3.3.4   Probability

So far we have only considered the possible outcomes of experiments. We have not considered whether certain events are more likely than others. Considering the example in the previous section it may well be true that in the past products similar to type A have generally sold well whilst products similar to type B have low sales. Thus, sample points representing high sales of A and low sales of B might be more likely (or probable) than points representing low sales of A and high sales of B. It will now be necessary to try to establish formal definitions of probability.

There are many definitions of probability but perhaps the most widely used is the *relative frequency approach to probability* according to which the probability of an event is defined as the proportion of the time that such an event would occur in the long run. For example, if we toss a fair coin we would expect the proportion of times that such an event would occur in the long run to equal ½. Thus the *probability* of obtaining a head should equal ½. If, say, twenty similar products to product A had been launched in the past and sixteen had resulted in high sales this could provide justification for assuming that the probability of future high sales equalled $16/20 = 0.8$.

There are, however, certain situations in which we are faced with an event of which we have no direct previous experience or historical information to base our estimate of probability upon. Suppose we were faced with the task of assessing the probability of high sales of a novel product; perhaps one based on a new technology. In such a situation we might have to rely on a *subjective* evaluation of probability by a businessman.

This subjective estimate of probability may depend on a number of factors, such as his feel for market conditions, experience in the industry and intuition. Practically, we might solicit subjective probabilities from a number of experts. The way that we handle such probabilities will be discussed in detail in the chapter on Decision Making.

Now if p_i are the probabilities associated with the different sample points that correspond to a particular event A, then the probability of the event A will equal the sum of the probabilities associated with the different sample points: i.e. $P\{A\} = \sum_A p_i$ where $P\{A\}$ is the probability of event A.

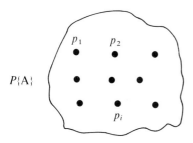

Figure 3.4

For example consider the case of the coin which was tossed twice. If we represent Tails by 0, Heads by 1, possible events could be shown as in Figure 3.5.

In the long run each sample point would be expected to occur ¼ of the time. Thus we can assign a probability of ¼ to each of our sample points. Suppose we are interested in the probability of obtaining a total of one head and one tail from our two tosses. Two sample points (TH) and (HT) correspond to this event and their probabilities are each 1/4. Thus the probability of getting a total of one head and one tail is ¼ + ¼ = ½.

Clearly all probabilities must ≥ 0. A probability of zero assigned to a particular event indicates that it is impossible whereas a

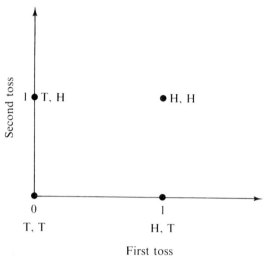

Figure 3.5

probability of one makes the event certain.

If an experiment has n outcomes and the probability of the ith outcome $= p_i$ then since one outcome must occur

$$\sum_{i=1}^{n} p_i = 1.$$

3.3.5 Probability Theorems

(i) Addition Theorems
Consider the sample points associated with the outcome of two experiments and corresponding to events A_1 and A_2. Thus any

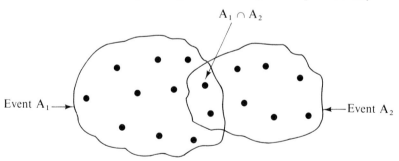

Figure 3.6

sample point in A_1 corresponds to event A_1 occurring and any sample point in A_2 corresponds to event A_2 occurring. The event that both A_1 and A_2 occur is given by $A_1 \cap A_2$. The event that at least one of A_1 or A_2 occurs is given by $A_1 \cup A_2$.

Suppose we are interested in the probability that *at least one* of the two events A_1 and A_2 has occurred (i.e. $P(A_1 \cup A_2)$).

Now $P(A_1) + P(A_2)$ gives the probabilities of sample points lying in the two regions combined, except that points in the common region of A_1 and A_2 would be summed twice, (i.e. the region $A_1 \cap A_2$). Thus it will be necessary to subtract $P(A_1 \cap A_2)$—i.e. probability of sample points falling in this common region.

Then $P(A_1 \cup A_2) = P(A_1) + P(A_2) - P(A_1 \cap A_2)$.

Events are said to be *mutually exclusive* if they have no sample points in common (i.e. occurrence of one event means that the other cannot possibly take place). For example, if a single card is drawn from a pack it is impossible for the events 'the card is a Jack' and 'the card is a King' to both take place.

For mutually exclusive events $P(A_1 \cap A_2) = 0$, and hence $P(A_1 \cup A_2) = P(A_1) + P(A_2)$.

Example

We draw a card at random from a properly shuffled pack.
(1) What is the probability of drawing a Jack or a King?
(2) What is the probability of drawing an Ace or a Spade?

(1) Drawing a Jack or a King are mutually exclusive events
$\therefore P(\text{Jack} \cup \text{King}) = P(\text{Jack}) + P(\text{King})$,
$\quad P(\text{Jack}) = 4/52 = 1/13$,
$\quad P(\text{King}) = 4/52 = 1/13$,
$\therefore P(\text{Jack} \cup \text{King}) = 1/13 + 1/13 = 2/13$.

(2) Drawing an Ace or Spade are not mutually exclusive events.
$\quad P(\text{Ace}) \qquad\quad = 1/13$
$\quad P(\text{Spade}) \qquad = \frac{1}{4}$
$\quad P(\text{Ace} \cap \text{Spade}) = 1/52$ (i.e. the Ace of Spades)
$\therefore P(\text{Ace} \cup \text{Spade}) = P(\text{Ace}) + P(\text{Spade}) - P(\text{Ace} \cap \text{Spade})$
$\qquad\qquad\qquad\quad = 1/13 + \frac{1}{4} - 1/52$
$\qquad\qquad\qquad\quad = 4/13$

(ii)   Conditional Probability

There are many occasions when it can be rather misleading to attempt to evaluate the probability of a given event without specifying the sample space with which we are concerned.

For instance, we may have a number of machines available, all of which can produce the same kind of transistor. Suppose that the machines are of different ages and each produces differing proportions of defective transistors. If one now chooses a transistor at random, the probability that it is defective will depend on which machine's output it was selected from. Suppose D corresponds to the event that a defective transistor is produced, and M_1 to the event that the transistor is produced by machine M_1. Then the probability that a transistor is found to be defective, given that it was selected from the output of machine M_1 is written $P(D \mid M_1)$.

In general we write $P(A \mid S)$ as the probability of event A relative to sample space S.

(iii)   Multiplication Theorem: Dependent and Independent Events

Suppose ten transistors are produced by machine M_1 and three are found to be defective. Suppose five transistors are produced by machine M_2 and one is defective. The sample space for this situation is shown in Figure 3.7.

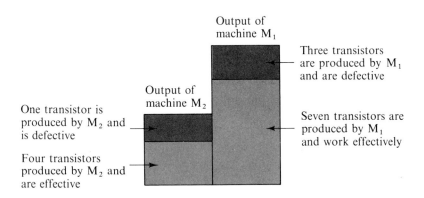

Figure 3.7

Now as we have previously explained the probability that a transistor from machine M_1 is defective is written $P(D|M_1)$. Similarly the probability that a transistor produced by M_2 is defective is $P(D|M_2)$.

Suppose we wished to calculate the probability that a transistor produced by M_1 is defective (i.e. $P(D|M_1)$); then we are only interested in the proportion of sample space corresponding to output from machine M_1, cf. Figure 3.8.

Output M_1

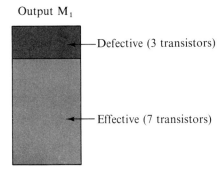

Defective (3 transistors)

Effective (7 transistors)

Figure 3.8

Now, it can be seen that $P(D|M_1) = 3/10$; i.e. it is equivalent to that proportion of sample space corresponding to output of M_1 that relates to defective items. The sample space corresponding to defective output of M_1 is $D \cap M_1$, i.e. that part of sample space that corresponds to both output of M_1 and defectiveness.

Thus, $P(D|M_1) = \dfrac{P(D \cap M_1)}{P(M_1)}$.

Similarly, we can see by examining sample space corresponding to M_2 that $P(D|M_2) = 1/5$.

Thus, $P(D|M_2) = \dfrac{P(D \cap M_2)}{P(M_2)}$.

Suppose the situation is now slightly different and, having found a defective transistor, we want to know the probability that it was produced by machine M_1. This would be written $P(M_1|D)$. Thus this time we are interested in sample space corresponding only to defectiveness (Figure 3.9).

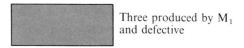

Three produced by M_1 and defective

One produced by M_2 and is defective

Figure 3.9

$P(M_1|D)$ = 3/4 and using the same argument as before,
$$P(M_1|D) = \frac{P(M_1 \cap D)}{P(D)}.$$

Thus, in general, for dependent events A and B,
$$P(A|B) = \frac{P(A \cap B)}{P(B)}$$

or $P(A \cap B) = P(A|B) \cdot P(B)$.

If the event B has absolutely no influence on whether event A will occur then the two events are said to be *independent*. In this case $P(A|B)$ simply equals $P(A)$. So, for independent events,
$$P(A \cap B) = P(A) \cdot P(B).$$

We shall now consider a few specific examples to try to illustrate this analysis.

For example, a box contains three 50-watt light bulbs and two 100-watt light bulbs. If two light bulbs are selected from the box at random what is the probability that both light bulbs will be 50-watt ones?

(a) With replacement after drawing the first light bulb.

(b) Without replacement after drawing the first light bulb.

Suppose A_1 represents the event that the first bulb drawn is a 50-watt one.

Suppose A_2 represents the event that the second bulb drawn is a 50-watt one.

Then the probability that both light bulbs are 50-watt ones is written as $P(A_1 \cap A_2)$.

(a) Now if the first bulb is replaced after being drawn it cannot affect the result of drawing the second bulb in any way.

Thus $P(A_1) = 3/5$

and $P(A_2) = 3/5$

For independent events $P(A_1 \cap A_2) = P(A_1) \times P(A_2)$
$$= 3/5 \times 3/5 = 9/25.$$

(b) If the first bulb is not replaced then the events are not independent. If a 50-watt bulb is removed on the first draw, then there remains four bulbs, two of which are 50-watt ones.

Hence $P(A_2 | A_1) = 2/4 = \frac{1}{2}$.

Now $P(A_1 \cap A_2) = P(A_1) \times P(A_2 | A_1)$,
$$= 3/5 \times 2/4 = 3/10.$$

3.4 Exercises on Probability Theory

Exercise 3.2

Two cards are drawn from an ordinary deck of 52 cards, the first being replaced before the second card is drawn.

(a) What is the probability that both cards will be spades?

(b) What is the probability that the cards will be either both spades or both hearts?

(c) If the first card is not replaced what is the probability of getting 2 spades?

(d) What is the probability that the first card will be a spade or a seven?

Exercise 3.3

A system consists of two components A and B. Failure of any one component will result in system failure. The probability of component A failing in a year is 0.7, and the probability of component B failing is 0.8. (Failure of A and B is independent). What is the probability (a) that the system remains sound for the year (b) both components fail during the year (c) at least one component fails during the year.

Exercise 3.4

Compare the probability of rolling a 4 with one die with the probability of rolling a total of eight with two dice.

Exercise 3.5

An electrical system consists of three components. One arrangement possible is to arrange three components each with a probability of 0.95 of remaining sound in series, i.e.

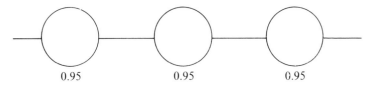

0.95   0.95   0.95

Figure 3.10

Breakdown of this system occurs if any one of the three components fail. Another possible arrangement is to arrange three components each with a probability of 0.60 of remaining sound in parallel.

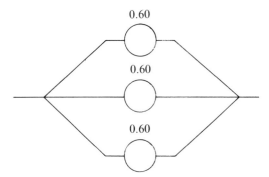

0.60

0.60

0.60

Figure 3.11

Breakdown of the system now occurs only if all of the three components fail. Which of these systems is more liable to breakdown? (In practice, of course, function and technical matters will constrain the choice of possible systems arrangement.)

3.5   Probability Distributions

3.5.1   Introduction

Having introduced basic ideas on probability in the previous section we will now proceed to the important subject of probability distributions.

If a value that a certain quantity may take is governed by chance then it is referred to as a *random variable*. For example, if a coin is tossed twice then the number of heads obtained from these two tosses (x) depends on chance and may take the values $x = 0$, $x = 1$ or $x = 2$.

It is clear, however, that probabilities can be associated with each of the values of the random variable described above. The specification of all the values of the random variable together with their associated probabilities is a *probability distribution*.

Supposing f(x) represents the probability of the random variable taking the value x; in our example x represents the number of heads obtained and
f(0) = ¼
f(1) = ½
f(2) = ¼

This is the probability distribution for our example. This example is an example of a *discrete* probability distribution (i.e. the random variable in question has a finite number of values).

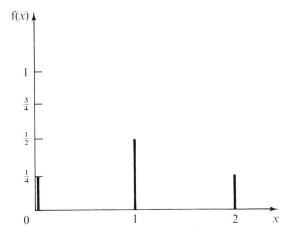

Figure 3.12

Exercise 3.6

Suppose a die is tossed twice. Let the random variable, x, represent the sum obtained from the two tosses. What is the probability distribution for x?

We shall now consider two specific types of discrete distribution called the *Binomial* and *Poisson* distributions.

3.5.2   The Binomial Distribution

This is a probability distribution which is very useful in practice. It is applicable to the type of situation in which the outcome of an experiment falls into one of two possible categories and we are interested in discovering the number of times one of the outcomes (number of 'successes') occurs in a given number of experiments (or trials). For example, a machine for producing electrical components may produce components which can be categorized as either effective (i.e. satisfactory for their chosen purpose) or defective. We may be interested in discovering the probability of finding a given number of effective components in a batch of a certain size.

More generally, this result is given by the Binomial distribution. If there are n trials and the probability of achieving a 'success' in any given trial is P, then the probability of obtaining r successes in the n trials is given by[1]

$$f(r) = \frac{n!}{r!\,(n-r)!}\; P^r\,(1-P)^{n-r}.$$

Supposing the machine which produces electrical components has a probability of 0.8 of producing an effective component. What is the probability that exactly three components in a batch of five will be effective?

Using the Binomial distribution we have $n = 5$ $r = 3$ $P = 0.8$.

$$\text{Hence } f(3) = \frac{5!}{3!\,2!}\,(0.8)^3\,(0.2)^2,$$
$$= 0.2048.$$

(It is implicitly assumed in the above that all trials are *independent*.)

Exercise 3.7

In the above example what is the probability of obtaining four or more effective components?

(i)   Properties of the Binomial Distribution
The mean of the Binomial distribution $\mu = n \times P$
and the standard deviation $\sigma = \sqrt{[nP(1-P)]}$

(ii)   Use of the Binomial Distribution
Unless n and r are both quite small then working out values for probabilities becomes very tedious. Instead values are read off directly from statistical tables. All good sets of statistical tables carry Binomial distribution tables[2].

3.5.3   The Poisson Distribution

The Poisson distribution is an approximation of the Binomial distribution which is valid when we are considering *rare* events.

Consider a situation in which the number of trials (n) of the experiment is large, the probability of success (P) is small and the product $n \times P = \lambda$ remains fixed at some intermediate value. Then it can be shown that the Binomial distribution approximates to:

$$f(r) = \frac{e^{-\lambda}\lambda^r}{r!} .$$

The following are examples of situations where the Poisson distribution may be applicable:

(1)   The number of customers arriving at a petrol station in a minute.
(2)   The number of atoms of a given quantity of radioactive material that decays in unit time.
(3)   The number of failures in a year of a widely used contraceptive device.

One great advantage of the Poisson distribution is that in many situations it may be impossible to determine n and P although λ may be known. For example, supposing it has been found that the average number of road deaths in a particular region is 3.8 per month. Now, we do not know the number of monthly journeys nor do we know the probability of a death occurring on any single journey. We do, however, know λ and hence are in a position to work out the probability of a given number of deaths occurring in a particular month.

Example

Supposing we are interested in calculating the probability that there will be exactly two deaths in a given month.

Since $f(r) = \dfrac{e^{-\lambda}\lambda^r}{r!}$ in this case $\lambda = 3.8$ and $r = 2$,

hence $f(2) = e^{-3.8}\dfrac{(3.8)^2}{2!} = 0.1615.$

Exercise 3.8

What is the probability that there will be at least one death during any given month?

Properties of the Poisson distribution
Mean of the Poisson distribution $= \lambda$ and standard deviation $= \sqrt{\lambda}$

3.5.4   Continuous Distributions

There are many situations where the random variable in question can possess an infinite number of values within a given range rather than a series of discrete values. Such distributions are called *continuous* distributions. Examples of continuous distributions are the heights of a large population and the weights of ball bearings produced by a given process. Because there are an infinite number of possible values it is futile to attempt to attach a probability to any specific value. (For example, no one will have a height of exactly 6 ft if measurements are made accurately enough and to a sufficient number of decimal places). Instead we can make statements related to the probability of a given random variable falling into a particular interval. For example, we can sensibly discuss the probability of an individual having a height between 5 ft 11 in. and 6 ft.

Thus, given a continuous probability distribution f(x) as in Figure 3.13, we can reason as follows.

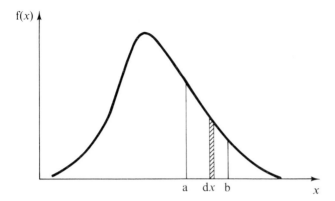

Figure 3.13

If we take a point x then the probability that a random variable has a value between x and $x + dx$ will simply be given by f(x)dx. Now this is the area of the thin strip which is shaded in the diagram. We can extend this line of reasoning to show that the probability of the random variable having a value between a and b is simply the area under the curve between a and b. Obviously, the total area under the curve (representing the certainty that the random variable must take one of its possible values) must equal one.

3.5.5 The Normal Distribution

The most important continuous probability distribution is the normal distribution. This distribution is often found in many practical situations (e.g. weights of chocolate bars from a properly adjusted machine, heights of adults in a large population, marks obtained by students in examinations, experimental errors).

This distribution is characterized by its bell-shaped curve and is symmetric with coincident mean, median and mode.

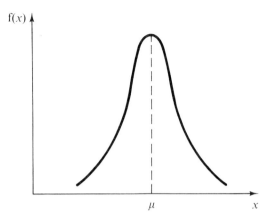

Figure 3.14

Normal distributions are completely determined by the specification of two parameters; mean (μ) and standard deviation (σ).

Incidentally, the probability distribution for the normal distribution is given by:

$$f(x) = \frac{1}{\sqrt{2\pi}} \exp{-\tfrac{1}{2}\left(\frac{x-\mu}{\sigma}\right)^2}$$

This is a somewhat complicated function but we shall not need to directly employ this expression to make use of the normal distribution. Thus for every different combination of μ and σ values we have a different distribution which would appear to limit the convenience with which we can use this distribution since it would be quite impractical to construct separate tables for each different combination of μ, σ values. Figure 3.15 shows the normal distribution for $\mu = 50$ and for different values of σ.

It is possible to transform all distributions to a standard one with mean 0 and standard deviation 1 by using the transformation $Z = \frac{x-\mu}{\sigma}$ (This transformed distribution then becomes $f(Z) = \frac{1}{\sqrt{2\pi}} \exp{\frac{-Z^2}{2}}$).

Using this transformation we can relate any point on a normal distribution to a corresponding point on the standard normal

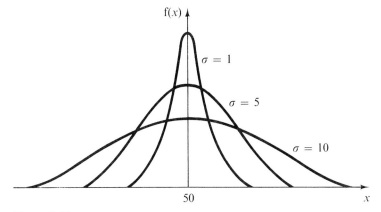

Figure 3.15

curve. It is this standard normal curve which is given in statistical tables.

These tables can be used as follows. Suppose we have a normal distribution with mean $\mu = 10$ and standard deviation $\sigma = 5$ and we wish to determine the probability of obtaining a value between 12 and 15. This probability is presented by the shaded area in the diagram (Figure 3.16). To do this we transform values on this

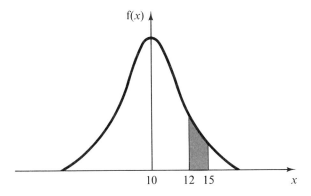

Figure 3.16

distribution to corresponding values on the standard normal distribution. Remember $Z(12) = (12 - 10)/5 = 0.40$. Looking this value up in our standard tables: (Figure 3.17).

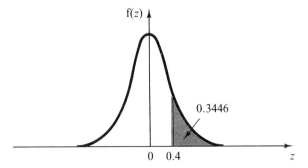

Figure 3.17

Tables show us that the probability of Z being greater than 0.4 equals 0.3446.

The value 15 corresponds to $Z(15) = (15-10)/5 = 1$ on the standard distribution.

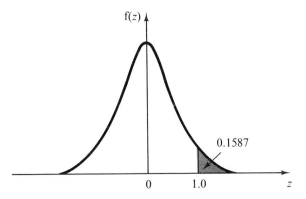

Figure 3.18

Tables show that the probability of Z being greater than $1.0 = 0.1587$ (see Figure 3.18). Hence the probability of Z being between 0.4 and $1.0 = 0.3446 - 0.1587 = 0.1859$.

Example

A machine produces chocolate bars; the weights of these chocolate bars are found to be normally distributed with mean weight of

120.0 g and standard deviation 0.4 g.

What proportion of chocolate bars might we expect to have weights between 119.5 g and 120.5 g?

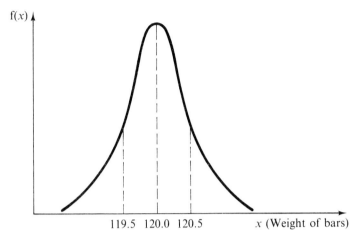

Figure 3.19

Making the transformation to the standard normal curve,

$$Z(120.5) = \frac{120.5 - 120.0}{0.4} = 1.25$$

From tables $P(Z > 1.25) = 0.1056$

Hence the proportion of bars with weights greater than 120.5 g = 0.1056

By symmetry, the proportion of bars with weights less than 119.5 g = 0.1056

Hence the proportion outside range 119.5—120.5 grams = 0.2112

∴ Proportion within range = $1 - 0.2112 =$ 0.7888

Exercise 3.9

The company risks being fined if a Weights and Measures Inspector finds chocolate bars of weight less than 119.0 grams. If a production run of 1000 bars with the machine adjusted as above is carried out, how many bars of weight less than 119.0 grams would we expect to produce?

3.6   Exercises in Probability Distributions

Exercise 3.10

If sixty per cent of the students in a particular college are male what is the probability that if five students are chosen at random more than three will be male?

Exercise 3.11

A maker of electrical resistors tests them for quality in the following way. Five resistors are chosen from the batch. If more than one of them is found to be defective then the entire batch is scrapped; otherwise the batch is accepted. What is the probability that the batch will pass the test:
(a) If the batch contains 10% defective resistors;
(b) 20% defective resistors; (c) 50% defectives?

Exercise 3.12

An average of three people are admitted to the Casualty Department of a large hospital during each weekend. If only five beds are provided for such cases, how often will it be necessary to divert patients to an alternative hospital?

Exercise 3.13

Electrical resistors with resistances between 140 and 160 Ω are required for a particular piece of electrical machinery. If resistors are supplied whose resistances are normally distributed with a mean of 148 Ω and standard deviation 6 Ω what proportion of these resistors would be expected to be unsuitable for this purpose?

Exercise 3.14 (more difficult)

A liquid is known to contain bacteria with a mean number of bacteria per cm^3 equal to 3. Ten one-cm^3 test tubes are filled with the liquid. Assuming the Poisson distribution is applicable to the number of bacteria found in each cm^3 calculate the probability:

(a) that all ten test tubes will show growth (i.e. contain at least one bacterium each).
(b) Exactly seven test tubes will show growth.

Exercise 3.15

The machine for producing resistors referred to in Exercise 3.13 can be adjusted to produce resistors of any mean value between 100 and 200 Ω. The resistance, however, will still be normally distributed and standard deviation remains at 6 Ω. If it is desired that exactly 5% of resistors should be produced with resistance greater than 150 Ω; at what mean value of resistance should the process be set?

3.7 The Exponential Distribution

This is a distribution which has many important applications particularly in the fields of queueing and replacement. For instance the duration of telephone calls and the times between breakdowns of a piece of equipment have shown often to follow an exponential distribution.

The exponential distribution is given by

$$f(t) = \lambda e^{-\lambda t}, (t > 0).$$

The mean of the distribution $= \dfrac{1}{\lambda}$.

For example suppose that breakdowns of a piece of equipment are exponentially distributed with a mean time between breakdowns of 2 hours

Since $\lambda = \dfrac{1}{mean} = \frac{1}{2}$

$\therefore f(t) = \frac{1}{2}e^{-\frac{1}{2}t}$

3.8 Use of Probability Distributions

The probability distributions described in this chapter can be considered as models of particular statistical processes. Each is based on certain basic assumptions (e.g. binomial distribution — events must be independent, Poisson distribution — events must be rare etc.). Thus it will be quite apparent that the validity of using a given distribution in a particular instance will depend on how well these basic criteria are met.

4

Statistical Methods II

4.1 Sampling

4.1.1 Introduction

In many situations where we analyse statistical information we consider only a selection of all the observations which could possibly be taken. This procedure is called *sampling*.

A *population* is defined as the totality of all observations of a statistical quantity that could possibly be made. A population may be finite (e.g. voting intentions of electors in a particular constituency, effectiveness of a given batch of components) or infinite (e.g. readings of air temperature in a particular area).

A *sample* is that part of the population which is observed. Sample information is useful because we can use the information gained from the sample to draw valid conclusions about the population which we are considering. Obviously, we use samples because it requires much less effort and expense to analyse part of the population rather than all of it. In situations where the population is infinite it would, in any case, be impossible to test the entire population. There are other situations such as testing whether a given batch of bombs are working effectively or testing to destruction particular components where inspection of the whole population would be self-defeating.

We generally use samples when carrying out quality control tests on electronic components. From tests upon part of the output we make conclusions about the quality of the entire output.

Again, if we are intending to market a new product, any market survey which we are likely to carry out will cover only a part (i.e. a sample) of the potential population of users.

Naturally, we pay a price for making conclusions about populations based on sample information only. This is because we now base our conclusions on only *part* of the available information and it is possible that we make incorrect deductions about the population on this basis. This is a topic which we shall expand on in later sections.

4.1.2 Random Samples

It is important to realize that if we are to make valid deductions about our population based on sample information then the sample should, as fairly as possible, represent the population being considered. The type of sample which most fulfils this requirement is a *random sample*. A sample of size *n* which is drawn from a particular population is said to be random if it was obtained by a procedure which gave every other possible combination of *n* items the same probability of being drawn. This is the type of sample obtained if the names of everyone in a room are put into a hat, the hat is thoroughly shaken and say, five names are drawn out. A sample that is not random may be *biased*; conclusions about particular populations based on biased samples may be particularly hazardous. In any case, there are no statistical methods available to analyse non-random samples.

One of the most celebrated cases of erroneous conclusions being drawn from biased samples concerns the 1936 U.S. Presidential election. A magazine called the Literary Digest conducted an opinion poll of voters' intentions for the forthcoming election. The method adopted was to select voters randomly from the telephone directory and then question them over the telephone. This opinion poll predicted a Republican landslide. (Republicans 60% of the votes, Democrats 40%). In the event, there was a landslide to the Democratic Party with their candidate obtaining 60% of votes cast against the Republican Party candidate's 40%. Although a very large sample (2 million voters) was taken erroneous predictions were made because the sample was biased. In 1936, a much higher proportion of Republican voters owned telephones than Democratic voters. Thus, any sample based on the use of telephone directories was bound to contain a built-in bias towards the Republican Party.

Another, possibly apocryphal, story of a biased sampling procedure was that used by an opinion pollster who conducted a survey of attitudes towards gambling in a station where a number of special trains were waiting to leave for Ascot Races.

Even if a sample is random, however, it is still possible that misleading conclusions may be made about the population simply because chance statistical fluctuations have made the sample unrepresentative. For example, 20% of a given batch of 1000 electrical resistors may be defective. If we examine a sample of ten resistors from this batch, however, it is quite possible (though not likely) that all will be effective. This is a topic which we shall consider further.

4.1.3 Symbolism for Populations and Samples

The symbols used to denote the different characteristics of populations and samples have been established by convention. Population mean and standard deviation are designated by μ and σ respectively and are called *parameters*; sample mean and standard deviation are designated by $\bar{x}$ and s and called *statistics*. The symbol n is used to denote the number of items in a sample.

4.1.4 Sampling Distributions: The Central Limit Theorem

The ideas introduced in this section are crucially important and it is essential that their implications should be fully grasped. They enable us to draw valid statistical conclusions about population parameters based on sample information.

Suppose we take a random sample of, say, forty chocolate bars from a large batch produced by a particular machine. Then let us proceed to find the mean weight of the bars in this sample of forty. (Call this mean weight $\bar{x}_1$). Then suppose we take a second sample of forty bars and again determine the mean weight, $\bar{x}_2$. We can continue this process taking a third, fourth, fifth, etc. sample of 40 and obtaining values, $\bar{x}_3$, $\bar{x}_4$, $\bar{x}_5$, etc. for the mean weights of the respective samples. If we continue further with this process of repeated sampling we can theoretically conceive of obtaining a distribution of mean weights for every sample of 40 bars that could be taken. This distribution is called the sampling distribution. The distribution will have its own mean $\mu_{\bar{x}}$ and own standard deviation $\sigma_{\bar{x}}$.

Now suppose the original probability distribution of weights of individual bars (*x*) produced by the machine is non-normal and has mean μ and standard deviation σ (see Figure 4.1).

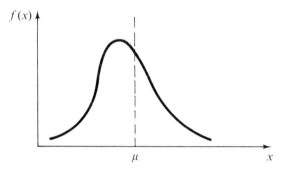

Figure 4.1   Probability distribution of weights of individual bars

Then the Central Limit Theorem states that whatever the initial probability distribution of weights of the bars, the distribution of the sample means approximates to a *normal* distribution with mean $\mu_{\bar{x}} = \mu$ (i.e. the mean of the original distribution) and with standard deviation $\sigma_{\bar{x}} = \sigma/\sqrt{n}$ (where *n* is the sample size).

This approximation becomes increasingly good as the sample size *n* increases. This is shown in Figure 4.2.

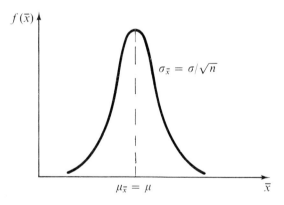

Figure 4.2   Probability distribution of mean weight of samples of bars

For convenience $\sigma_{\bar{x}} = \sigma/\sqrt{n}$, which is the standard deviation of the distribution of the sample means, is called the *standard error*. The value of the standard error is therefore considerably smaller than the standard deviation of the original distribution. This is, however, intuitively plausible since within a sample it is likely that very high values would be averaged down and very low values averaged up. Hence, it is entirely reasonable to expect less spread amongst the sample means than between the individual items in the original distribution.

The importance of the above result is that it enables us to use sample statistics to make valid inferences about population parameters without knowing anything about the shape of the probability distribution of the population.

4.1.5 Examples of the Use of the Central Limit Theorem

Suppose the probability distribution of wages in a country is asymmetric with a mean of £2000 and standard deviation £600 (see Figure 4.3).

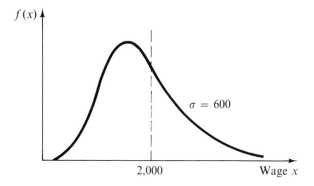

Figure 4.3   Probability distribution of wages

If random samples of 25 people are chosen and the average wage $\bar{x}$ calculated, for each sample, then it will be found that the sample mean will be approximately normally distributed with a mean of 2000 and standard error $= \dfrac{600}{\sqrt{25}} = 120$ (Figure 4.4).

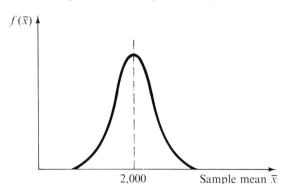

Figure 4.4   Probability distribution of sample mean

It is possible to calculate the probability that a sample mean wage greater than £2100 is observed.

$$Z\ (2100) \ = \ \frac{2100\ -\ 2000}{\dfrac{600}{\sqrt{25}}} \ = \ \frac{100}{120} \ = \ 0.833$$

From tables $P\ (Z\ >0.833)\ =\ 0.202$

The importance of this result is that, had we not known the initial probability distribution of wages, we could have made statistical deductions from our sample information by means of the central limit theorem.

Exercise 4.1

The weights of chocolate bars produced by a particular production process possess a non-standard probability distribution with mean 140 g and a standard deviation of 24 g.

A sample of 20 bars is withdrawn from a particular batch by the Weights and Measures Inspector. The company face prosecution if the mean weight of the sample should turn out to be less than 134 g. What is the probability of this occurring? Suppose it is possible to adjust the mean weight of bar produced by the process without affecting the standard deviation. If it is wished to reduce the risk of prosecution to 0.01 where should the mean be placed?

4.2 Estimation

Managers will, from time to time, need to make estimates of population parameters based only on sample information. For instance, it may be necessary to estimate the likely mean sales of a particular line based on sample information from a test marketing exercise.

Suppose we have carried out an experiment on 25 light bulbs and we find that the mean lifetime $\bar{x}$ = 300 hours. On the basis of this sample information, what can we say about the mean lifetime of the population of bulbs from which this sample was taken? If we were simply going to make a single figure estimate we could take the value of this sample mean (i.e. 300) as the best estimate of the population mean available. This is called a *point estimate.*

This estimate, however, gives no feel for the degree of precision with which we are making the statement. (Is there, for instance, a significant chance the population mean could differ widely from 300 or is it likely that it will turn out in any event to be fairly close to 300?) We can do this by providing an *interval estimate* which gives the probability that a parameter will fall in a particular interval.

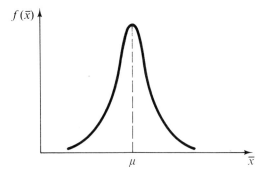

Figure 4.5

Now from the Central Limit Theorem, the sample $\bar{x}$ was obtained from a normal distribution with mean μ and standard error $\sigma/\sqrt{n}$. (Fig. 4.5)

From our normal tables we know that 95% of the normal curve is within 1.96 standard deviation of the mean. Hence, 95% of the time a sample mean $\bar{x}$ will be within $1.96\ \sigma/\sqrt{n}$ of μ. It follows logically, therefore, that 95% of the time that μ will be within $1.96\ \sigma/\sqrt{n}$ of $\bar{x}$. Hence there is a 95% probability that μ is between $\bar{x}\ -\ 1.96\ \sigma/\sqrt{n}$ and $\bar{x}\ +\ 1.96\ \sigma/\sqrt{n}$.

This is called the 95% *confidence interval*.

Now if we know from experience that the standard deviation for the type of light bulbs that we are investigating is 25 hours, then our 95% confidence interval becomes

$$300\ -\ 1.96\ \times\ \frac{25}{\sqrt{25}}\ \text{to}\ 300\ +\ 1.96\ \times\ \frac{25}{\sqrt{25}}$$

i.e. 290.2 to 309.8.

This means that we are 95% certain that the population mean has a value between 290.2 and 309.8. If the population standard deviation is unknown we can use the sample standard deviation as an estimate providing the sample is large (i.e. above about 30).

Exercise 4.2

Calculate (i) the 90% confidence interval (ii) the 99% confidence interval for the above example.

Exercise 4.3

A random sample of 100 components was taken from the output of a machine for producing electrical resistors. The mean resistance of the sample was 22.0 Ω with standard deviation 2.0 Ω.

Construct the 95% confidence interval for the mean resistance of the entire batch.

4.3　Testing Statistical Hypotheses

4.3.1　Introduction

It is important in statistics to be able to draw conclusions from statistical information. This procedure is called *hypothesis testing*. For example, supposing a drug company intend to promote a new drug. Results of initial trials tend to show improved results from use of the drug. It is possible, however, that results observed in the tests have occurred by statistical chance and not because the new drug is actually any improvement. Before the drug company goes to the expense of building plant for the new drug and promoting it, it would like to have a fair degree of certainty that the new drug really is an improvement. The procedure used to do this sometimes causes the beginner some conceptual difficulties. Basically, the way we attempt to proceed is to make conservative assumptions then see if enough statistical evidence exists to disprove them. This conservative assumption usually involves accepting the *status quo* — in the drug company it would involve assuming no difference in effectiveness between the two drugs. This is called the *null hypothesis* (H_o). The *alternative hypothesis* (H_1) is accepted once the null hypothesis is thoroughly discredited. In the case of the drug company, the alternative hypothesis corresponds to the new drug being conclusively superior to the existing drug.

We can use as an analogy the system of criminal justice in England. Under this system an accused person is assumed innocent until proven guilty. Thus the null hypothesis (H_o) is that the accused person is innocent. Until this hypothesis is conclusively rejected we cannot accept the alternative that the accused is guilty (H_1).

Note, however, that although a not guilty verdict may be brought (i.e. H_o is accepted) it does not mean that we are convinced that the accused is actually innocent. It may simply mean that there is not enough evidence to reject the hypothesis of his innocence *beyond all reasonable doubt*.

4.3.2 Type I and Type II Errors

Decision	H_o Correct	H_1 Correct
Accept H_o	Correct decision	Type II error
Reject H_o	Type I error	Correct decision

As a result of making a statistical test of a hypothesis it is possible to make two incorrect decisions.

(i) Rejecting the null hypothesis when it is in fact true (called type I error). In the case of the drug company, this corresponds to concluding that the new drug is significantly better than the old one when in reality there is no difference between them. In the legal analogy, it corresponds to finding an innocent man guilty. (The probability of a type I error is usually designated as α).

(ii) Accepting the null hypothesis when, in fact, it is false. In the drug company example, this corresponds to concluding that no significant difference exists between the two drugs when, in fact, such a difference does exist. In the legal situation, this corresponds to failing to convict a guilty man. (The probability of a type II error is usually designated as β).

Now for a specific test it is impossible to reduce the size of a type I error without increasing the probability of a type II error and vice versa. Thus, if we decide to relax the rules of evidence to make it less likely that a guilty person can be acquitted it is inevitable that we increase the risk of convicting an innocent person.

Exercise 4.4

In the legal example which of the two types of error is more likely? Explain why this should be so.

4.3.3   Significance Level of Statistical Tests

A machine for producing capacitors was specified to produce capacitors with mean capacitance 500 μF and standard deviation of 81 μF. It is suspected that the mean capacitance produced by this machine has now significantly changed. A sample of 250 capacitors is selected and their capacitance measured.

Now if we set up our null and alternative hypothesis:

Null hypothesis H_0 :   Mean capacitance produced by
                                      machine is unchanged ($\mu = 500 \ \mu$F)

Alternative   Mean capacitance produced is
hypothesis H_1 :   significantly different

Supposing the test adopted is that H_0 should be rejected (and consequently H_1 accepted) if the mean capacitance falls outside the range 488—512 μF. The range for rejection of the null hypothesis is called the *critical region*.

(i)   Type I error
Now if we wish to calculate the probability of a type I error for this

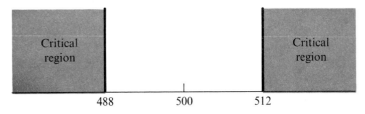

Figure 4.6

test we need to calculate the probability of getting a sample mean either ≤ 488 or ≥ 512. Now, assuming H_o is true (i.e. mean capacitance $= 500\,\mu F$), then according to the central limit theorem the probability distribution for the sample mean will be normal with mean 500 and standard error

$$= \frac{81}{\sqrt{250}} = 5.12.$$

We have obtained just *one* observation from the distribution and we are interested in the probability that this observation came from the parts of the distribution within the critical region.

Since we have a normal curve:

$$Z(512) = \frac{512 - 500}{5.12} = 2.34.$$

$$Z(488) = \frac{488 - 500}{5.12} = -2.34.$$

From normal tables, the probability $(Z \geq 2.34) = 0.0096$.
By symmetry, the probability $(Z \leq -2.34) = 0.0096$.
Probability of committing a type I error $= 2 \times 0.0096 = 0.0192$.

When the statistical experiment results in a sample value falling in the critical region and consequently, rejection of the null hypothesis takes place, the result is said to be *significant*. The probability of committing a type I error is the *significance* level of the test. Obviously, the smaller the probability of a type I error (i.e. the smaller the probability of incorrectly rejecting our null hypothesis) the greater the degree of confidence that we can have in our result. In other words we are considerably more confident of a result which we have proved at the 1% significance level than one proved at only the 5% significance level.

It is not possible to lay down hard and fast rules about which significance level should be adopted. This will depend on the individual case and the seriousness with which we view the rejection of a true null hypothesis.

(ii)   Type II error

Unlike the case of the type I error there is no single value of type II error for a given test. A type II error in this example corresponds to failure of the test to conclude that the mean capacitance of capacitors produced by the process has actually changed. Clearly, if there is a major change in mean the probability of a type II error occurring will be less than if a small change in mean has occurred.

Suppose for example the mean capacitance of the capacitors has changed to 520 μF.

Then assuming the standard deviation is unchanged the distribution of sample means is as shown in Figure 4.7.

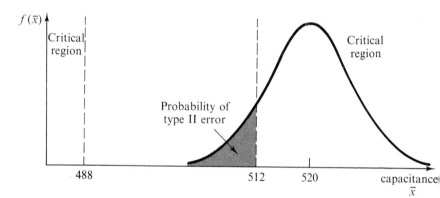

Figure 4.7

$$Z(488) = \frac{488 - 520}{5.12} = -6.25$$

This corresponds to a negligible proportion of the distribution falling in the region $Z \leq -6.25$

$$Z(512) = \frac{512 - 520}{5.12} = -1.56.$$

From normal tables $P (Z \leq -1.56) = 0.059$.

Thus, this corresponds to probability of 5.9% for a type II error.

Suppose the mean of the process has a much smaller change (say $= 504$) then we have the following distribution of sample means (Figure 4.8).

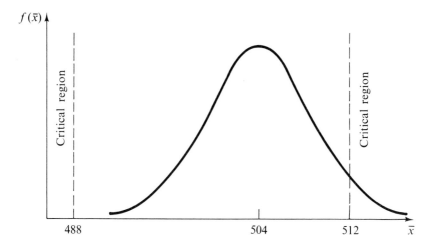

Figure 4.8

Working as before $Z (488) = \dfrac{488 - 504}{5.12} = -3.13 \; P(Z \leq -3.13)$ is negligible

$$Z(512) = \frac{512 - 504}{5.12} = \frac{8}{5.12} = 1.56.$$

From normal tables $P(Z \geq 1.56) = 0.59$.

Hence, there is only a probability of 0.059 that the sample mean falls in the critical region. Probability of a type II error $= 0.941$ or 94.1%.

Thus the probability of a type II error depends on the change that has taken place. This is quite sensible; we would expect our test to identify that a major change has taken place with more certainty than a minor change. Practically, it is more important that major changes should be recognized by the test.

The *power* of the tests correspond to the probability of correctly rejecting the null hypothesis for different values of population

mean μ (i.e. $1 -$ type II error).
Thus for $\mu = 520$ Power of test $= 0.941$,
$\qquad \mu = 504$ Power of test $= 0.059$.

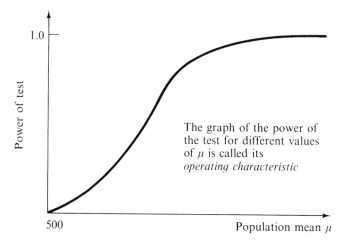

The graph of the power of the test for different values of μ is called its *operating characteristic*

Figure 4.9

Exercise 4.5

A manufacturer of torches is testing to see if the average life of torches that he is producing is above or below the standard of 2,000 hours. In order to check this out the manufacturer proposed to take a sample of 200 torches and determine the mean lifetime of each torch in the sample. He plans to use a 1% significance level. It is known from experience that standard deviation of this type of torch is likely to be 500 hours.
(a) What are the null and alternative hypotheses for this test?
(b) What is the probability of a type I error for this test? What does this mean?
(c) Where should the critical region be constituted?
(d) Suppose the mean life of the torches in fact differs from the standard by 200 hours, what is the probability that this will be detected?

Exercise 4.6

An electrical manufacturer produces microcircuits in batches of 1,000 and guarantees to customers that not more than 20% of any batch should be defective. Should a customer discover a batch containing more than 20% defective then he has the right to return the batch and ask for (an expensive) special delivery.

The microcircuits are tested for quality in the following manner; a random sample of five microcircuits is taken from each batch and tested for quality. If more than one defective microcircuit is found in the sample then the entire batch is destroyed. Otherwise it is sent off to a customer.

Which null and alternative hypothesis do you consider that the above statistical test investigates? Discuss what are the type I and type II errors for the above test and derive general mathematical expressions for them. From the manufacturer's point of view what cost does the commission of each of these types of error involve?

4.3.4 Testing Sample Means

As seen in the foregoing section we often wish to test out an hypothesis regarding a population mean based on sample information.

Consider a company that have been using an electric motor in their washing machines over a number of years supplied by manufacturer A. They have used these components so long that the population parameters of the motors' lifetime, mean μA (1,180 h) and standard deviation $\sigma A(90)$ can be considered to be known.

The company are then offered an alternative motor by manufacturer B. These motors are considerably cheaper than those offered by A and it is claimed that mean lifetimes are the same. The company, however, decide not to switch to motor B until they are certain that this type of motor does not have a shorter mean life than A.

Tests on 100 motors of type B yield the result $\bar{x}_B = 1,140$ h and $s_B = 80$. Now if we set up the null hypothesis corresponding to no significant difference in lifetimes between motors A and B, then the null hypothesis H_1 is represented by $\mu_B = 1,180$ and the alternative hypothesis H_1 by $\mu_B \leq 1,180$. We do not know σ_B the population standard deviation of type B. Since we have a large sample, however, it is permissible to use s_B the standard deviation of the sample as an estimate for σ_B.

Using the central limit theorem and assuming H_0 is true we have observed one value from a normal distribution of sample means with mean 1,180 and standard error $80/\sqrt{100}$. In this situation we are only concerned with the possibility that the lifetime of B is *shorter* than that of A. Hence there will only be one critical region for the test and thus this test is known as a *one-tail* test.

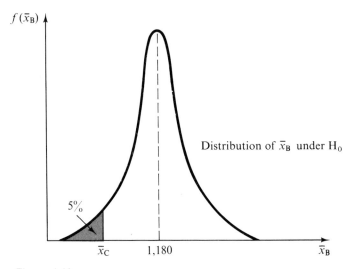

Figure 4.10

The location of the critical region for the test will depend on the choice of significance level adopted. The choice of significance level is always a subjective decision and will depend on the seriousness of making a type I error. Supposing we decide on a 5% significance level (i.e. decide to accept a 5% chance of a type I error).

Now 5% of normal curve is less than $Z = -1.64$.

∴ If $\bar{x}_C$ indicates the beginning of the critical region,

$$-1.64 = \frac{\bar{x}_C - 1,180}{8}$$

$$\therefore \bar{x}_C = 1,167$$

In other words if the null hypothesis was true there would only be a 5% chance of observing a value less than 1,167. Hence, at 5% significance level, we can conclude that the motor B definitely has a shorter lifetime than motor A.

4.3.5 Testing Differences between Two Sample Means

A different situation occurs when we have to decide whether observed differences between two sample means indicate that they could have been drawn from populations with the same mean or whether the difference is so great that this is an indication that both samples have come from populations with unequal means.

Now suppose we take a random sample from the distribution of population I, and let the value of the sample mean be $\bar{x}_1$. Let us take a further random sample from the *output* of population 2, and let the sample mean obtained be $\bar{x}_2$.

When considering the value of $\bar{x}_1 - \bar{x}_2$ we are interested in finding out whether this value is great enough to justify the conclusion that the samples were drawn from populations with different means.

Now it can be shown that if sample sizes are n_1 and n_2 and the population means of the original distribution μ_1 and μ_2 then, providing the samples are large, the statistic $\bar{x}_1 - \bar{x}_2$ will be normally distributed with mean $\mu_1 - \mu_2$ and standard deviation

$$\sigma_{\bar{x}_1 - \bar{x}_2} = \sqrt{\left(\frac{\sigma_1^2}{n_1} + \frac{\sigma_2^2}{n_2}\right)}^* \quad \begin{array}{l} (\sigma_1, \sigma_2 \text{ are standard deviations of} \\ \text{populations I and 2).} \end{array}$$

Now if the original populations have identical means (i.e. $\mu_1 = \mu_2$) then the distribution $\bar{x}_1 - \bar{x}_2$ will have zero mean.

Supposing the company in the previous example had no experience with any brand of motor and wished to establish whether significant differences existed between any brands before deciding which type to purchase. Supposing samples of 100 were taken from those supplied by manufacturers of type Y and type W and that the following results were obtained.

* This is called the standard error of the difference between the two means.

$$\bar{x}_Y = 1160\ h \qquad\qquad \bar{x}_W = 1140\ h$$
$$s_Y = 90\ h \qquad\qquad s_W = 80\ h$$

Now, if we make the null hypothesis the assumption that no difference exists between brand Y and W then we have

$$H_0 : \mu_Y - \mu_W = 0.$$
$$H_1 : \mu_Y - \mu_W = 0.$$

Now the standard error of the difference between means

$$\sigma_{\bar{Y} - \bar{W}} = \sqrt{\left(\frac{\sigma_Y{}^2}{n_Y} + \frac{\sigma_W{}^2}{n_W}\right)}.$$

Since we have large samples we can take sample standard deviations s_Y and s_W as estimates of population standard deviation σ_Y and σ_W

Thus, $\sigma_{\bar{Y} - \bar{W}} = \sqrt{\left(\dfrac{(90)^2}{100} + \dfrac{(80)^2}{100}\right)} = 12.04.$

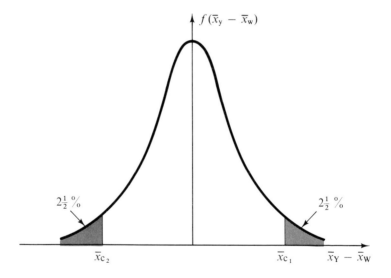

Figure 4.11

Thus if the null hypothesis is valid, the difference in sample means $\bar{x}_Y - \bar{x}_W$ is normally distributed with mean zero and standard error $= 12.04$.

This time we are interested in whether *either* brand of motor has a longer life. Thus, this time there will be two critical regions, and this is called a *two-tail* test.

If we choose a 5% significance level for our test we know there is a probability of 0.025 that standard normal variate $Z \geq 196$; similarly there is a probability of 0.025 that standard normal variate $Z \leq -1.96$.

$$1.96 = \frac{\bar{x}_{C_1} - 0}{12.04} \text{ , where } \bar{x}_{C_1} \text{ is boundary of r.h.s. critical region.}$$

$$\therefore \bar{x}_{C_1} = 23.6$$

$$-1.96 = \frac{\bar{x}_{C_2} - 0}{12.04} \text{ , where } \bar{x}_{C_2} \text{ is boundary of l.h.s. critical region.}$$

$$\bar{x}_{C_2} = -23.6 \text{ (approx.)}$$

Since observed difference $+20$ does not lie inside critical region we can accept the null hypothesis. In other words this experiment has provided insufficient evidence for concluding that a significant difference in lifetimes exists between brands W and Y.

Exercise 4.7

Two research laboratories have independently produced drugs for treating a certain degenerative disease. The first drug was tested on a group of 80 randomly selected sufferers of the disease. This group had an average remission of 5.4 months with standard deviation 1.2 months.

The second drug was tested on a similar group of 60 randomly selected patients. This group had average remission of 6.2 months with standard deviation 1.5 months.

Has this test shown that the second drug provides a significantly longer period of remission?

4.4 The Chi-Squared Distribution

Many statistical experiments involve a number of possible outcomes. Often we are interested in whether the frequency that certain outcomes occurred over a number of trials is consistent with a particular hypothesis. For example, if we were involved in a game of dice we might well be concerned as to whether the number of times that each face of the die is observed is consistent with the hypothesis that the die is fair!

Let's take a specific example; a die is rolled 60 times in a gaming club and the following results were obtained:

Face	1	2	3	4	5	6	Total
No. of observations	14	8	4	11	6	17	60

Are these results consistent with the die being fair or have we grounds to suspect that the die might be loaded in some way? In this type of situation the χ^2 *statistic* is very useful. This statistic is defined as:

$$\chi^2 = \sum_{\substack{\text{all} \\ \text{possible} \\ \text{outcomes}}} \frac{(\text{observed frequency} - \text{expected frequency})^2}{\text{expected frequency}}$$

Clearly, the poorer the agreement between observed and expected values then the less likely it is that the hypothesis used to calculate the expected values is true. This in turn corresponds to a high value of the χ^2 statistic.

Even if H_o should be true, however, we would expect to obtain a non-zero value of χ^2. After all we would expect some divergence from expected values purely as a result of chance fluctuations. Even if the die was fair we would not expect each face to show *exactly* ten times out of the sixty experiments.

In addition, we might reasonably expect that the larger the number of possible outcomes the larger the chance of obtaining spuriously high χ^2 values. In fact, the number of possible outcomes (minus one) is defined as the *number of degrees of freedom for the experiment*.

For instance, in the case of the dice game the number of degrees of freedom equals the number of possible outcomes (six) minus one (i.e. five).

Statistical methods have been developed which can be used to calculate the likely distribution of χ^2 given that the observed values are consistent with the hypothesis from which the expected values have been calculated. Different distributions are obtained depending on the number of degrees of freedom considered.

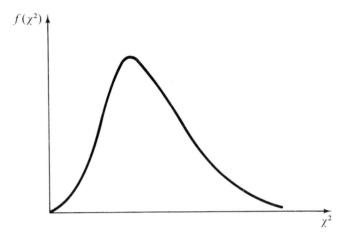

Figure 4.12

It can be seen from the shape of this curve that there is only a small chance of obtaining a large value of χ^2 if the null hypothesis is valid. We can use the above distributions to set appropriate significance levels to our statistical tests and this procedure will be described for our example.

For the earlier example:

H_o : Die is fair,
H_1 : Die is biased.

If H_o is true then each face of the dice might be expected to occur ten times.

Face	1	2	3	4	5	6	Total
Observed Frequency	14	8	4	11	6	17	60
Expected	10	10	10	10	10	10	60

$$\chi^2 = \sum_{i=1}^{6} \frac{(O_i - E_i)^2}{E_i},$$

where O_i and E_i are observed and expected frequency of each occurrence.

$$\text{Then } \chi^2 = \frac{(14-10)^2}{10} + \frac{(8-10)^2}{10} + \frac{(4-10)^2}{10} + \frac{(11-10)^2}{10}$$

$$+ \frac{(6-10)^2}{10} + \frac{(17-10)^2}{10}$$

$$= 1.6 + 0.4 + 3.6 + 0.1 + 1.6 + 4.9$$

$$= 12.2.$$

As previously mentioned, there are five possible degrees of freedom in this experiment. Suppose we decide that 5% is an appropriate significance level for this test. Turning to our tables we find that, if H_o is true, then there is only a 5% chance of obtaining a χ^2 value greater than 11.07. In other words, if the die really was fair in only five similar experiments out of 100 would we expect to

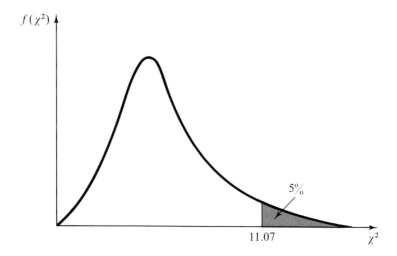

Figure 4.13

obtain a value greater than 11.07. Thus, we can reject the null hypothesis at the 5% significance level.

4.4.1 Limitations of χ^2 Test

The continuous curve given in the χ^2 tables is an approximation to the true discrete values of χ^2. Experience tells us that this approximation is generally satisfactory so long as the expected frequency of all observations is five or greater. Where this does not hold, observations can be combined with adjacent ones until this condition is satisfied.

4.4.2 χ^2 Test and Goodness of Fit of Curve

The χ^2 test can be used for the goodness of fit of curves. It may be used to test the adequacy of the fit of a given observed distribution to a standard statistical distribution or it might be used to test the adequacy of a particular empirical distribution. For example, it could be used to test whether observed data are consistent with a given empirically derived production function.

Example

A company which manufacturers tubes for television receivers conducted a test of a sample batch of 1,000 tubes and recorded the number of faults in each tube in the following way:

No. of faults per tube	0	1	2	3	4	5	6
Frequency of occurrence	620	260	88	20	8	2	2

The company are interested in discovering whether the distribution of the numbers of faults per tube can be described by a Poisson distribution (this would be consistent with the faults occurring randomly).

Let null hypothesis H_0 : Poisson distribution is applicable.
Let alternative hypothesis H_1: Poisson distribution is not applicable.

From the observed data mean $\mu = 0.55$
    i.e. Under H_o: $\mu = 0.55$.

We can now calculate the expected frequency of each number of faults/tube occurring under our null hypothesis:

No. of Faults	Observed Frequency	Expected Frequency under H_o	$\dfrac{(O_i - E_i)^2}{E_i}$
0	620	$1,000 \times e^{-0.55} = 577$	3.20
1	260	$1,000 \times 0.55 e^{-0.55} = 317$	10.25
2	88	$1,000 \times \tfrac{1}{2} \times (0.55)^2 e^{-0.55} = 87$	0.01
3	20	$1,000 \times 1/6 \times (0.55)^3 e^{-0.55} = 16$ ⎫*	8.90
4 or more	12	$1,000 -$ above $= 3$ ⎬	
Total	1000	1000	22.36

* Categories combined since expected number of observations in 4 or more category is less than 5.

Now when calculating the number of degrees of freedom appropriate to such cases we have to subtract the numbers of parameters of the distribution which have been estimated from the data. In this case, only one parameter (the mean) has been calculated from the data:

i.e. Number of degrees of freedom = Number of possible outcomes − Number of parameters calculated from data − 1

$$= 4 - 1 - 1 = 2.$$

If a 0.1% significance level is taken we find that χ^2 value for 2 degrees of freedom is 13.81. Hence, we may reject the hypothesis that this data is consistent with the Poisson distribution at a very high level of certainty.

Exercise 4.8

In an experiment on breeding flowers of a certain species, the following results are obtained:

120 magenta flowers with green stigma
48 magenta flowers with red stigma
36 red flowers with green stigma
13 red flowers with red stigma

Mendelian theory predicts that these flowers would occur in the ratio 9:3:3:1 respectively. Are these results consistent with the predictions of Mendelian theory?

Exercise 4.9

The following data represents an investigation of the distribution of the sexes of the children of 32 families of 4 children:

No. of sons	0	1	2	3	4
No. of families	4	9	8	8	3

Is this data consistent with the idea that male and female children are equally likely and produced randomly?

5

Forecasting

5.1 Introduction to Forecasting

A forecast is an estimate or prediction of the future. Most organizations require good forecasts if they are to make sensible decisions and plan effectively for the future, e.g.

> A firm which is considering the possible launching of a new product would need to have good forecasts of likely level of sales.
>
> The Government requires forecasts of birth rates when deciding on levels of provision of nursery school places, beds in maternity hospitals, etc.
>
> The Electricity Board will require forecasts of future electricity consumption when planning its programme of capital expenditure. Accurate forecasts of future copper prices are essential for appropriate planning in the electrical engineering industry.

One of the oldest known forecasting approaches was that of the Delphic oracle who combined subjective judgments with analysis based on the colour of birds' entrails! Although today we have much more sophisticated analytical methods, good forecasting on many occasions still requires the exercise of appropriate subjective judgement.

5.2 Requirements of a Forecast

5.2.1 Accuracy

Requirements for accuracy of a forecast will vary according to the decision for which the forecast is required. Decisions concerning a product which involves very heavy fixed costs and whose profits are concentrated in the last few per cent of sales would be examples of cases where very accurate forecasts would be required.

5.2.2 Time Horizon

The time horizon for the forecast will depend on the time period that the decision must be taken over. Such time periods might be

(a) *Immediate* (0—3 months) e.g. replenishment of stocks of a standard item.
(b) *Short-term* (1—6 months) e.g. purchase of fashion goods for retail outlets.
(c) *Medium-term* (3—24 months) e.g. leasing of plant and equipment.
(d) *Long-term* (2—10 years) corresponding to strategic decisions such as changing a product line or a major expansion.
(e) *Very long term* (10 years plus) corresponding perhaps to a major strategic decision such as merger or introducing completely new technology.

5.2.3 Speed and Regularity of Decisions

Some situations require quick decisions and it is important that the forecasting procedure should take account of this. It is obviously of little value to adopt a sophisticated forecasting procedure involving six months of data collection when a decision is required in two months.

5.2.4 Level of Detail

Again the forecast should provide appropriate detail for the decision which is to be taken. For instance, a clothing manufacturer making fashion goods for the spring sales will require forecasts of demand for each size of garment not just total aggregate sales.

5.3 Forecasting Techniques

Although there are many forecasting methods available, all fit into one of three broad categories.

5.3.1 Time Series Models

The basic idea of the time series model is that past trends should be identified and then extrapolated into the future. This method, of course, relies on the assumption that the general forecasting environment is reasonably stable, so that past movements provide a sensible guide as to future trends. The sort of situation where such a technique could be valuable might be where a short-term forecast of the sales of a well established product is being made. Such techniques are less applicable in the longer term during which a major socio-economic change may take place. The technique could also be invalid in the short-term if a major change in the commercial environment occurs (e.g. suppose market conditions for the product are changed by a heavy promotional campaign or a change in Government economic policy).

5.3.2 Causal Models

Instead of attempting to extrapolate past trends, this type of model attempts to relate the variable being forecast (dependent variable) to other variables with which it is associated (independent variables). If a reliable relationship is obtained and if it is possible to make accurate predictions of the independent variables then an accurate forecast of the dependent variable becomes possible. For example, it may be possible to relate sales of electricity to independent variables such a price of electricity, price of alternatives (e.g. gas), GNP, sales of electrical appliances and so on.

The relationships between these variables are quantified using past data and it is possible to apply various tests to assess how well the model fits. If forecasts or assumptions about the independent variables can be made then the model may be used to obtain forecasts for the dependent variable.

This type of model can be useful in rather longer term situations than the time series model. Unlike the time series model, it may still be valid if there is a major change in the economic environment, e.g. supposing the market environment for a particular item was substantially altered by a heavy promotional campaign. So long as the relationship contained a term involving expenditure on promotion then such a model ought still to be valid.

The article reproduced at the end of this lesson provides a very good indication of the reliability of causal and time series models to forecasts of car ownership.

5.3.3 Qualitative Forecasts

In certain situations it may be necessary to attempt to make a forecast in the absence of any relevant qualitative data. For example, launching a completely new product or assessing the likely market penetration of a totally new production process are situations where hardly any relevant data may exist. Such forecasts have to be based on subjective assessments of the situation and usually involve the experts in a given area. Attempts have been made to systematize such forecasting methods, and techniques such as morphological analysis, delphi methods, scenario analysis, etc. have been developed. Space will not permit further discussion of these techniques here.[1]

5.4 Time Series Models

5.4.1 Approach

An initial approach involves examining the basic data in an attempt to recognize relevant trends or patterns. Examples of possible movements are presented below:

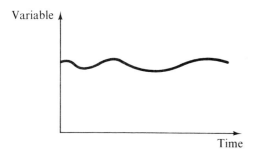

Figure 5.1

(a) This is a *horizontal* or *stationary* pattern. It seems that there are no underlying regular trends. The value of the variable comprises random fluctuations about a constant mean.

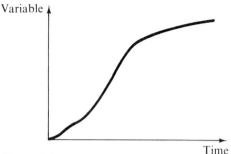

Figure 5.2

(b) In this situation we have a clear example of a non-linear *trend* over time. The sales of a new product, for example, could well follow such a pattern.

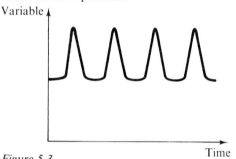

Figure 5.3

(c) In this example, the variable shows regular fluctuations over time. Such variations are called *seasonal* variations. If the variations, however, occur at intervals greater than one year such variations are then called *cyclic* variations.

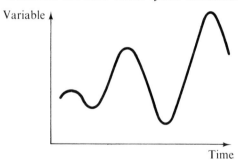

Figure 5.4

(d) This curve gives an example of a variable showing very strong and irregular fluctuations.

It is, of course, possible for a variable to show more than one of these sources of variation. For example, a variable may show trend, seasonal and cyclic variation simultaneously.

5.4.2 Simple Time Series Models

In this section we shall introduce two simple time series techniques, moving average and exponential smoothing.

(i) Moving average
A moving average forecast is based on the average of a number of historical data points. If there is a significant trend in the data this forecast will lag behind. By choosing an appropriate number of historical data points this method can eliminate the effect of the seasonal variation. For example, if quarterly data is available and we take four data points in our moving average, then the effect of seasonal variation should be eliminated.

More formally, if N is the number of time periods chosen and if F_{t+1} is the forecast for time period $t+1$ and V_t, V_{t-1}, V_{t-2} *are the value of the variables in time periods t, $t-1$, $t-2$ etc.;* then

$$F_{t+1} = \frac{V_t + V_{t-1} + V_{t-2} + \ldots + V_{t-N+1}}{N},$$

$$= \frac{1}{N} \sum_{i=t-N+1}^{t} V_i.$$

e.g. Supposing the sales of a particular product during the period January—April were 78, 70, 68 and 73. Then using a four month moving average the forecast for May is given by:

$$\frac{78 + 70 + 68 + 73}{4} = 72.$$

Now suppose the actual sales for May turn out to be 75 then the forecast for June becomes:

$$\frac{70 + 68 + 73 + 75}{4} = 72.$$

It should be noted that the larger the number of observations which are included in the moving average the greater the degree of smoothing that will be achieved. In addition, equal weighting is given to all N observations included in the forecast and all observations prior to time period $t - N + 1$ are ignored entirely.

(ii) Exponential smoothing
This technique involves the use of a *weighted* moving average, giving more weight to recent observations and correspondingly less weighting to earlier observations.
The forecast for period $t + 1$ is given by:

$$F_{t+1} = \alpha V_t + \alpha(1 - \alpha) V_{t-1} + \alpha(1 - \alpha)^2 V_{t-2} + \ldots$$
$$+ \alpha(1 - \alpha)^n V_{t-n} \qquad (5.1)$$

Where F, V have same meaning as before, α is a parameter taking a value between 0 and 1. The $\alpha (1 - \alpha)^n$ term has the effect of progressively reducing the impact of earlier observations on the forecast.
Now Equation (5.1) can be rewritten as

$$F_{t+1} = \alpha V_t + (1 - \alpha) [\alpha V_{t-1} + \alpha(1 - \alpha)V_{t-2} + \alpha(1 - \alpha)^2 V_{t-3} \ldots$$
$$\text{and } F_t = \alpha V_{t-1} + \alpha(1 - \alpha)V_{t-2} + \alpha(1 - \alpha)^2 V_{t-3} \ldots$$
$$\text{Hence } F_{t+1} = F_t + \alpha(V_t - F_t).$$

i.e. New forecast = last period's forecast + α (difference between actual value of variable and forecast value during last time period).
There are a number of advantages associated with exponential smoothing.
(1) It gives relatively more weight to recent data.
(2) It can incorporate all past data. Data is not suddenly disregarded, it simply receives a progressively lower weighting.
(3) It requires storage of substantially less data (only last period's forecast and actual values need to be recorded).
The value given to the smoothing constant α will depend on the

relative weight which it is intended to give to more immediate values. The value chosen for α is usually settled by a process of trial and error.

e.g. Suppose the January sales of a product are 4,200. Since this is the first month of sales involving this product the forecast for February is also 4,200. Supposing we take the value of the smoothing constant α to equal 0.2 and actual sales for February = 4,100.

Now March forecast = February forecast + 0.2 (February actual − February forecast).

Then March forecast = 4,200 + 0.2 (4,100 − 4,200)
$\qquad\qquad\qquad$ = 4,180.

If March actual $\qquad$ = 4,300,
Forecast for April $\quad$ = 4,180 + 0.2(4,300 − 4,180)
$\qquad\qquad\qquad$ = 4,204.

Exercise 5.1

The demand for a product for the first six months of the year is given by:

$\qquad$ January, 48; February, 60; March, 50;
$\qquad$ April, 72; May, 80; June, 60.

(a) Calculate the six-month moving average for the remainder of the year, making forecasts one month in advance. In the event, actual sales were given by:

$\qquad$ July, 66; August, 72; September, 80;
$\qquad$ October, 61; November, 65; December, 75.

(b) Carry out the forecast for the last six months of the year using exponential smoothing with $\alpha = 0.2$. Which of these techniques provided the most accurate forecasts in this example?

5.4.3 Time Series Forecasting using Decomposition Analysis

Moving average and particularly exponential smoothing techniques may well give reasonable results for short-term forecasts that do not require a high degree of accuracy.

If the variable in question is undergoing significant rising or falling trends, or experiences seasonal or cyclical effects then any forecast based on either moving averages or exponential smoothing methods will inevitably lag behind reality. In practice, it may be necessary to take account of trend, seasonal and cyclical factors in the same forecasting model.

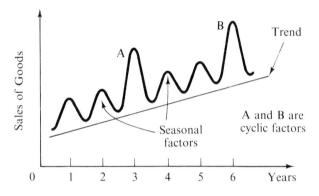

Figure 5.5

The trend factor represents the long-term underlying movement in the time series. In Figure 5.5, it can be seen that the underlying trend is a gradual linear increase. Non-linear trends present greater difficulty in analysis.

A *seasonal variation* is a fluctuation which must recur on an annual basis. For example, greeting card manufacturers may find that a boom in sales occurs around Christmas, motor car manufacturers receive a boom during the middle of the year, sales of alcoholic drink may decline after New Year.

Cyclical variation corresponds to the type of fluctuations that recur over a period of years on a regular basis. The national economy which is related to the business cycle may exhibit this sort of fluctuation. In Figure 5.5, A and B represent cyclical fluctuations.

One form of the decomposition model is:

$$V_i = T_i \times S_i \times C_i + I_i.$$

Where V_i is forecast value of variable for time period, i;
  T_i is value of trend factor for time period, i;
  S_i is value of seasonal factor for time period, i;
  C_i is value of cyclic factor for time period, i;
  I_i is random element.

The approach adopted is to use past data to estimate the value of the trend. If this is then eliminated it leaves us with seasonal, cyclic and random elements. The seasonal and cyclic elements are then separated.

The seasonal and cyclic factors are obtained by moving average techniques whilst the trend factor is obtained from the use of regression relationships[2] (see Section 5.5.1).

For example, suppose we are trying to forecast the sales of a particular piece of machinery, suppose values of trend factor $T_i = 500$, seasonal variation $S_i = 1.40$, cyclic factor $C_i = 1.50$. Then, ignoring the random element:

$$V_i \text{ (values of sales of machinery)} = 500 \times 1.40 \times 1.50,$$
$$= 1,050.$$

Exercise 5.2

Suppose in the next month the value of the trend term $T = 500$ and the seasonal variation and cyclic terms 1.3 and 1.6 respectively. What is the new value of the forecast?

5.5 Causal Models

We have mentioned earlier that the basis of causal models is the establishment of a relationship between the variable which we wish to forecast (dependent variable) and other variables whose future values we can determine with reasonable accuracy (independent variables).

The simplest type of causal model is one in which we believe that a linear relationship exists between a given variable and the dependent variables. A technique called *linear regression* can be used for such cases. If we suspect that the linear relationship exists between the dependent variable and two or more independent variables we use a technique called *multiple linear regression*.

5.5.1   The Scatter Diagram

Where a relationship is suspected between two variables it is useful
to plot a scatter diagram (sometimes called a *scattergram*). This
gives some overall impression of the nature of the relationship. For
example, consider the following table of energy consumption and
national income for a number of countries for 1971.

Country	*Energy Consumption per head* (t.c.e.)	*National Income per head* (US$ 000s)
Belgium	6.0	2.6
Denmark	5.4	2.8
France	4.4	2.7
Germany, W.	5.5	2.9
Ireland	3.4	1.3
Italy	3.0	1.6
Japan	3.9	2.0
Netherlands	5.5	2.4
U.K.	5.5	2.1
U.S.A.	11.6	4.1

(Note: units of energy consumed are tons of coal equivalent (t.c.e.) i.e.
energy from all sources is converted to a common measure based on the
amount of coal required to provide equivalent energy.)

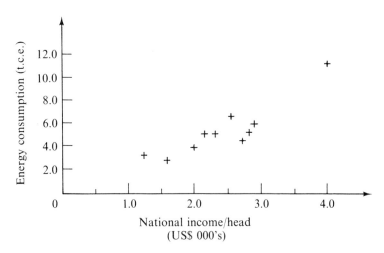

Figure 5.6

The scatter diagram suggests an approximately linear relationship between energy consumption per head and national income per head.

This suggests that the use of linear regression techniques might be appropriate in this case. In other cases, we may find that the scatter diagram indicates either there is no relationship between the two variables in question or that the relationship is definitely not linear, as in the examples shown below.

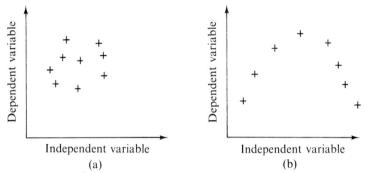

Figure 5.7   *(a) Scatter diagram suggesting that dependent and independent variables are not related*
(b) Variables are related, but not linearly

5.5.2 Fitting the Regression Equations: General

We should be aware that there is no such thing as a *correct* regression equation. Instead the analyst, using his knowledge of the problem or by looking at a plot of the data, suggests that a particular type of relationship might be appropriate. This equation is then fitted to the data and is then tested to see to what extent it 'explains' the data. This is particularly important in multiple linear regression in which we suspect a relationship between a given dependent variable and a number of independent variables. If the degree of explanation of the data is very high there may not be much practical point in looking for an equation which would fit better, although there is no guarantee that one does not exist.

5.5.3   Fitting the Regression Equation: Simple Linear Regression

Let us consider further the relationship between energy consumed per head and national income per head. Let Y denote energy consumed per head and X represent national income per head. If we use the subscript i to represent individual measurement so that each point on the diagram is an X_i, Y_i *pair (X* indicates that national income is the independent variable).

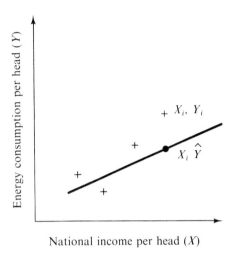

Figure 5.8

If we look at the diagram we see that the general trend can be expressed by a linear function.

$$\hat{Y} = a + bX_i ,$$

where $\hat{Y}$ is the estimated value of the Y_i at a particular value of X_i.

Now the individual Y_i can be expressed by:

$$Y_i = a + bX_i + \epsilon_i ,$$

where ϵ_i represents an 'error term' or residual of the variation of the Y_i which is not accounted for by the regression equation. The coefficients a and b are called *regression coefficients* and they themselves are random variables since they depend on the particular sample of data we happen to have available. The central problem of linear regression analysis is to find which values of a and b give the best fit to the data. Now the residuals, ϵ_i, measure the extent to which $a + bX_i$ departs from Y_i and, if we take the sum of squares of these residuals, we shall have a measure of total deviation of the data from the regression line.

Let $\quad E = \Sigma \epsilon_i{}^2$
$$E = \Sigma[Y_i - (a + bX_i)]^2$$

then by definition, we find the a and b values which minimize E. This is called the *principle of least squares*. To minimize E we must take

$$\frac{\partial E}{\partial a} = 0 \text{ and } \frac{\partial E}{\partial b} = 0.$$

(See Chapter 6, Optimization).

If we do this we obtain, after some manipulation,

$$\Sigma Y_i = na + b\Sigma X_i \qquad (5.2)$$
and $\quad \Sigma X_i Y_i = a\Sigma X_i + b\Sigma X_i{}^2 \qquad (5.3)$

These equations may be solved to yield,

$$b = \frac{n\Sigma X_i Y_i - \Sigma X_i \Sigma Y_i}{n\Sigma X_i{}^2 - (\Sigma X_i)^2},$$

or alternatively, if we divide through by n, we get:

$$b = \frac{\Sigma X_i Y_i - \bar{X}\Sigma Y_i}{\Sigma X_i{}^2 - \bar{X}\Sigma X_i},$$

Having found b we can determine a.

From Equation 5.2:

$$a = \Sigma Y_i/n - b\Sigma X_i/n,$$
i.e. $\quad a = \bar{Y} - b\bar{X}$.

If we take our example of energy consumed per head *(Y)* against national income per head *(X)* (Section 5.5.1) we find that:

$$\Sigma Y_i = 54.2$$
$$\Sigma X_i = 24.5$$
$$\Sigma X_i Y_i = 147.88$$
$$\Sigma Y_i{}^2 = 345.6$$
$$\Sigma X_i{}^2 = 65.53$$

Hence, $b = \dfrac{147.88 - \dfrac{24.5}{10} \times 54.2}{65.53 - \dfrac{24.5}{10} \times 24.5}$,

$$= \frac{147.88 - 132.79}{65.53 - 60.03} ,$$

$$= \frac{15.09}{5.50} = 2.74 .$$

and $a = \bar{Y} - b\bar{X}$,
$$= 5.42 - 2.74 \times 2.45,$$
$$= 5.42 - 6.71,$$
$$= -1.29.$$

This implies that for every thousand dollars increase in national income per head we might expect energy consumption to rise by 2.74 tons of coal equivalent.

5.5.4   Use of Regression Equation for Forecasting

Using the previously derived regression equation we can make estimates of per capita energy consumption given national income per head.

For example, supposing we are attempting to forecast the energy consumption per head for a nation with national income of $4,000 per capita. Then our forecast using the regression which we have already derived ($Y = -1.29 + 2.74X$) becomes:

$$Y = -1.29 + 2.74 \times 4,$$
$$= 9.67 \text{ tons of coal equivalent.}$$

Thus, the regression relationship can be used to provide forecasts providing we assume that the existing regression relationship holds good over the range considered. Over a wider range of values for national income per head than that included in the basic information (i.e. if we attempt to *extrapolate* the relationship) it is quite possible that a good fit will not be achieved. This problem is common to all forecasting situations.

Exercise 5.3

Consider the following table of personal disposable income and consumer expenditure for the U.K. for the period 1965—1974 (in thousands of millions of pounds):

Year	Consumer's Expenditure	Personal Disposable Income (000s millions £)
1965	22.9	25.0
1966	24.2	26.6
1967	25.4	27.8
1968	27.4	29.7
1969	29.0	31.6
1970	31.5	34.6
1971	35.1	38.5
1972	39.6	44.1
1973	45.1	50.9
1974	51.7	59.2

(a) Plot a scatter diagram of this data.
(b) Attempt to fit a linear regression equation to this data.
(c) Use the regression relationship you have derived to derive a forecast for 1975 if personal disposable income for this year was expected to be £65 thousand million pounds.

5.5.5 Regression Coefficients and Chance

There are many practical situations in which the points on our scatter diagrams represent only a sample from a very much larger population of points which might have been observed. This puts us in the position of having to question whether the line we fit is very much affected by the particular sample of points we have observed. This involves us in investigating the likely sampling errors in (a) and (b)[3].

5.5.6   Correlation and the Significance of the Regression

A measure of the quality of fit of any regression line is how well it accounts for the variation of the individual values of Y (Y_i) from the mean value of $Y(\bar{Y})$.

Let us consider the regression line given in Figure 5.9. We have observed a particular data point X_i, Y_i marked with a circle. We have also identified the corresponding point on the regression line X_i, $\hat{Y}$ and the mean of all the Y_i values indicated by $\bar{Y}$. Thus, if we use $\bar{Y}$ to estimate Y_i, then we find that the total deviation of Y_i from the mean value is $Y_i - \bar{Y}$. Now the regression line explains $\hat{Y} - \bar{Y}$ of this deviation. This is called the *explained variation*. The remaining variation $Y_i - \hat{Y}$ is called the *unexplained or residual variation*.

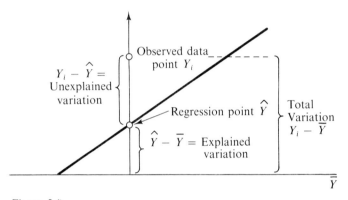

Figure 5.9

As can be seen from Figure 5.9:

$$Y_i - \bar{Y} = (\hat{Y} - \bar{Y}) + (Y_i - \hat{Y}).$$

If we square to eliminate positive and negative effects and then sum it can be shown that:

$$\Sigma(Y_i - \bar{Y})^2 = \Sigma(\hat{Y} - \bar{Y})^2 + \Sigma(Y_i - \hat{Y})^2$$

This is an important result since it states that:

Total variation² = Explained variation² + Unexplained variation.²

It would seem reasonable to define the 'efficiency' of a regression equation by the proportion of total variation which it accounted for. This ratio of explained variation to total variation is called the *coefficient* of *determination* (r^2) where

$$r^2 = \frac{\Sigma(\hat{Y} - \bar{Y})^2}{\Sigma(Y_i - \bar{Y})^2} \;.$$

To find r^2 we can calculate $\hat{Y}$ at each value of X_i and then substitute it into the above equation summing over all n values (X_iY_i).

The square root of the coefficient of determination is called the *correlation coefficient*. There are alternative derivations of r which will give the correct sign. A positive value of r indicates a positive slope in the regression line and vice versa.

An alternative derivation of r gives:

$$r = \frac{\Sigma X_i Y_i - \bar{X}\,\Sigma Y_i}{\sqrt{[(\Sigma X_i^2 - \bar{X}\Sigma X_i)(\Sigma Y_i^2 - \bar{Y}\Sigma Y_i)]}}$$

The value of r must be in the range $-1 \le r \le 1$.
If we take our earlier example,

Y represents energy consumption per head,
X represents national income per head,
Then $\Sigma Y_i = 54.2$,
$\quad \Sigma X_i = 24.5$,
$\quad \Sigma X_i Y_i = 147.88$,
$\quad \Sigma Y_i^2 = 345.6$,
$\quad \Sigma X_i^2 = 65.53$.

Hence $r = \dfrac{147.88 - \dfrac{24.5}{10} \times 54.2}{\sqrt{[(65.53 - \dfrac{24.5}{10} \times 24.5)(345.6 - \dfrac{54.2}{10} \times 54.2)]}}$

$r = \dfrac{147.88 - 132.79}{\sqrt{[(65.53 - 60.03)(345.6 - 293.8)]}}$

$\quad = \dfrac{15.09}{\sqrt{(5.5 \times 51.8)}}$

$\quad = 0.894$

Thus, the coefficient of determination, $r^2 = 0.799$

Thus the regression equation explains approximately 80% of the variation of energy use. One might suspect that other factors such as energy price and industrial structure might be significant also. In fact, one might well consider the use of multiple regression techniques (see Section 5.5.6) to take account of these other factors explicitly. Nevertheless this analysis suggests that this simple model should give reasonable forecasts.

It must also be remembered that the coefficient of determination, r^2, measures only how well one variable *describes* the changes in another not how much the change in one variable is *caused* by changes in the other.

Exercise 5.4

Find the coefficient of determination and coefficient of correlation for the example on the relationship of consumers' expenditure and personal disposable income. What does this relationship tell you about the reliability of the fit of the regression equation?

5.5.6   Multiple Linear Regression

The general form of the multiple linear regression equation is:

$$Y = a + bX_1 + cX_2 \ldots + gX_i + \ldots.$$

For example, supposing economic theory led us to believe that the value of sales of a given product A (Y) was related to consumer disposable income (X_1), price of product A (X_2), price of close substitutes (X_3), and net advertising expenditure on item A (X_4), then we could attempt to construct the multiple regression equation

$$Y = a + bX_1 + cX_2 + dX_3 + eX_4.$$

It has been mentioned previously that there is no mathematically 'correct' regression equation and this point is of particular importance when we are considering multiple regression. Considerable effort and expertise may be devoted in practice to deciding how many and which independent variables ought to be introduced into the regression equation.

Having proposed a particular regression equation it is then necessary to compute the coefficients of this equation. It is possible to do this algebraically, although even if only two or three independent variables are involved, this is a laborious process. For more variables, this task becomes impracticably burdensome. Thus, a computer is used for this purpose. Most scientific computers have a standard program (or *package*) available for which the user has only to supply the data in the appropriate form.

5.5.7 Index of Determination for Multiple Regression Equations

An index of determination R^2 can be defined which is exactly equivalent to the coefficient of determination in simple linear regression. It is denoted by R^2 to show that it relates to multiple regression. As in the case of linear regression, this statistic measures what proportion of the total variation of the dependent variable is 'explained' by the regression equation. In practice, it may often be possible to increase the value of R^2 by adding additional variables to our regression equation. It may be, however, that the improvement in explanatory power of the equation is not worth the additional complexity involved.

There are some additional difficulties associated with multiple linear regression.[2]

5.6 Time Series versus Causal Models

The extract from a newspaper article published in early 1978 and presented below illustrates quite well some of the problems relating to the choice between time series and causal models for forecasting (note 'extrapolatory' methods in this article means time series methods). This article points out that previous Government forecasts of car ownership levels which were based on time series models had tended to over-estimate levels of car ownership. It is proposed that a causal model which takes into account variables such as income levels, family circumstances and fuel price variations ought to be used.

Extract—GOVERNMENT　　GIVES　　WAY　　ON　　ROAD FORECASTS

'The Government yesterday accepted the central criticism of its traffic forecasting methods in an independent report and immediately published scaled-down predictions of future car ownership levels.'

'Mr William Rodgers, Transport Secretary, in welcoming the report of the Advisory Committee on Trunk Road Assessment, agreed to establish at once a standing committee to monitor developments in forecasting and road evaluation. He said he would start immediately to judge schemes in the light of the committee's findings.'

'Sir George Leitch, chairman of Short Brothers and Harland, who was chairman of the advisory committee responsible for the report, will be chairman of the new standing committee.'

'Further Government reaction to the 150,000-word report is expected in the first of a series of annual White Papers on roads, publication of which will probably begin in March, Mr Rodgers said.'

'The changes in Government forecasts are intended as interim measures to allow further consideration to be given to the report's suggestion that future forecasts should be based on 'causal' rather than 'extrapolatory' methods.'

'The difference is that a causal model permits the inclusion of more sophisticated determinants in judging the extent of car ownership, such as income level, family circumstances and fuel price variations. In the department's revised forecasts, an element of causality is introduced for the first time, using data from the family expenditure survey.'

'Introducing the report which was commissioned last February, Sir George said the committee was in favour of "more openness, better balance, greater flexibility and a fuller recognition of the uncertainties". Such an approach would win greater public acceptability of the methods used, he said.'

'The section on forecasting is the most critical in the report and, having conducted a series of 'before and after' studies, the committee concludes that the department has tended in the past 'to over-predict traffic, in certain cases significantly'.'

Exercise 5.5

(a) Explain why you think that the use of time series models may have led the Government to over-estimate future car ownership levels.

(b) Can you suggest any other situations where use of time series models may lead to inaccurate estimates being made?

6

Optimization Techniques

6.1 Optimization

Managers are often in situations where they wish to maximize the attainment of an objective. For example, a manager might know that the relationship between the profit gained on a particular product and the price charged is given by the expression below:

Profit $(Z) = 400P - 20P^2 - 100$,

where P is price charged (see Figure 6.1).

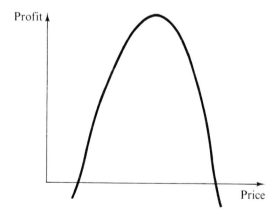

Figure 6.1

The manager's objective may be to obtain *maximum* profit. We call the process of discovering which price would yield maximum profits *optimization*.

Let us consider another situation. Supposing a manager knows the relationship between total stockholding cost and the quantity (Q) that he orders each time. Suppose that this relationship turns out to be:

$$\text{Total stockholding cost} = 5Q + \frac{500}{Q}.$$

This relationship is shown in Figure 6.2.

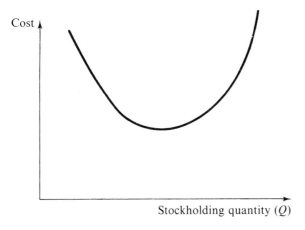

Figure 6.2

The manager's objective might well be to minimize the total stockholding cost. The process of devising which level of stockholding (Q) achieves this objective is again an example of *optimization*.

The two situations described above are simply two problems taken from a wide variety of optimization problems encountered in management. In general, we approach these problems in two ways. (1) Develop an appropriate mathematical model to describe the system that we are considering. (2) Apply the appropriate optimization technique.

Exercise 6.1

The number of items of a luxury good sold (N) is given by:

$$N = 200 - 1.3p \text{ (where } p \text{ is the price in pounds).}$$

If the goods cost the company £50 each to produce, construct a model which relates total profit obtained to the price sold.

6.2   The Concept of a Function

A function is a rule that establishes a relationship between different variables. In the first example in Section 6.1, for instance, we note that there is a functional relationship between profit and price. This can be written as:

$$\text{Profit} = f \text{ (price),}$$
$$\text{or } Z = f (P).$$

where Z is profit and P is price.

Writing the relationship in this way implies that P is the *independent* variable and Z is the *dependent* variable. This means that once values are assigned for the independent variable the corresponding value for the dependent variable is established through this relationship.

Since the profit is a function of only one variable it can be said that this is a *single variable* function.

Now, of course, for practical purposes we are interested in knowing the exact functional relationship between variables, not simply the fact that such a relationship exists.

The exact functional relationship in this case is, as we have already seen:

$$Z = 400P - 20P^2 - 100.$$

This is an example of a *non-linear* function (a linear function contains only constants and variables to the first power).

Suppose a company makes two products, de luxe desks and

standard desks. De luxe desks are sold for £100 each and standard desks are sold for £60 each. Then the total revenue obtained will be a function of the number of de luxe (N_D) and number of standard desks (N_S) sold.

Thus we can write $R = f(N_D, N_S)$

The exact relation is of course

$$R = 100 N_D + 60 N_S$$

This is an example of a *multivariable, linear* function.

Exercise 6.2

Construct an example of a non-linear multivariable function.

6.3   Slope of Line and Rate of Change

Let us consider the cost of printing a given publication. Typically, such costs are in the form of a fixed (set-up) cost together with a constant additional (or marginal) cost for each item produced. Suppose set-up cost is £100 and the marginal cost is £1.2.

Total cost is simply a function of the number produced and the exact functional relationship is in fact:

$$C = 100 + 1.2 N,$$

where C is the total cost of production and N is the number produced.

This relationship is represented in Figure 6.3.

Clearly N is the independent and C the dependent variable.

The term *slope* is used to measure the degree of steepness or rate of change of a function. In general this is defined as the change in dependent variable caused by a one unit change in one of the independent variables.

We can see that in the case of the straight-line relationship which

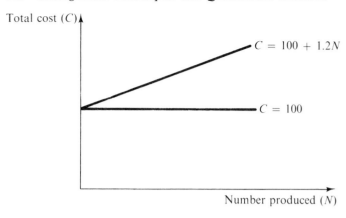

Figure 6.3

we are currently considering, the slope is simply given by the coefficient of the independent variable. Thus, in this case, the slope is + 1.2 (the plus sign indicates that C increases when N increases, and decreases when N decreases).

If the cost of publication were simply £100 and did not depend at all on the number of items produced then this could be represented simply by $C = 100$.

This is also shown in Figure 6.3 and is simply a horizontal line with zero slope.

Let us now consider another situation. Suppose (as is likely) that the sales of a particular product is a function of the price charged for it.

Suppose the exact relationship is given by

$$N = 200 - 2 \times P \qquad P \leq 100$$
$$N = 0 \qquad\qquad\quad P \geq 100$$

This relationship is shown graphically in Figure 6.4.

In this case the slope is − 2. Note the *negative* slope which in this case means that sales decrease with increasing values of price and vice versa.

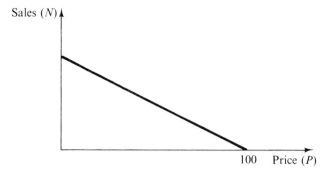

Figure 6.4

Exercise 6.3

Suppose that a salesman is paid a fixed sum of £200 per month together with a bonus of £5 for all items sold. Devise an appropriate model for his salary. What is the slope of the line?

6.4   The Concept of the Slope of a Curve (at a point)

In all three models discussed in the previous section it will be noted that the slope remained constant at all points on the lines. This is always the case for linear functions.

For non-linear functions, however, we face a quite different situation, in that the slope changes from point to point.

Let us take the stock management example in Section 6.1. We recall that total cost of the stock system is a function of order quantity and that the exact relationship is given by:

$$C = 5Q + \frac{500}{Q} .$$

As we can see from Figure 6.2 the value of the slope of this curve will be different at different points.

Suppose we employ the symbol $\triangle$ to indicate a very small change in the value of a variable. Then if $\triangle X$ represents the change in the value of the independent variable X, and $\triangle Y$ indicates the consequential change in dependent variable Y, then $\triangle Y/\triangle X$ represents the consequential change in the dependent variable Y caused by a one unit change in the independent variable X.

If we consider the linear relationship:

$$C = 100 + 1.2N$$

in the last section, it is quite clear that the ratio $\dfrac{\triangle C}{\triangle N}$ remains the same, regardless of the particular element of curve chosen.

If we now look at the stockholding cost example

$$C = 5Q + \frac{500}{Q} :$$

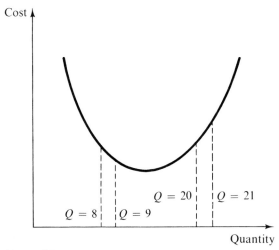

Figure 6.5

For $Q=8$, $C = 40 + \dfrac{500}{8} = 102.50,$

For $Q=9$, $C = 100.56,$

Between $Q=8$ and $Q=9$

$$\frac{\triangle C}{\triangle Q} = \frac{100.56 - 102.50}{9-8} = -1.94.$$

For $Q = 20$, $C = 125.0$,
For $Q = 21$, $C = 128.8$,

$\therefore$ Between $Q = 20$ and $Q = 21$

$$\frac{\triangle C}{\triangle Q} = \frac{128.8 - 125}{21 - 20} = +3.8$$

Thus we have demonstrated quite clearly that the slope of the curve is different at different points. The negative slope between $Q = 8$ and $Q = 9$ indicates cost is falling as order size increases on this part of the curve, the positive slope between $Q = 20$ and $Q = 21$ indicates that the cost is rising on this part of the curve. Also the rate of increase at this point is greater than the rate of fall on the earlier section.

Exercise 6.4

Using the stockholding cost example, compare the slope between $Q = 3$ and $Q = 4$ with that between $Q = 11$ and $Q = 12$. What conclusion do you draw from your results?

6.5 The Concept of a Derivative

The term *derivative* is used to indicate the rate of change or slope of a function. This corresponds to the ratio of $\triangle Y / \triangle X$ for an infinitesimal change, $\triangle X$, in the independent variable X.

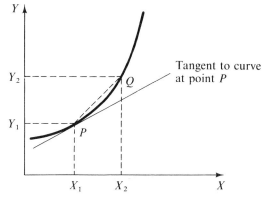

Figure 6.6

Let us consider Figure 6.6, supposing P and Q are points X_1, Y_1 and X_2, Y_2. Now the average slope between the two points will be that of the line joining the points P and Q, i.e.

$$\frac{Y_2 - Y_1}{X_2 - X_1} = \frac{\triangle Y}{\triangle X} \;.$$

It is, however, quite possible to consider the slope of progressively smaller portions of the curve (i.e. smaller and smaller intervals of $\triangle X$). As we keep on reducing the interval $\triangle X$ we eventually end up with a line which does not cut the curve at all but simply touches the curve at the point P.

This line is called the *tangent* to the curve, and the derivative at a point is simply equal to the slope of the tangent at that point of the curve.

Hence, if we can calculate the derivative at any point on a curve then we have the value of the slope at that point.

The derivative of Y with respect to X is written dY/dX

More formally, $dY/dX = \triangle Y/\triangle X$ as $\triangle X \to 0$

The process of finding the derivative of a function is called *differentiation*.

6.6　Rules for Differentiation

(1)　*Constants*

In Section 6.3 we had a model $C = 100$. In this context, the cost was always 100 irrespective of the number produced and the line had no slope. Hence $dC/dN = 0$.

In general terms, the derivative of a constant is zero.

(2)　*Linear function*

In Section 6.3 we had a linear model $C = 100 + 1.2N$. We remember the slope of this line is 1.2. More formally, suppose N increases by $\triangle N$:

Then

$$C + \triangle C = 100 + 1.2 (N + \triangle N),$$
$$\triangle C/\triangle N = 1.2.$$

As $\triangle N \to 0$, then $dC/dN = 1.2$

In general, the derivative of aX with respect to $X = a$.

(3) *General power function*
Given a general power function $Y = kX^n$ *where k and n are* constant; the derivative is given by:

$$\mathrm{d}Y/\mathrm{d}X = n\, k\, X^{n-1}.$$

If we take the example in Section 6.1,

$$Z = 400P - 20P^2 - 100$$

we get therefore $\mathrm{d}Z/\mathrm{d}P = 400 - 40P$.

If we wish to verify this more formally:
Suppose P increases to $P + \triangle P$, resulting in a corresponding increase in Z of $\triangle Z$.

$$
\begin{aligned}
\text{Then } Z + \triangle Z &= 400(P + \triangle P) - 20(P + \triangle P)^2 - 100, \\
Z + \triangle Z &= 400P + 400\triangle P \\
&\quad - 20(P^2 + 2P\triangle P + \triangle P^2) - 100, \\
\triangle Z &= 400\triangle P - 40P\triangle P - 20\triangle P^2.
\end{aligned}
$$

As $\triangle P \to 0$, the term $\triangle P^2$ becomes negligible.

Hence $\dfrac{\mathrm{d}Z}{\mathrm{d}P} = \dfrac{\triangle Z}{\triangle P}$ as $\triangle P \to 0 = 400 - 40P$.

(4) *Derivative of a Product*
If $Y = RS$ and R and S are functions of X

then $\dfrac{\mathrm{d}Y}{\mathrm{d}X} = \dfrac{R\mathrm{d}S}{\mathrm{d}X} + \dfrac{S\mathrm{d}R}{\mathrm{d}X}$.

e.g. Consider the function $Y = X^3 (3X + 2)$

Applying the above relationship

$$\frac{\mathrm{d}Y}{\mathrm{d}X} = X^3.3 + 3X^2 (3X + 2)$$

$$= 12X^3 + 6X^2$$

(5) *Derivative of a quotient*

Suppose $Y = R/S$ and R and S are functions of X,

then $dY/dX = \dfrac{SdR/dX - RdS/dX}{S^2}$.

e.g. Suppose we have the function

$$Y = X^3/(3X + 2)$$

Then $dY/dX = \dfrac{(3X+2)\,3X^2 - X^3(3)}{(3X+2)^2}$

$$= \dfrac{9X^3 + 6X^2 - 3X^3}{(3X+2)^2}$$

$$= \dfrac{6X^2(X+1)}{(3X+2)^2}$$

Exercise 6.5

Find the derivatives of the following functions:

(1) $Y = 3X^2 + 2X + 4$,

(2) $Y = 3X^2 + 2/X^2 + 4$,

(3) $Y = (4X+3) \times 5X^2$,

(4) $Y = (4X+3)/5X^2$.

6.7 Application of the Concept of Differentiation to Optimization

We have established that the derivative of a function is a general expression for its slope. If we now return to the problem of Section 6.1 — what price to charge to maximize profits — we can clearly see that profit is maximized where the slope is horizontal. This is illustrated in Figure 6.7.

Now the slope is zero when horizontal, and this must therefore correspond to the point at which the derivative is zero.

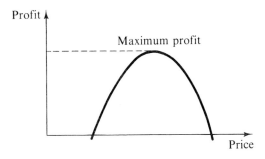

Figure 6.7

Profit $Z = 400P - 20P^2 - 100$

As we have already seen, $\dfrac{dZ}{dP} = 400 - 40P$

If the derivative (i.e. dZ/dP) $= 0$
$400 - 40P = 0$
$\therefore P = 10$

This result can be easily verified by calculating resultant values of profit around $P = 10$. Thus:

P	Z	P	Z
8	1820	10	1900 (optimum)
9	1880	10.1	1899.8
9.5	1895	11	1880
9.9	1899.8		

If we now go on to consider the second example which is raised in Section 6.1 (i.e. the stockholding situation):

$$C = 5Q + 500/Q,$$

where C is stockholding costs, Q is quantity ordered.

As can be seen from Figure 6.8, minimum cost is reached where the slope is horizontal, i.e. the derivative is zero.

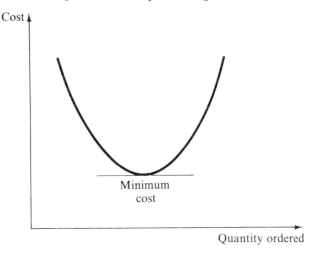

Figure 6.8

Since $C = 5Q + 500/Q$,
$dC/dQ = 5 - 500/Q^2$.

Now $dC/dQ = 0$ where $5 - 500/Q^2 = 0$.
i.e. $Q^2 = 100$ or $Q = 10$,

and the minimum cost corresponding to $Q = 10$

$$= 5 \times 10 + \frac{500}{10} = 100$$

As a check:

If $Q = 9$, $C = 45 + \dfrac{500}{9} = 45 + 55.56 = 100.56$.

$Q = 11$, $C = 55 + \dfrac{500}{11} = 55 + 45.45 = 100.45$.

This is consistent with $Q = 10$ being a minimum.

6.8   Distinguishing between Maxima and Minima

We have seen in the previous section that in both minimization and maximization cases, the optimum was at the point at which the slope or derivative equalled zero. Although it was obvious in these particular contexts which was a mimimum and which was a maximum, it is valuable to have some mathematical means for distinguishing the two.

The way we do this is by looking at the *second-order derivative* of the function at the suspected maxima or minima. The second derivative written d^2Y/dX^2 is simply the derivative of the first-order derivative, and gives the rate of change of the first order derivative.

This second-order derivative should be *positive* for a minimum and negative for a *maximum*. This should be intuitively plausible if we remember that at a minimum the slope of the curve is changing from negative to positive, therefore the change in slope is positive. For a maximum the reverse is the case.

Looking at the profit maximization example:

$$dZ/dP = 400 - 40P,$$
$$\therefore d^2Z/dP^2 = -40.$$

This second derivative will be negative for $P = 10$ (in fact negative for all values of P) and this, therefore, corresponds to *maximization*.

Taking the stock system example:

$$dC/dQ = 5 - 500/Q^2,$$
$$\therefore d^2C/dQ^2 = 1000/Q^3.$$

This is positive for $Q = 10$ (and indeed positive for all physically possible values of Q). Hence this corresponds to *minimization*.

Finally, in more complex situations, there may be more than one maximum or minimum (see Figure 6.9):

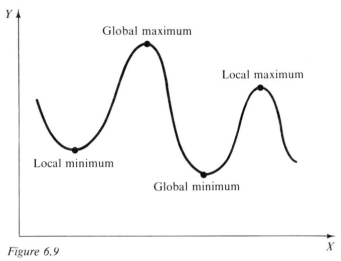

Figure 6.9

In this situation we call the overall maximum (or minimum) the *global* maximum (or minimum). Other maxima (or minima) are called *local* maxima (or minima). To discover which are global or local optima it is necessary to calculate the value of Y at these different optima and compare them.

Exercise 6.6

Suppose the cost function of producing X pounds of a certain pet food is given by:

$$X^3 - 6X^2 + 2X.$$

What size of batch will minimize cost per pound of production?

Exercise 6.7

In Exercise 6.1 determine what price will maximize profit.

6.9   Optimization of Multivariable Functions

In the previous sections, the situations we have attempted to optimize have involved single variable functions. In Section 6.2, however, we introduced the concept of the multivariable function. Optimization of such a function is more difficult and involves the use of *partial derivatives*.

A partial derivative of a multivariable function is a derivative with respect to one of the independent variables, the other variables being treated as constant.

The partial derivative of a function Y with respect to X is written

$$\frac{\partial Y}{\partial X}$$

For example, suppose we have a variable Y which is a function of two independent variables X, Z: $Y = XZ + X^2$.

Then $\dfrac{\partial Y}{\partial X} = Z + 2X$ (note Z is treated as a constant),

and $\dfrac{\partial Y}{\partial Z} = X$ (the X is treated as constant).

The rules for finding an optimum for such a two-variable function are very similar to those for a single-value function. In this case, both partial derivatives must equal zero at the optimum.

Let us take a specific example. In Section 6.2 we were considering a firm that made both de luxe and standard desks. Suppose N_D, N_S are the numbers of de luxe and standard desks sold. Suppose the company is interested in establishing a pricing policy for the two desks that maximizes profits for the product line as a whole. Suppose that the standard desks cost £20 to produce and the de luxe desks cost £30. Then if the price of standard desks is P_S and that of de luxe desks is P_D, overall profit is given by:
Profit $= N_D (P_D - 30) + N_S (P_S - 20)$

Over time, the company have observed that an increase in price for the de luxe desk is usually accompanied by a drop in sales for this desk, but an increase in sales for the standard desk. This is because the two products are *substitutable*. (The same effect occurs when an increase in the price of coffee results in a rise in the sales of tea.) Conversely, a rise in price of the standard desk results in a drop of sales for this desk, but an increase in the sales of the de luxe desk. Suppose the relationships between numbers sold and price are as follows:

$$N_D = 100 - 2P_D + 0.5P_S,$$
and $$N_S = 160 - 3P_S + 0.4P_D.$$

Then if we substitute into the equation for profit (Z) we get:

$$Z = (100 - 2P_D + 0.5P_S)(P_D - 30)$$
$$+ (160 - 3P_S + 0.4P_D)(P_S - 20)$$
$$Z = 100P_D - 2P_D{}^2 + 0.5P_SP_D - 3000 + 60P_D - 15P_S$$
$$+ 160P_S - 3P_S{}^2 + 0.4P_DP_S - 3200 + 60P_S - 8P_D.$$

i.e. $Z = -2P_D{}^2 - 3P_S{}^2 + 0.9P_SP_D + 152P_D + 205P_S - 6200.$

Now we know that at the optimum the partial derivatives of profit with respect to both independent variables must be zero.

Now $\dfrac{\partial Z}{\partial P_D} = -4P_D + 0.9P_S + 152 = 0$ at optimum,

$\dfrac{\partial Z}{\partial P_S} = -6P_S + 0.9P_D + 205 = 0$ at optimum,

Solving these equations we get $P_D = 47.28,$
$$P_S = 41.26.$$

These, then, are the prices to charge to maximize profits.

In fact, although the above is clearly a maximum, we need additional tests to determine in more complex situations whether the point is a maximum or minimum. These tests are somewhat complex and the student is recommended to consult[1].

6.10   Constrained and Unconstrained Optimization

So far we have handled situations involving single and multivariable functions which are *not subject to any constraint*. In other words, there were no pre-set limits to the values of the dependent variables.

Suppose, however, we have an advertising budget of £10,000 which we wish to divide up between TV and newspaper advertising. Suppose A_{TV} is the amount spent on TV advertising and A_N is the amount spent on newspaper advertising. We know that sales are given by the following function:

$$2A_{TV}{}^2 + 3A_N{}^2 + 4A_{TV}A_N + 5A_{TV} + 6A_N.$$

Obviously, if we had the job of maximising the function alone then the result would be unbounded. However, we have a budget limitation in that $A_N + A_{TV} = 1000$. This type of optimization problem involving equality constraints can be solved using a technique called *Lagrange multipliers*.

Other optimization problems can involve inequality constraints. These can be handled using a technique known as mathematical programming which is discussed in the following chapter.

Exercise 6.8

In the example in Section 6.9 suppose the cost of producing the de luxe desk rises to £35. Calculate the new optimum price to charge.

7

Linear Programming

7.1 Introduction

Consider the following problems:

(1) A manufacturer has resources of raw materials, plant and machinery, and manpower which he can use to produce a number of different products. He wishes to know how many of each type of product he should produce to maximize his profits.

(2) A manufacturer is attempting to make a particular kind of animal feed from a number of different constituents. He wants to do this at minimum cost. There are, however, certain constraints concerning the nutritional contents of the diet that must be met.

(3) A marketing manager wants to determine how best to allocate a fixed advertising budget amongst a number of advertising media such as T.V., radio, newspapers and magazines. He wishes to contact the maximum number of people subject to fulfilling certain constraints about covering minimum numbers in particular socio-economic categories.

All the above problems are optimization problems in that the decision-maker is trying to maximize or minimize some quantity. In the first example, the manufacturer wants to maximize profit; in the second example we wish to minimize costs and, in the third example, to maximize total audience coverage. Unlike most of the examples discussed in the previous chapter, however, on this occasion we are working under constraint. In the first example, we are constrained by limited resources of manpower, plant and raw materials available. In the diet problem, we have to meet certain nutritional constraints. In the final problem, we have limited financial resources and have to meet various audience targets.

Many problems of this type, where we are attempting to optimize a quantity subject to constraint, can be tackled using linear programming methods. Such methods have been successfully employed to tackle diverse problems from production scheduling to plant location in a wide range of industries.

7.2 Graphical Solution

7.2.1 A Simple Example

Let us consider a simple example. A small farmer grows two cereals — wheat and barley. He makes £120 profit from each hectare of land on which wheat is grown and £100 profit from each hectare on which barley is grown. His total production, however, is limited by the amount of land that he has available, together with constraints in the availability of fertilizer and manpower. The size of the farm is twelve hectares. Each hectare of wheat grown requires five cwt of fertilizer and each hectare of barley needs two cwt of fertilizer. There is a total of only fifty cwt of fertilizer available. The planting of a hectare of wheat requires two man-weeks of labour; while planting a hectare of barley takes six man-weeks. In all there are sixty man-weeks of labour available at the appropriate time of year. We also make the assumption that it is possible for the farmer to sell everything that he produces.

Let W be the number of hectares of wheat that he decides to produce, and B the number of hectares of barley. Then total profit is given by:

$$120W + 100B.$$

This function is called the *objective function*.

There are, however, a number of constraints we have to deal with. (In addition, it is obvious that B and W must be greater than or equal to zero, since negative values are physically impossible.)

(i) Land constraint
The farmer has only a total of twelve hectares available. Thus, total amount of land used for wheat and total amount used for barley must not exceed twelve hectares:

$W + B \le 12$.

We can draw a graph of the equation $W + B = 12$. All points on this line just meet the constraints. All points to one side of the line give values of $W + B < 12$, and all points on the other give values of $W + B > 12$. In this case, points on the side of the line adjacent the origin fulfil the condition $W + B < 12$. (If in doubt which side to choose, check whether or not the origin meets the constraints.) Thus, all positive values of B and W which satisfy this constraint lie between these lines and the axes. (Such solutions are called *feasible solutions*.) This area is shaded in on the diagram.

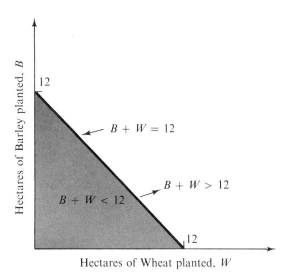

Figure 7.1   Land constraint

(ii) Fertilizer constraint

We have only fifty cwt of fertilizer available and we know that each hectare of wheat takes five cwt of fertilizer and each hectare of barley two cwt of fertilizer. Hence, W hectares of wheat requires $5W$ cwts of fertilizer, B hectares of barley requires $2B$ hectares of fertilizer. Hence:

$5W + 2B \le 50$.

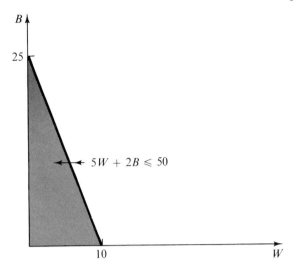

Figure 7.2 Fertilizer constraint

We can draw this again on Figure 7.2 and we have again shaded in all feasible solutions.

(iii) Manpower Constraint

We have a total of sixty man-weeks of labour available at the appropriate time of year. Planting a hectare of wheat takes two man-weeks of labour, whilst a hectare of barley requires six man-weeks. Thus, the manpower constraint is:

$$2W + 6B \leq 60.$$

This is shown in Figure 7.3.

We have drawn the equation $2W + 6B = 60$. Feasible solutions lie between this line and the axes and this area has been shaded in.

Now the only *feasible* solutions to the problem as a whole are those which satisfy *all* the constraints, as shown on Figure 7.4.

It can be seen that only points in the polygon, A, B, C, D, E satisfy all the constraints. Therefore, all feasible solutions lie in this area and the region is called the *feasibility polygon*.

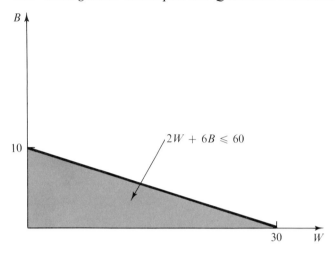

Figure 7.3   Manpower constraint

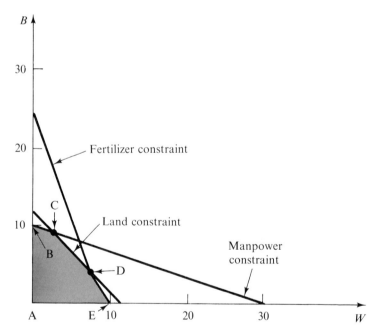

Figure 7.4   Feasible region

7.2.2 Finding an Optimum

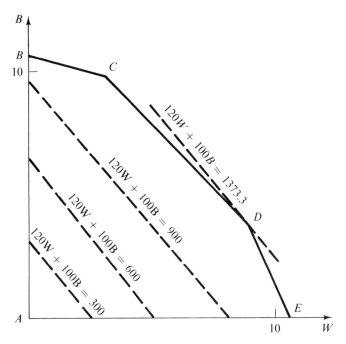

Figure 7.5

We have now managed to identify all possible solutions to this problem as lying within the feasibility polygon, A, B, C, D, E. We are not, however, interested in merely finding a feasible solution, we want the best possible solution. (For example, the point A corresponds to planting nothing, leaving all resources idle, and hence obtaining no profit. While quite clearly feasible, this would not be of much interest in practice.) Now our profit function is given by:

$$\text{Profit} = 120W + 100B.$$

It is possible to construct a whole series of parallel lines where $120W + 100B$ are equal to different values of profit. Any point on one of these lines in the feasible region corresponds to solutions with the same value of profit. Thus all points on the line $120W + 100B = 300$, correspond to feasible solutions whose profit = £300.

Thus, each of the parallel lines in Figure 7.5 is called an *isoprofit* line. Now the further away from the origin that the isoprofit line is drawn, the greater will be the value of the profit.

Hence, the maximum value of profit will be given by the isoprofit line furthest out from the origin that just touches the feasible region. This must inevitably occur at a vertex and will be at the point D in our example.

Thus, the optimum solution will occur at one of the vertices of the feasibility polygon. This means that instead of having to consider the infinite number of solutions represented by all the points within the feasibility polygon, we can restrict our search for solutions to the much more limited number of vertices of the feasibility polygon. The solutions at these vertices are called *basic feasible solutions.*

If, in fact, we consider the basic feasible solutions for this polygon we get the following:

Vertex (basic feasible solution)	No. of Hectares of Wheat (W)	No. of Hectares of Barley (B)	Profit
A	0	0	0
B	0	10	1000
C	3	9	1260
D	$8\frac{2}{3}$	$3\frac{1}{3}$	$1373\frac{1}{3}$
E	10	0	1200

Thus the optimal solution is at D, resulting in a profit of £1373⅓.

7.2.3   Introduction of 'slack' variables

It is possible to replace the inequality constraints outlined in the last section with equality constraints by the introduction of a number of additional slack variables. If we do this we get the following:

(i)	Land constraint	$W + B + S_1$	$= 12.$
(ii)	Fertilizer constraint	$5W + 2B + S_2$	$= 50.$
(iii)	Manpower constraint	$2W + 6B + S_3$	$= 60.$

Since S_1 corresponds to the difference between the land actually planted ($W + B$ hectares) and total available land (12 hectares) it therefore corresponds to unutilized land. For this reason it is called a 'slack' variable. Similarly, S_2 corresponds to unused fertilizer and S_3 to unused manpower. If we examine the value of our slack variables at each of the basic feasible solutions, we obtain the following:

Vertex (basic feasible) solution)	W Hectares of Wheat	B Hectares of Barley	S_2 'Slack' Land	S_2 Slack' Fertilizer	S_3 'Slack' Manpower
	Profit				
A	0	0	0	12	50	60
B	1000	0	10	2	30	0
C	1260	3	9	0	17	0
D	1373⅓	8⅔	3⅓	0	0	22⅔
E	1200	10	0	2	0	40

It will be noted from the above that at each vertex (basic feasible solution) there are exactly three non-zero variables. It will also be noted that there is no basic feasible solution that fully utilizes all available resources and this is a common feature of such problems. Even at the optimal solution D, there are 22⅔ weeks of unused manpower.

The variables that have positive values in any given basic feasible solution are called *basic variables*. The variables with values of zero are called *non-basic*. The set of basic variables is called the *basis*. Thus, it will be noted that at basic feasible solution C; W, B and S_2 are basic variables (in the basis) while S_1 and S_3 are non-basic. At D; W, B and S_3 are in the basis whilst the non-basic variables are S_1 and S_2.

In general, if we have a linear programming problem with m constraints and n variables (including slacks) each basic feasible solution will have m basic variables and $n-m$ non-basic variables. In the above problem, we had three constraints and five variables (including slacks). Then, we would expect three basic variables and two non-basic variables in each basic feasible solution. It has already been observed that this is, in fact, the case.

7.2.4 Form of the Problem
There are two features of the above problem that should be noted:

(i) Linearity

It will be noted that the objective function and all the constraints are linear (i.e. consist only of variables of the first power, that is X; not X^2 or $X^{1/2}$).

(ii) Equilibrium

It is assumed that the system is in equilibrium and none of its fundamental variables are changing over time.

Exercise 7.1

A well-known company produces both de luxe and standard toys. The company wishes to use its limited resources of machine time, warehouse space and painter time to produce a mix of products that will maximize its profits. Resources required to make each toy are given below:

Resource	Standard Unit	De luxe Unit	Capacity (h)
Machine hours	2	3	24,000
Warehouse space	4	3	36,000
Painter time	0	1	6,000

If profit from each de luxe toy is £3 and profit from each standard toy is £1, what is the most profitable mix of products that can be produced?

7.3 A Minimization Case

The procedure for handling minimization problems is very similar to the maximization case. As before, we identify the feasible region. We then need to choose the vertex corresponding to a minimum rather than a maximum.

Let us work through a specific example. A food merchant has received an order from a customer for a shipment of at least 2,000 kg of animal food. The customer requires that at least 1,000 kg of the food should be protein and he is not prepared to accept more than 175 kg of fat. The dealer can make up the food by purchasing different quantities of ingredients A and B. The following table gives the percentage by weight of carbohydrate and fat in the two ingredients:

	Ingredient A	*Ingredient B*
Protein	25%	75%
Animal fats	5%	10%

The cost of each ingredient is £1 per kg for ingredient A and £4 per kg for ingredient B. The problem is to determine optimum amounts to be purchased of each of the two ingredients.

Let Q_A, Q_B be the quantities purchased from each of the two suppliers.

We therefore wish to minimize $Q_A + 4Q_B$

We have, however, to take cognizance of the following constraints:

(i)   Quantity constraint
We must supply a total quantity of food of at least, 2,000 kg.

Hence, $Q_A + Q_B \geq 2000$.

(ii)   Protein constraint
We must supply at least 1,000 kg of protein. We know that each kg of ingredient A can supply 0.25 kg of protein and that each kg of ingredient B can supply 0.75 kg of protein. Thus, Q_A kg of ingredient A will provide $Q_A/4$ kg of protein, and Q_B kg of ingredient B provide $3Q_B/4$ kg of protein. Hence

$$\frac{Q_A}{4} + \frac{3Q_B}{4} \geq 1000,$$

or $Q_A + 3Q_B \geq 4000$.

(iii)   Fat constraint
We know that we are limited to providing a total of 175 kg of fat. Each kg of ingredient A contains $\frac{1}{20}$ kg of fat and each kg of ingredient B contains $\frac{1}{10}$ kg of fat. Hence,

$$\frac{Q_A}{20} + \frac{Q_B}{10} \leq 175.$$

or $Q_A + 2Q_B \leq 3500$.

Having specified these three constraints we can then identify the feasible region.

We have shaded in the feasible region XYZ (in Figure 7.6). We wish to minimize the cost function $Q_A + 4Q_B$. We can draw a whole series of isocost lines for different values of the expression $Q_A + 4Q_B$. Clearly, the closer this can be drawn to the origin, the lower the overall cost. It is again clear that this minimum cost must occur at one of the vertices of this feasibility polygon. This turns out to be vertex Z. ($Q_A = 2,500$ kg; $Q_B = 500$ kg and total cost £4,500.) A complete enumeration of the vertices of the feasibility polygon gives the table below.

Vertex	Q_A	Q_B	Cost	
Z	2,500	500	£4,500	← minimum cost
X	1,000	1,000	5,000	
Y	500	1,500	6,500	

Exercise 7.2

Vitamins A and B are found in food stuffs F_1 and F_2. One ounce of F_1 contains 3 units of vitamin A and 4 units of vitamin B. One ounce of F_2 contains 6 units of vitamin A and 3 units of vitamin B. Each ounce of F_1 and F_2 cost 4p and 5p respectively. The minimum daily requirements per person of vitamins A and B is 80 units and 100 units respectively. Assuming that anything in excess of the minimum requirements of A and B is not harmful, find the mixture of foods F_1 and F_2 which meets the daily requirement for vitamins at minimum cost.

7.4   Analytical Methods of Solution

The graphical method illustrates some of the important features of solutions to linear programming problems. (Idea of feasibility

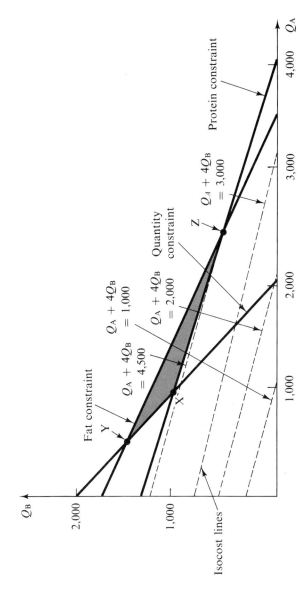

Figure 7.6 The feasible region

polygon, fact that the optimum solution always occurs at a vertex.)

It is quite clear, however, that if the farmer's problem had involved planting three possible crops, then the use of the graphical method to find a solution would have presented considerable difficulty. Four or more possible crops would have been quite impossible to handle with this method. Since almost all problems of practical interest involve a large number of different variables, it will clearly be necessary to derive a mathematical approach to this type of problem.

Let us look again at the farmer's problem, writing the constraints in equality form:

Maximize $Z = 120W + 100B$

Subject to (1) Land constraint, $\quad W + B + S_1 \quad\quad = 12,$
$\quad\quad\quad$ (2) Fertilizer constraint, $\quad 5W + 2B + S_2 \quad = 50,$
$\quad\quad\quad$ (3) Manpower constraint, $2W + 6B + S_3 \quad = 60.$

$\quad W, B, S_1, S_2$ and $S_3 \geq 0,$

where W, B are number of hectares of wheat and barley grown, S_1, S_2 and S_3 are surplus land, fertilizer and manpower respectively. Clearly the 'slack' variables S_1, S_2 and S_3 make no contribution to profit.

We can start our analysis by identifying a first basic feasible solution corresponding to one of the vertices of the feasibility polygon.

An obvious basic feasible solution given the above equation is:

$\quad S_1 = 12, S_2 = 50, S_3 = 30, W = 0, B = 0.$

This corresponds to doing nothing, making no profit and leaving all resources completely idle (the point A on the feasibility polygon). The *basic* variables are S_1, S_2 and S_3 while W and B are *non-basic* variables. Now, it is possible to express the objective function in terms of the non-basic variables and to express the basic variables in terms of the non-basic variables.
If we do this we get:

$\quad$ Objective function $Z = 0 + 120W + 100B,$

subject to (1) $S_1 = 12 - W - B$
(2) $S_2 = 50 - 5W - 2B$
(3) $S_3 = 60 - 2W - 6B$
(obtained by re-arranging the constraint equations).

Now we might consider whether it is possible to improve the objective function by giving one of the non-basic values a non-zero value (this would involve it taking the place of one of the existing basic variables in the basis).

We note that W has a large positive coefficient. There are, thus, clear advantages in bringing this variable into the basis. However, the size of the value that we can give it is limited by the requirement that no variable can have a negative value.

If we look at equations (1), (2) and (3) above, and remembering that B still has the value zero:

From (1) max. value of $W = 12$

(2) max. value of $W = \dfrac{50}{5} = 10$

(3) max. value of $W = \dfrac{60}{2} = 30$

Thus, 10 is the maximum value we can assign to W without violating any of the non-negativity constraints. Thus W now becomes basic and replaces S_2 which now has a zero value and leaves the basis.
Our new solution, therfore, is:

$$W = 10, \ B = 0, \ S_1 = 2, \ S_2 = 0, \ S_3 = 40, \ \text{profit} = 1200$$

This corresponds to the vertex E in the feasibility polygon (Figure 7.5).

We can now repeat the process writing the objective function in terms of non-basic variables and expressing each basic variable as a function of the non-basic variables.

From equation (2) $W = 10 - \dfrac{2}{5}B - \dfrac{S_2}{5}$.

Hence, in order to keep the objective function in terms of non-basic variables, we must substitute for W.

Thus $Z = 120\left\{10 - \dfrac{2}{5}B - \dfrac{S_2}{5}\right\} + 100B$

i.e. $Z = 1200 - 48B - 24S_2 + 100B$
$\phantom{\text{i.e. }}Z = 1200 + 52B - 24S_2$

The constraint equations become:

(1a) $S_1 = 12 - \left(10 - \dfrac{2}{5}B - \dfrac{S_2}{5}\right) - B$

$ = 2 + \dfrac{2}{5}B + \dfrac{S_2}{5} - B$

$ = 2 - \dfrac{3}{5}B + \dfrac{S_2}{5}$

(2a) $W = 10 - \dfrac{2}{5}B - \dfrac{S_2}{5}$

(3a) $S_3 = 60 - 2\left(10 - \dfrac{2}{5}B - \dfrac{S_2}{5}\right) - 6B$

$ = 60 - 20 + \dfrac{4}{5}B + \dfrac{2}{5}S_2 - 6B$

$ = 40 + \dfrac{2}{5}S_2 - \dfrac{26}{5}B$

We note that the variable, B, still has a large positive coefficient, thus we can increase our profit by giving B a positive value and bringing it into the basis.

We can find the maximum possible value that can be ascribed to B by looking at constraint equations (1a, 2a, 3a).

From (1a) max. value of $B = \dfrac{10}{3}$,

 (2a) max. value of $B = 25$,

 (3a) max. value of $B = \dfrac{200}{26} = \dfrac{100}{13}$.

Thus, the maximum possible value that B can take without violating any of the non-negativity constraints $= \dfrac{10}{3}$.

Our new basic feasible solution is $B = 3\frac{1}{3}$, $W = 8\frac{2}{3}$, $S_1 = 0$,
$S_2 = 0$, $S_3 = 40 - \dfrac{26}{5} \times \dfrac{10}{3} = \dfrac{68}{3} = 22\frac{2}{3}$.

This corresponds to the vertex D on the feasibility polygon. We have already seen by the graphical method that this corresponds to the optimum. This can be verified by expressing the objective function in terms of the non-basic variables.

This gives the following:

$$B = \frac{5}{3} \{2 + \frac{S_2}{5} - S_1\}$$

Substituting for B in the objective function we get:

$$Z = 1200 + 52 \times \frac{5}{3} \{2 + \frac{S_2}{5} - S_1\} - 24S_2,$$

$$= 1200 + \frac{520}{3} + \frac{52}{3}S_2 - \frac{260}{3}S_1 - 24S_2,$$

$$= 1373\frac{1}{3} - \frac{20}{3}S_2 - \frac{260}{3}S_1.$$

It is quite clear that it is impossible to improve the basis by giving S_1 or S_2 non-zero values. Since they both have negative coefficients the effect would be to reduce the overall profitability.

7.4.1 The Simplex Method

The procedure outlined in the preceding section is rather tedious. The simplex method involves writing out basic feasible solutions in the form of a tableau, and the application of a few simple rules ensures that we move to a different basic feasible solution which is nearer to the optimum. Mathematically, this is equivalent to the procedure that has been carried out in the preceding section.

Taking the farmer's problem once again, we can easily identify an initial basic feasible solution:

$W = 0$, $B = 0$, $S_1 = 12$, $S_2 = 50$ and $S_3 = 60$.

We then construct the following tableau in which basic variables are expressed as a function of non-basic variables, and the objective function is written in terms of non-basic variables. The purpose of the column (Θ) will be outlined shortly.

				Variables				
Basic Variable	Value (b)	W	B	S_1	S_2	S_3	(Θ)	
S_1	12	1	1	1	0	0	12	
S_2	50	5	2	0	1	0	10	←pivot row
S_3	60	2	6	0	0	1	30	
obj. Z	0	120	100	0	0	0		

$\uparrow$
pivot column

We then go through the following procedure:

(1) Examine the signs of the coefficients in the objective function. Select the largest positive coefficient (in this case, 120 belonging to column W) in the tableau above. This column is the *pivot* column and the variable associated with this pivot column (i.e. W) will be the variable that enters the basis.

(2) We now calculate the "(Θ)" for each row (this is simply equal to b/corresponding element of pivot column). These values are given under col (Θ). The row with the minimum (Θ) value is designated the *pivot row* and the variable which corresponds to this row will now leave the basis (this is S_2 in this case).

(3) The pivot row and pivot column intersect at the *pivot element*. This element is marked with a $\square$ in the tableau. Then divide all elements in the pivot row by the pivot element. This gives the new pivot row. All elements in the new pivot column are zero except for the pivot element.

Thus the new tableau becomes:

Basic Variable	Value (b)	W	B	S_1	S_2	S_3	
S_1		0					
W	10	1	$\frac{2}{5}$	0	$\frac{1}{5}$	0	← new pivot row
S_3		0					
Z		0					

$\uparrow$
new pivot column

All the other elements are calculated according to the following rules:

New element = Old element − corresponding element in old pivot col. x corresponding element in new pivot row

Taking the element at the top left-hand corner we get:

Old element = 12, corresponding element in old pivot column = 1
corresponding element in new pivot row   = 10

New element = $12 - 10 \times 1 = 2$

In this way we can calculate the remaining elements in the tableau:

	Basic Variable	Value (b)	W	B	S_1	S_2	S_3	(Θ)	
	S_1	2	0	3/5	1	− 1/5	0	10/3	← pivot row
	W	10	1	2/5	0	1/5	0	25	
	S_3	40	0	26/5	0	− 2/5	1	100/13	
obj.	Z	− 1200	0	52	0	− 24	0		

↑
pivot column

The above tableau corresponds to the vertex E on the feasibility polygon with profit of £1200 ($W = 10$ hectares, $B = 0$ hectares). If we repeat the above sequence of steps, we find that B has a large positive coefficient and thus should be the new pivot column. The values of (Θ) indicate that S_1 is the pivot row. Hence, B takes the place of S_1 in the basis and, applying the rules we have already derived, we get the following tableau:

	Basic Variable	Value (b)	W	B	S_1	S_2	S_3
	B	10/3	0	1	1⅔	− ⅓	0
	W	8⅔	1	0	− ⅔	⅓	0
	S_3	22⅔	0	0	− 8⅔	4/3	1
obj.	Z	− 1373⅓	0	0	− 86⅔	− 6⅔	0

This is equivalent to vertex D on the feasibility polygon (i.e. $W = 8\frac{2}{3}$, $B = 3\frac{1}{3}$, $Z = 1373\frac{1}{3}$). This corresponds to the optimum solution since the coefficients of all the non-basic variables are negative.

Thus the simplex method starts from any given vertex on the feasibility polygon. Each iteration will yield an improved solution and hence an optimum may be reached in a finite number of steps.

Exercise 7.3

Solve Exercise 7.1 using the simplex technique.

7.4.2   Shadow Prices

There is considerable additional information that can be obtained from an examination of the optimal solution which we obtained in the previous two sections.

It will be remembered that in the optimum solution the objective function was:

$$Z = 1373\frac{1}{3} - 86\frac{2}{3} S_1 - 6\frac{2}{3} S_2$$

where S_1 and S_2 were non-basic variables (i.e. had zero value).

As we have already remarked, it would not be worth our while to introduce S_1 and S_2 in the basis giving them non-zero values. Every unit of S_1 included in our solution would reduce profit by £$86\frac{2}{3}$ pounds, every unit of S_2 would reduce profit by £$6\frac{2}{3}$.

Now S_1 corresponds to 'slack' land, thus adding a hectare of this is exactly equivalent to reducing the supply of land by one unit. Reducing the supply of land by one hectare, therefore, leads to loss in profit of £$86\frac{2}{3}$. Conversely, increasing the supply of land by one hectare will increase profit by £$86\frac{2}{3}$. Thus, if the farmer is able to rent land for less than £$86\frac{2}{3}$ a hectare, it would be profitable for him to do so. This value £$86\frac{2}{3}$ is called the *shadow price* of land.

A similar argument will establish the shadow price of fertilizer as £$6\frac{2}{3}$ a cwt. It can also be seen that the shadow price of manpower is zero. This means that another man-week of labour is worth precisely nothing. The reason for this is quite clear. In our optimal solution we already have 22⅔ man-weeks of spare manpower. With so much surplus resource already available it would be quite pointless to pay for any more.

Exercise 7.4

What are the shadow prices of machine hours, warehouse space and painter time in Exercise 7.1?

7.4.3 Simplex Method: Treatment of Greater Than or Equal To Constraints

Consider now the minimization case that we looked at in Section 7.3. This problem was Minimize $Q_A + 4Q_B$ subject to the following constraints:

Quantity constraint, $Q_A + Q_B \geq 2000$,
Protein constraint, $Q_A + 3Q_B \geq 4000$,
Fat constraint, $Q_A + 2Q_B \leq 3500$.

We can turn the minimization problem into a maximization one by maximizing the negative of the objective function (this is equivalent to minimization).

If we turn inequality constraints into equality constraints by the addition of 'slack' variables, we obtain the following:

$Q_A + Q_B - S_1 = 2000$,
$Q_A + 3Q_B - S_2 = 4000$,
$Q_A + 2Q_B + S_3 = 3500$,

where S_1 is the quantity supplied above the minimum, S_2 is the number of units of protein supplied above the minimum. S_3 is the amount of fat below the limit which is supplied.

S_1, S_2, S_3 are all ≥ 0.

We cannot in this case, however, easily identify an initial basic feasible solution as we could in the previous problem. If we simply try:

$$Q_A = 0, \; Q_B = 0 \text{ we get } S_1 = -2000,$$
$$S_2 = -4000,$$
$$S_3 = 3500.$$

This 'solution', however, violates the non-negativity constraints on S_1 and S_2 and thus must be regarded as a non-starter.

A way around this is to introduce 'dummy' variables Z_1 and Z_2 into the first two constraint equations. If this is done we get the following set of constraints:

$$Q_A + Q_B - S_1 + Z_1 = 2000, \quad \text{(I)}$$
$$Q_A + 3Q_B - S_2 + Z_2 = 4000, \quad \text{(II)}$$
$$Q_A + 2Q_B + S_3 = 3500. \quad \text{(III)}$$

It is possible to identify an initial basic feasible solution.

$$Q_A = Q_B = S_1 = S_2 = 0,$$
$$Z_1 = 2000, \; Z_2 = 4000, \; S_3 = 3500$$

We must, however, devise a way to ensure that no dummy variable makes an appearance in the optimal solution. We can do this by introducing Z_1 and Z_2 into the objective function and giving them large negative coefficients. This will automatically ensure that they are removed from the basis at an early stage.

Thus, the objective function becomes:

Maximize
$$Z = -Q_A - 4Q_B - MZ_1 - MZ_2$$

Where M is a very large positive number. Writing out our simplex tableau we must first obtain our objective function in terms of non-basic variables:

From I $\; Z_1 = 2000 - Q_A - Q_B + S_1$
$\quad$ II $\; Z_2 = 4000 - Q_A - 3Q_B + S_2$

$$Z = -Q_A - 4Q_B - M(2000 - Q_A - Q_B + S_1) - M(4000 - Q_A - 3Q_B + S_2)$$
$$Z = -6000M + (2M - 1)Q_A + 4(M - 1)Q_B - MS_1 - MS_2$$

Basic Variable	Value (b)	Q_A	Q_B	S_1	S_2	S_3	Z_1	Z_2	(Θ)	
Z_1	2000	1	1	-1	0	0	1	0	2000	
Z_2	4000	1	$\boxed{3}$	0	-1	0	0	1	4000/3	←pivot row
Z_3	3500	1	2	0	0	1	0	0	1750	
obj. Z	$6000M$	$(2M-1)$	$4(M-1)$	$-M$	$-M$	0	0	0		

↑
pivot column

∴ Q_B takes place of Z_2 in basis.

Basic Variable	Value (b)	Q_A	Q_B	S_1	S_2	S_3	Z_1	Z_2	(Θ)	
Z_1	$\tfrac{2}{3}000$	$\boxed{\tfrac{2}{3}}$	0	-1	$\tfrac{1}{3}$	0	1	$-\tfrac{1}{3}$	1000	←pivot row
Q_B	$\tfrac{4}{3}000$	$\tfrac{1}{3}$	1	0	$-\tfrac{1}{3}$	0	0	$\tfrac{1}{3}$	4000	
S_3	$\tfrac{5}{6}000$	$\tfrac{1}{3}$	0	0	$\tfrac{2}{3}$	1	0	$-\tfrac{2}{3}$	$\tfrac{5}{2}000$	
Z	$(\tfrac{2}{3}000M+ \tfrac{16}{3}000)$	$(\tfrac{2}{3}M+\tfrac{1}{3})$	0	$-M$	$(\tfrac{M}{3}-\tfrac{1}{3})$	0	0	$-\tfrac{1}{3}(M-1)$		

↑
pivot column

∴ Q_A takes place of Z_1 in basis.

Basic Variable	Value (b)	Q_A	Q_B	S_1	S_2	S_3	Z_1	$\bullet Z_2$	(Θ)	
Q_A	1000	1	0	$-3/2$	$\tfrac{1}{2}$	0	$3/2$	$-\tfrac{1}{2}$	2000/3	
Q_B	1000	0	1	$\tfrac{1}{2}$	$-\tfrac{1}{2}$	0	$-\tfrac{1}{2}$	$\tfrac{1}{2}$	2000	
S_3	500	0	0	$\boxed{\tfrac{1}{2}}$	$\tfrac{1}{2}$	1	$-\tfrac{1}{2}$	$-\tfrac{1}{2}$	1000	←pivot row
Z	5000	0	0	$\tfrac{1}{2}$	$-3/2$	0	$-M-\tfrac{1}{2}$	$-M+3/2$		

↑
pivot column

∴ S_1 takes place of S_3 in basis

The above tableau corresponds to vertex X.

Basic Variable	Value (b)	Q_A	Q_B	S_1	S_2	S_3	Z_1	Z_2
Q_A	2500	1	0	0	2	3	0	-2
Q_B	500	0	1	0	-1	-1	0	1
S_1	1000	0	0	1	1	2	-1	-1
Z	4500	0	0	0	-2	-1	$-M$	$-M+2$

The above tableau corresponds to vertex Z and is optimal.

Since, however, we maximized the negative of the objective function; the lowest cost solution is £4500 with Q_A = 2500 and Q_B = 500.

Exercise 7.5

Interpret the shadow prices in the above example.

Exercise 7.6

Use the simplex method to solve Exercise 7.2. Discuss the shadow prices.

7.5   The Use of Computer Packages

7.5.1   Applications

As we have seen, the availability of the simplex method enables us to tackle considerably larger problems than was possible using graphical methods. Many problems of industrial interest, however, involve hundreds (or sometimes even thousands) of variables and constraints. Thus, some aid with the computation is essential if we are to handle this type of problem.

Many computing facilities provide linear programming packages. Each package will specify the required format of input data. Inset 1 shows the input format for the farmer's problem. This package was then used to solve the farmer's problem.

```
***** PROBLEM NUMBER  1 *****

        TITLE
        FARMER
        REGULAR
        VARIABLES
        W  B
        MAXIMIZE
        120W+100B
        CONSTRAINTS
   1.   W+B.LE.12
   2.   5W+2B.LE.50
   3.   2W+6B.LE.60
        RNGOBJ
        RNGRHS
        PRINT
        CHECK
        OPTIMIZE
```

Inset 1

7.5.2 Results

(i) Optimal solution

A summary of results is shown in inset 2. As expected, the optimum
is identical to that obtained earlier (i.e. 8⅔ hectares of wheat *(W)*,
3⅓ hectares of barley *(B)*, 22⅔ man-weeks of slack manpower {
this is slack row 3 in inset (2)}. Maximum profit is again £1373⅓.
Shadow prices are shown as opportunity costs in this print out. As
before we get the shadow price of land = £86⅔. Shadow price of
fertilizer is £6⅔.

```
USING REGULAR
FARMER


                      SUMMARY OF RESULTS

VAR   VAR      ROW STATUS        ACTIVITY        OPPORTUNITY
 NO  NAME       NO                LEVEL             COST
  1  W          --    B        8.6666667        0.0000000
  2  B          --    B        3.3333333        0.0000000
  3  SLACK-- D-   1   LB       0.0000000       86.6666667
  4  SLACK-- D-   2   LB       0.0000000        6.6666667
  5  SLACK-- D-   3   B       22.6666667        0.0000000


    MAXIMUM VALUE OF THE OBJECTIVE FUNCTION =       1373.333333


    CALCULATION TIME WAS     .0010 SECONDS FOR   3 ITERATIONS.
```

Inset 2

(ii)   Sensitivity analysis
Two sensitivity analyses are provided in this print-out:
(a) the optimality range for right-hand-side constants,
(b) optimality range for cost coefficients.

```
USING REGULAR
FARMER
```

```
                              RNGRHS
                              ******
              (OPTIMALITY RANGE FOR RIGHT-HAND-SIDE CONSTANTS)
                         NON-SLACK RESOURCES ONLY

  BI    XOUT      MIN  BI      ORIGINAL BI      MAX  BI     XOUT
                  --------     -----------      -------
                  Z-LOWER          Z            Z-UPPER


   1     2        10.000         12.000         14.615        5
                  1200.0         1373.3         1600.0

   2     5        33.000         50.000         60.000        2
                  1260.0         1373.3         1440.0


       CALCULATION TIME WAS    .004 SECONDS
```

Inset 3

(a)   Optimality range for right-hand-side constraints (inset 3)
We have seen that the shadow price of land is £86⅔ per hectare.
This means that the availability of an additional hectare of land is
worth £86⅔. There must clearly, however, be some limit to this. If
say, 100 hectares of additional land were available, these could not
be worth $100 \times$ £86⅔. Some other constraint would be reached
before it would be possible to utilize all 100 additional acres.

Inset 3 provides this sensitivity analysis; the value of shadow
price for land is only valid between 10 and 14.615 hectares. For
land availability outside this range, a different basis will make up
the optimum solution. Similarly, the relevant range for fertiliser
supply is 33—60 cwt.

(b)   Optimality range for cost coefficients (inset 4)
At present, the farmer receives £100 for each hectare of barley
grown. Suppose the price of barley were to rise and the price of
wheat to remain constant. It is likely that a point would be reached

```
                              RNGOBJ
                              ******
             (OPTIMALITY RANGE FOR COST COEFFICIENTS)
                       BASIC VARIABLES ONLY
```

CJ	XIN	MIN CJ	ORIGINAL CJ	MAX CJ	XIN
		-------	----------	-------	
		Z-LOWER	Z	Z-UPPER	
2	3	48.000	100.00	120.00	4
		1200.0	1373.3	1440.0	
1	4	100.00	120.00	250.00	3
		1200.0	1373.3	2500.0	

```
   CALCULATION TIME WAS   .004 SECONDS
```

Inset 4

where it would become profitable to abandon production of wheat. According to inset 4, this would occur when the price of barley rose to £120. Conversely, if the price of barley fell while that of wheat remained constant, we could reach the point where we abandoned attempts to grow barley and concentrated our resources on production of wheat. This would occur when the price of barley fell to £48.

As far as wheat is concerned the solution will remain optimal for wheat prices between £100 and £250 per hectare.

Exercise 7.7

If you have an available computer package, use it to solve Exercise 7.1

7.6   Linear Programming in Practice

7.6.1   General Approach

In the previous section we have seen that the availability of a linear programming computer package can make the calculation of a solution to a linear programming problem a relatively straightforward matter. The problems that we are likely to come across in real life, however, will not be so clearly defined as the examples we have discussed so far in this chapter. Thus, the major difficulties encountered are likely to arise in the problem definition and formulation phases, and in the interpretation of the solution obtained. Definition and formulation of a linear programming problem can be considered to consist of the following steps:

(i)   Definition of objectives
It is important at the outset to try to define objectives that we have in mind clearly. Properly defined objectives will facilitate the remainder of the problem formulation. For example, in the farmer's problem, the objective was to set appropriate areas of wheat and barley so as to maximize total profit.

(ii)   Definition of variables
This should also include designating appropriate dimensions and units. In the farmer's problem, the variables *W, B hectares* of wheat and barley should be defined.

(iii)   Formulation of constraints
All constraints must be clearly identified (note constraints can be greater than ($\geq$), less than ($\leq$) or equal to ($=$)). Incorrect specification of constraints may lead to infeasible solutions being considered or feasible (and possibly optimal solutions) being excluded.

(iv)   Formulation of objectives
The objective function should be formulated to yield an appropriate pay-off measure for all feasible solutions.

7.6.2 A More Difficult Example: Benzadol Chemical Company

The Benzadol Chemical Company has been formed by the merger of two separate companies — Benzadron Pharmaceutical Company and Aspadol Drugs Company, Ltd. The primary motive for the merger was to integrate production of hexatendrine, a by-product of the Benzadron production process which is an important ingredient in the manufacture of aspadol. A less important reason was to rationalize the use of computer time which is intensively used by both processes for quality control.

Benzadol policy has been to operate the two former companies as separate profit centres but this has caused considerable argument over what is a reasonable price to charge for the transfer to hexatendrine from Benzadron to Aspadol and also the price to charge for usage of computer time.

Table 7.1 shows the resource utilization for each division, together with available supplies of computer time and labour.

Table 7.1 Resources Used

		Benzadron Division	Aspadol Division	Capacity Available (per day)
Inputs	Computer Time (mins)	9.6	6.4	480
	Labour (man-hours)	6	5	260 (each division)
	Direct Costs (raw materials)	£4.8	£2.5	—
Outputs	Benzadron (kg)	3	—	—
	Aspadol (kg)	—	4	—

The manufacture of 4 kg of aspadol requires 2 kg of hexatendrine. This is obtained entirely from the Benzadron Division which produces 1 kg of hexatendrine as a by-product to each 3 kg of benzadron manufactured. Any excess hexatendrine (i.e. surplus to the requirements of the Aspadol Division) is currently sold on the external market at £2.5 per kg.

Currently, benzadron sells at £2.6 per kg and aspadol at £3 per kg and Benzadol thinks it can sell as much as it is able to produce at these prices.

(1) How much benzadron and aspadol should be produced?

(2) If you were asked to set a price for hexatendrine and computer time, what prices would you use?

(3) If extra computer time can be bought from a computer bureau at £1 per minute, would you advise Benzadol to use it?

If we now go through the stages of attempting to formulate this problem:

(i) Definition of objectives

The motive of the merger between Benzadron Pharmaceutical Co. and the Aspadol Drug Co. was to integrate production of hexatendrine, and to rationalize the use of computer time, presumably in order that the new amalgamated company can increase overall profitability. Thus profit maximization would appear to be a reasonable objective.

(ii) The three products are aspadol, benzadron and hexatendrine. We can define:

X_A = kg of aspadol produced,
X_B = kg of benzadron produced.

We may not need to define a variable to represent production of hexatendrine since we have an exact relationship between this product and aspadol and benzadron.

(iii) Formulation of constraints
(a) Computer time
Each kg of output of aspadol requires 1.6 min of computer time; similarly each kg of output of benzadron requires 3.2 min. Hence this constraint becomes:

$$1.6X_A + 3.2X_B \leq 480 \tag{7.1}$$

(b) Labour
Each kg of aspadol produced requires 1.25 man-hours of labour. Similarly, each kg of benzadron requires 2 man-hours. Hence:

$$1.25X_A \leq 260, \text{i.e. } X_A \leq 208, \tag{7.2}$$
$$2X_B \leq 260, \text{i.e. } X_B \leq 130. \tag{7.3}$$

(c) Hexatendrine
Each kg of aspadol that is produced requires ½ kg of hexatendrine. The source of hexatendrine is the benzadron production; ⅓ kg of hexatendrine resulting from the production of 1 kg of benzadron. If the process is to continue the supply of hexatendrine must be greater than or at least equal to demand:

X_B kg of benzadron production results in $\dfrac{X_B}{3}$ kg production of hexatendrine

X_A kg of aspadol production requires supply of $\dfrac{X_A}{2}$ kilos of hexatendrine

Hence, $\dfrac{X_B}{3} - \dfrac{X_A}{2} \geq 0$ $\qquad\qquad\qquad$ (7.4)

(iv) Objective function

Aspadol sells for £3 per kg and benzadron sells for £2.6 per kg. In addition, any excess hexatendrine can be sold for £2.5. Now the amount of excess hexatendrine is $(\dfrac{X_B}{3} - \dfrac{X_A}{2})$ kg. The direct cost of producing aspadol is £⅝ per kg and the direct cost of producing benzadron is £1.6 per kg, thus profit per kg of aspadol is £2⅜ and per kg of benzadron £1.

Hence the objective function is:

- $Z = 2\tfrac{3}{8}\, X_A + X_B + 2.5\,(\dfrac{X_B}{3} - \dfrac{X_A}{2})$,

i.e. $= \dfrac{9}{8}X_A + \dfrac{11}{6}X_B.$

We can now simplify these equations by multiplying through by appropriate factors and turn inequalities into equalities by the addition of slack variables:

i.e. constraints become:

(1)	Computer time	$X_A + 2X_B + S_1$	$= 300$
(2)	Aspadol labour	$X_A + S_2$	$= 208$
(3)	Benzadron labour	$X_B + S_3$	$= 130$
(4)	Hexatendrine	$3X_A - 2X_B + S_4$	$= 0$

Objective function − Maximize $27X_A + 44X_B$.

(a) If we solve this linear programming using either the simplex method or a linear programming package, we end up with the following optimal solution:

$$X_A = 75$$
$$X_B = 112.5$$
$$S_2 = 133$$
$$S_3 = 17.5$$
$$S_1 = 0$$
$$S_4 = 0$$

Thus 37½ kgs of hexatendrine are produced and used in the optimal solution.

(b) The shadow price on the hexatendrine constraint is 6p per kg. This is the value of additional hexatendrine and could, therefore, be used as a suitable transfer price between the two divisions. The shadow price of computer time works out at 94p per min. and this would be a suitable internal price to set.

(c) The offer of additional computer time at £1 per min. should be rejected since the availability of additional units of computer time only allows profits to be increased by 94p.

Exercise 7.8

A chemical company has four divisions producing four products. Each division uses labour and a common raw material. Some divisions also use as inputs two compounds which are by-products of other divisions, but which cannot be bought or sold in the market. The table below gives the amount of inputs and outputs associated with each division when operated at unit output levels, where inputs appear with negative signs and outputs with positive signs. There are constant returns to scale.

	Division 1	Division 2	Division 3	Division 4
Output	1	1	1	1
Raw material	− 3	− 2	− 5	− 4
Labour	− 4	− 3	− 1	− 2
By-product 1	1	− 3	4	− 1
By-product 2	− 2	0	− 3	4

The outputs of divisions 1, 2, 3 and 4 sell at £5.30, £4.20, £5.50, £3.20 per unit respectively, and the raw material costs 30p per unit. The company has 500 units of labour available. At what levels should the company operate the four divisions to maximize profits? If the firm could acquire additional units of by-product 1 for 20p per unit would you advise the firm to buy some?

Exercise 7.9

A continuous chemical process plant consists of two process stages — preparation and finishing. The plant can be used for making three possible products X, Y and Z, one at a time. Making X and Y uses both the preparation and finishing stages while Z uses the finishing stage only. The amounts of raw materials needed per tonne of each final product are 2.0, 1.6 and 1.2 tonnes per tonne of X, Y and Z respectively. The maximum capacity of the preparation stage is 100 tonnes per day of raw materials processed, and of the finishing stage 150 tonnes per day of finished product. The incremental profit on each product, taking account of raw material costs, manufacturing costs and selling prices of products, are 10, 12 and 8 m.u. (money units) per tonne of X, Y and Z respectively.

(a) Using the L.P. simplex procedure, find the production plan which, over a period of time, will maximize the plant profitability.

(b) Suppose a further requirement is that there is a minimum demand for each product equivalent to 10 tonnes per day; deduce the optimal production plan for this new situation.

In each case interpret the results to demonstrate their validity.

8

Making Decisions

8.1 Decision-Making in Practice

A decision-maker is often faced with choosing between a number of different courses of action in order to achieve some goal. Managers are employed to take decisions that will, they hope, help to achieve some of the objectives of their organization.

Decisions can be classified as *strategic* (where a non-routine, novel, ill-structured problem is faced) or *operational* (where repetitive day-to-day routine problems are encountered).

It is important that senior management spend their time and expertise on strategic decisions and do not fritter their time away on routine problems. For this reason, a policy is often laid down for such routine situations which will provide a *programmed* decision. An example of this is a stock control system for a particular line which involves automatically placing an order for 200 items once the stock on hand has fallen to 100. For the more ill-structured and non-routine problems the manager will need to take a separate decision each time. Such decisions are called *non-programmed* decisions.

The experience, skill and flair of the manager is extremely important for good decision-making but decision-making can be helped by the use of decision analysis. Decision analysis can help to identify the relationship between a sequence of decisions and their outcomes. It can also help the manager take uncertainty into account in a more formal way. Subjective judgement is highly important but decision analysis introduces a technique for revising subjective judgements in the light of subsequent evidence.

We outline below three practical situations in which decision analysis has been applied.

(1) A UK company was involved in developing an automatic landing system for aircraft in conditions of limited visibility. The company were, however, uncertain whether the proposed landing system would offer an acceptable degree of safety in the presence of radio interference.

The company had the option available of proceeding with the project or not. If they did decide to proceed they had the further option available of developing an environmental monitor which, if successfully adopted, would warn of the presence of extraneous interference and hence ensure that the landing system was never used in unsafe conditions.

A further option which emerged was to commission a one-year intensive study and simulation by the aircraft manufacturer into the ability of the aircraft landing equipment to operate properly in the presence of extraneous influence. Decision theory was used to evaluate these alternative options.

(2) A surgeon feels from symptoms exhibited that there is a strong possibility that a patient is suffering from a given disease whose treatment requires major surgery. There still remains a slight element of uncertainty and he feels that he would like more information before taking an irrevocable decision. He therefore carries out a series of tests and revises his earlier subjective judgement on the outcome of these tests.

(3) A North Sea Oil exploration outfit were considering whether to spend £25,000 on fitting an additional safety device to one of their drilling platforms. Fitting this device should considerably reduce the probability of over-pressurization of a valve. If over-pressurization does occur it is possible that no harm may be done. On the other hand over-pressurization could cause a rupture in the valve and a subsequent explosion. An explosion could cause either a six- or twelve-month delay to the project. Decision analysis was used to work out the economic consequences of deciding either to fit or not to fit the safety device.

Further case studies on the practical application of decision theory can be found in[1].

8.2 Structure of Decisions

Although a decision-maker may be faced with many different types of decision a common *structure* may be recognized.

As we have mentioned in the previous section, he will be trying to achieve some goal or objective. In practice this may be to achieve as large a profit as possible, maximize his market share, minimize costs, cure his patient. It is possible that some conflict may arise between different objectives (e.g. between maximizing profit and market share).

Secondly, the decision-maker should systematically search for a range of possible options from which a set of alternative courses of action can be determined. It is important that all feasible courses of action are identified as it is possible that an unlikely strategy may best achieve an objective. The discipline of attempting to apply decision analysis should help to ensure that such options are not overlooked.

Next we need to know the value of the possible outcomes associated with each strategy in terms of the decision-maker's objectives. Such values are known as the pay-offs. The set of pay-offs available associated with the outcomes associated with each decision is known as the *pay-off matrix.*

For instance, we have to decide between investing £100 in two different electronics companies, A and B. Suppose next year the economy may show either high, medium or low growth. If growth is high then the investment in Company A will be worth £200, if medium, £120 and if low, £80. Investment in Company B will be worth £160, £120 and £100 for high, medium and low growth respectively. Then this can be represented in matrix form as follows:

| | State of Nature | | |
	High Growth	Medium Growth	Low Growth
Investment A	200	120	80
Investment B	160	120	100

As we show below, this formulation often proves useful for analysis of the problem.

8.2.1 Decision-Making Criteria

Decisions are invariably made in an uncertain context (i.e. the state of nature is unknown). Otherwise, decision-making would be straightforward. In the previous example, if our objective was to maximize the value of our investment and we *knew* that high growth would take place then we would choose Investment A. The presence of uncertainty, however, makes life more difficult. Investment A gives the highest possible pay-off should growth be high, but if, in the event, growth turns out to be low then it will provide a lower return than Investment B. For this reason we need to establish criteria against which we can evaluate the pay-offs associated with each strategy.

8.2.2 Criterion of Pessimism

This criterion corresponds to identifying the worst possible outcome in each strategy and then identifying the 'best of the worst' outcome in order to select the optimal strategy.

For the previous problem this corresponds to:

	High Growth	*Medium Growth*	*Low Growth*	*Worst (min.) Outcome*
Investment A	200	120	80	80
Investment B	160	120	100	100

Clearly, applying the criterion of pessimism the optimal strategy is Investment B since the worst possible outcome here is the investment being worth £100.

8.2.3 Criterion of Optimism

This is just the reverse of the previous procedure; we identify the best possible outcome associated with each strategy and then choose the maximum of the maximum values. This is called the maximax.

For the previous example:

	High Growth	*Medium Growth*	*Low Growth*	*Best (max.) Outcome*
Investment A	200	120	80	200
Investment B	160	120	100	160

Applying this criterion, this means that Investment A is the optimal strategy since this investment has associated with it an outcome of £200.

8.2.4 Criterion of Regret

Here the approach used is to identify the regret (or opportunity loss) associated with cash outcome if a particular decision is undertaken.

For example, suppose that in our example the economy shows high growth. If we had decided to undertake Investment A, then our opportunity loss would be zero since this investment gives maximum return (£200) if the economy shows high growth. On the other hand, had we chosen Investment B we would have received a return of £160.

This is, however, £40 less than the return we could have received had we chosen Investment A. Therefore the opportunity loss associated with choosing Investment B in this instance is £40. In this way, an opportunity loss matrix can be constructed.

| | State of Nature | | | |
	High Growth	Medium Growth	Low Growth	Maximum Regret
Investment A	0	0	20	20
Investment B	40	0	0	40

We can then identify the maximum regret (opportunity loss) associated with each strategy. For strategy A this is £20 and for strategy B this is £40. If one sets out to minimize the maximum regret, this would cause one to choose strategy A.

8.2.5 The Concept of Expected Value

This concept allows us to take uncertainty into account explicitly.

Supposing we take part in a lottery and that prizes of value V_1, $V_2 \ldots V_k$ are offered. Suppose, further, that the probability of a given ticket winning each of these prizes is given by $P_1, P_2 \ldots P_k$. Then the expected value of the lottery tickets is:

$$P_1V_1 + P_2V_2 + \ldots + P_kV_k.$$

The expected value of the lottery ticket is the amount which would be won on average if a ticket was bought in the same lottery on many occasions.

Suppose a man invests £100 in a particular company. According to an investment analysis the probability of the following returns are: £200   0.5

    £100   0.3

    £0   0.2

∴ Expected value of the investment

= £200 × 0.5 + £100 × 0.3 + £0 × 0.2,

= £130.

Since he has already had to invest £100 the *expected gain* from the investment = £130 − £100 = *£30.*

8.2.6 Decision-Making under Uncertainty and Expected Pay-Off

Suppose we know the probabilities of the possible outcomes. For example, supposing we know that the probability of high growth in the economy is 0.5, the probability of medium growth is 0.3 and the probability of low growth 0.2. Then if we decide to invest in investment A our expected pay-off or expected value of this course of action will be:

200 × 0.5 + 120 × 0.3 + 80 × 0.2,

= 100 + 36 + 16,

= 152.

The expected pay-off if we take decision B will be:

160 × 0.5 + 120 × 0.3 + 100 × 0.2,

= 80 + 36 + 20,

= 136.

Thus, the expected value of investment A is higher. This means that, on average, one would get a higher return from investment A than from investment B. Thus, if one was adopting a policy of maximization of expected values investment A would be chosen. Since the decision is to be taken on a once-only basis, expected value might not be the best criterion to use. We shall consider this question later in our section on utilities.

Exercise 8.1

You have decided to dispose of your second-hand car. Unfortunately, it has failed its M.O.T. test and will require £100 spending on it to pass its test. A car-breaker has offered you £50 for it in its present condition. Since it is a foreign car you have little idea of the strength of the second-hand market for this make. If the market is strong then with an M.O.T. you would get around £250, if moderate around £150 and if weak £80.

Without an M.O.T. you would get £120, £80 and £50 respectively for strong, moderate and weak markets. If you decide to advertise your car for private sale, however, you incur a further £10 in advertising expenses.

(a) Identify the three possible strategies and construct the appropriate pay-off matrix.
(b) Which strategy would you adopt (i) if you were adopting the criterion of pessimism (ii) the criterion of optimism (iii) the criterion of regret?
(c) Supposing the probability of a strong, moderate and weak market are given by 0.3, 0.3 and 0.4 respectively. Which decision maximizes your expected value?

8.3 Sequential Problems

In practice, many decision-making problems have a long-drawn-out structure in so far as they consist of a whole sequence of decisions. Thus, the problem becomes a *multi-stage* one because the outcome of one decision affects future decisions. For instance, if a manufacturer is in the process of marketing a new type of radio one decision he may have to make is whether or not to test market the product. Given various possible outcomes of this course of action he may then be required to decide between re-designing the product, an energetic advertising campaign or complete withdrawal of the product and so on. This type of sequential decision problem can best be represented by a *decision tree*. A decision tree is thus a schematic representation of a decision problem.

A decision tree consists of *nodes, branches, probability estimates* and *pay-offs*. There are two sorts of nodes: decision nodes and chance nodes. A decision node is usually represented by a square, $\square$, and indicates that a deliberate decision has to be made to choose one of the branches which emanate from that node (i.e. one of the available strategies must be chosen).

If we consider the investment example discussed in Section 8.2 and represented by Figure 8.1 at decision node DN ≠ 1 we have to decide which of the two available strategies investment A or investment B ought to be followed.

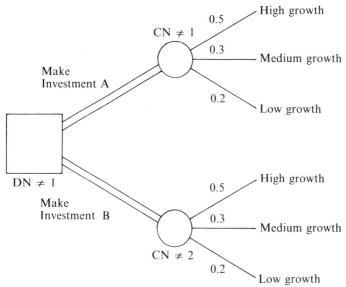

Figure 8.1

A chance node usually designated by a circle ○ shows the different possible events (states of nature, competitors actions or some other condition) which can result from a chosen strategy. For example in the investment example, high, medium or low economic growth may follow decisions to invest either in investment A or investment B.

Branches emanate from and connect various nodes. There are two types of branches, decision branches and chance branches. *Decision branches* (which may be represented by two parallel lines, =) represents a strategy or course of action. (Note two decision branches emanate from decision node DN ≠ 1). A *chance branch* (denoted by a single line, −) represents a chance-determined event. Associated probabilities are indicated alongside respective chance branches. Any branch that marks the end of the decision tree (i.e. it is not followed by either a decision or chance node) is called a *terminal* branch. A terminal branch can represent either a decision alternative or a chance outcome.

Pay-offs can be positive (i.e. revenue or sales) or negative (e.g. expenditure or costs) and they can be associated either with decision or chance branches.

It is possible for a decision tree to be *deterministic* or *probabilistic* and it can represent a single stage (one decision) or multi-stage (a sequence of decisions) situation.

8.3.1 Decision Tree Example

An oil company is attempting to decide what course of action to adopt with respect to a new exploration site. One option is to sell the rights of the site to a competitor for £5 million (£5m). A second option is to drill for oil immediately. The cost of carrying out this drilling operation will be £9m. If oil is discovered this will result in revenue of £40m to the company. If the well is dry there is, of course, no revenue. The probability of discovering oil if drilling takes place at once is 0.4. A third option is to carry out a seismic test, to see whether the rock structure is of oil-bearing form. (Cost, £1m).

It is reckoned that there is a 50:50 chance that a positive result will be obtained from such a test. In either case, the company have the option of carrying out the drilling operations with the same rewards for finding oil as before. If, however, a positive seismic test was obtained there is a 0.6 probability of finding oil if drilling goes ahead.

In the event of a negative seismic test this probability is reduced to 0.2. If a positive seismic test is obtained, however, the company have the option of selling its rights to the site for £7m.

8.3.2 Analysis of Example

The decision tree which corresponds to this example is given in Figure 8.2.

In order to analyse this tree we start working backwards from the end branches. Consider the section of tree in Figure 8.3. The expected value of the decision option to sell is quite clearly £7m. If

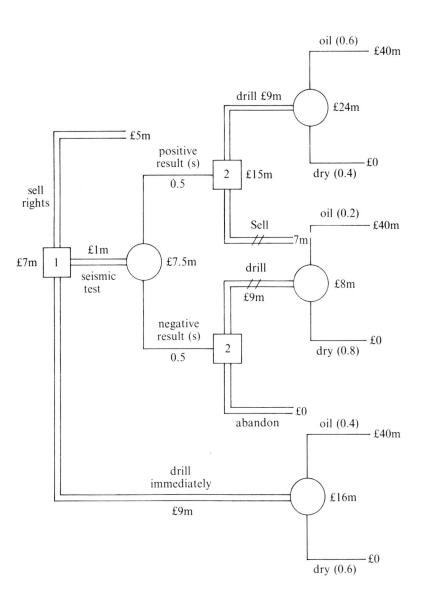

Figure 8.2   Decision tree for oil-field example

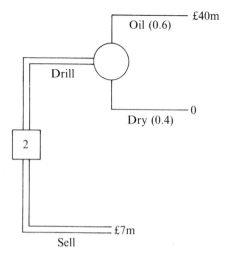

Figure 8.3

we look at the option to drill we see that this has a 0.6 probability of a £40m outcome and a 0.4 probability of zero.

Thus the expected value of this option is:

$$(0.6 \times £40m + 0.4 \times £0 = £24m) - £9m, \text{(the cost of drilling)}$$
$$= £15m.$$

Since this is greater than the £7m that can be obtained by selling the option, this becomes the preferred strategy.

Now, taking the branch of the tree which follows the negative seismic result, we have expected value of option of drilling:

$$0.2 \times £40m + 0.8 \times 0 - £9m = -£1m.$$

The expected value of abandoning the option is zero which dominates the option of drilling. Hence, the expected value of a negative result is zero. Now, let's get back to the first decision point.

Option 1 Selling rights has expected value of £5m.

Option 2 Seismic test; the expected value is:

0.5 × pay-off of positive result + 0.5 × pay-off of negative result − cost of test,

$$= \quad 0.5 \times \text{£15m} + 0.5 \times \text{£0} - \text{£1m,}$$
$$= \quad \text{£6.5m.}$$

Option 3 Drill immediately.
Expected return is $0.4 \times \text{£40m} + 0.6 \times 0 - \text{£9m}$ (cost of drilling),
$$= \quad \text{£16m} - \text{£9m,}$$
$$= \quad \text{£7m.}$$

Thus, the optimal strategy is to follow option 3 and drill immediately.

The example works in terms of cash pay-offs but it is possible to work with utilities in exactly the same way (see Section 8.4).

The results of such a decision tree exercise ought not to be accepted blindly. How sure are we that the costs and pay-offs are as described in the diagram?

Strategy 2 which would involve taking the seismic test, drilling if a positive result was obtained and abandoning if a negative result was obtained, has an expected value £0.5m less than strategy 3. However, this strategy has less risk about it. The really expensive decision is to drill. Drilling and finding no oil results in the £9m being spent with no return. If we drill immediately there is a 0.6 chance of this happening. If we undertake the seismic test and drill only if the result is positive there is only a 0.4 chance that the drilling will yield no oil. Thus, although the expected return of strategy 2 is lower it has rather less risk of a large loss. Of course, it can be argued that if we had worked in terms of utility throughout this risk would have been implicitly taken into account.

Exercise 8.2

Try to carry out the following decision tree exercise.

The Catastrophic Chemical Company regard Research and Development decisions as investment decisions and it is faced with a decision about a project to develop a series of sophisticated computer-controlled production facilities.

These facilities will give the firm an edge in the highly competitive market, but the R&D manager has doubts about the firm's technical capability to fulfil the project.

Under pressure from marketing and sales engineers, however, he will admit that the firm has an even chance of completing the project within three years. If the three-year period is exceeded the firm will lose money by incurring extra development costs and by lost market opportunities.

The R&D manager and the project engineers estimate the maximum cost for the research over the three-year period as £60,000 and that there is indeed an even chance of successful development within three years.

Should success not occur after three years they feel that there is the option of authorizing the sum of £20,000 to be spent over the next year in the hope of successful completion; the chances of the latter outcome is felt to be 0.4 since leading researchers would then have to be switched to other projects. If no viable production facilities were generated in four years they feel that they would have no option but to abandon the project. If, however, they were ready to launch at the end of four years then the group estimate a 0.2 chance of a pay-off of £180,000, a 0.4 chance of a pay-off of £100,000 and a 0.4 chance of a pay-off of £60,000.

Pay-offs resulting from a three-year development are, however, more attractive and are thought to be as follows: A 0.3 chance of £200,000, a 0.4 chance of £110,000 and a 0.3 chance of £70,000. If a project has to be abandoned they decide not to count as losses any inroads which competitors might make through the introduction of similar production facilities.

(1) Construct the decision tree facing the Catastrophic Chemical Company.
(2) Analyse the tree and determine the optimum decision.
(3) Comment on the decision above and discuss whether any subjective factors exist which ought to be considered.

Example 8.3
Betabrek Ltd.

Betabrek Ltd. are manufacturers of a popular breakfast cereal marketed in shops and supermarkets under the 'Betabrek' brand name. The company is concerned about the narrowness of its product range and detects possible fragmentation of the breakfast cereal market. It is therefore trying to diversify into the health food market where it feels the market is growing, and higher profit margins may be obtainable. Initially, it plans to use its existing distribution system, eventually also retailing through specialist health food outlets.

The manager who is responsible for launching the project has calculated that the value of a successful launch in present-day money terms would be £600,000. On the other hand, failure after the expenses of production and launching would entail losses equivalent to £900,000. Past experience suggests that the chances of a successful launch are around two in three.

The project team is now considering whether to try out the new product in a test market. Test marketing will give more information about the market but will not, in itself, change the likelihood of a successful launch. Two test markets are available with different costs and characteristics.

One of the test markets Proletaria would cost £50,000 to use. Consumers in this area are known to be unresponsive to new products, and success in Proletaria is thought to guarantee success in a national launch. On the other hand, the chances of success in Proletaria are rated at only $\frac{1}{3}$ while there is a 50% chance of success nationally even after failure in Proletaria.

Consumers in Patriciana, by contrast, are keen on new products and the chances of success there are put at 80%. There is, however, still at 25% chance of failure nationally even after success in Patriciana. There is still believed to be a $\frac{1}{3}$ chance of success nationally even after failure in Patriciana. The cost of using this test market is £100,000.

Analyse this situation and make recommendations for action by Betabrek Ltd.

8.4 The Concept of Utility

8.4.1 Limitations of Concept of Expected Value

So far, we have made considerable use of the concept of expected value. This concept, however, has grave limitations in certain cirumstances. Let us take the oil exploration example. Suppose a small Scottish-based company have been given exploration rights over this block. Adopting the approach of attempting to maximize expected value we should adopt the strategy of drilling immediately. This strategy, however, involves investing £9m with a 0.6 risk of failing to find any oil. If oil is obtained, however, the company might expect to receive a handsome profit. Suppose, however, the Company's assets only amounted to a total of £7m.

Then, even if it were able to finance the project, it would be taking a 0.6 chance of potential bankruptcy. Unless the company were already in absolutely desperate financial straits, it would seem to be totally unacceptable to embark on a course of action involving a 0.6 probability of bankruptcy.

Now the company could reduce the potential risk by spending £1m on a seismic test. But, even given a positive result from the test, if the company drills it will face a 0.4 probability of catastrophic failure. This is a situation which cannot be adequately covered by the expected value concept. The most sensible course of action for the company to follow might be to sell its interest in the block to a larger company who could afford to face a loss of £9m. It might be possible for the company to negotiate an interest in the contract but keep its amount of capital at risk to an acceptable level.

Thus, this is a situation not adequately covered by the use of the expected value concept.

Taking a further example, the expected value of an insurance policy must in most cases be negative (this must follow since pay-out of claims is generally less than the intake of premiums). In spite of this, however, most rational individuals still take out insurance policies, since they are not prepared to take the risk of, say, a total catastrophic loss caused by their house burning down or a car accident.

On the other hand, some large companies may follow a policy of bearing risk themselves on certain items e.g. accident damage to car fleet.

They may be in a position to do this, since an accident to any one car is not catastrophic as far as the company as a whole is concerned, and since the expected values of insurance policies are negative, then it is worth their while bearing the risk themselves.

8.4.2 Utility

In the previous section, we saw that a loss of £9m would cause the decision-makers' company to be declared bankrupt. If the company was able to withstand fairly comfortably the loss of £900,000, then we can say that the loss of £9m is more than ten times worse than the loss of £900,000. Obviously, we must develop our concept of utility in such a way that conversion of monetary units

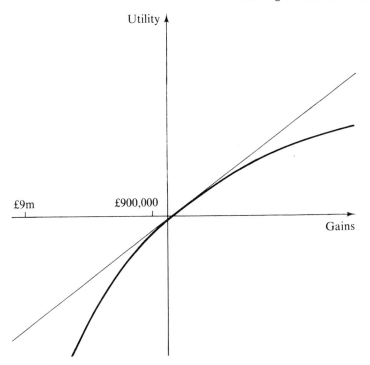

Figure 8.4

into utilities reflects such preferences.

Supposing we make the relationship between monetary gains and losses and utilities linear for gains and for small negative losses. Then, if we bend the curve down non-linearly as in Figure 8.4, we give large losses a disproportionately large negative utility. It is important not to make the curve bend down too steeply or to start the bending too quickly, since this could lead us into the situation where we attached such a heavy weighting to the possibility of loss that we never took any risks and thus never made any gains.

On the positive side of the curve, it is usual for the curve to eventually bend away from the straight line. This indicates that increasing units of money are resulting in smaller additional gains in utility.

The general shape of the utility curve in Figure 8.4 is one which is found quite commonly in practice. It corresponds to that of the *risk-averse* decision-maker. The straight line curve would correspond to that of a decision-maker who might be described as *risk-neutral*.

It would also be possible to construct a curve which bent upwards instead of downwards as in Figure 8.5. (risk-prone). This

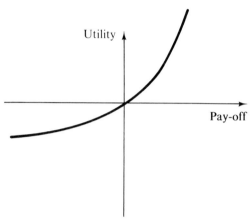

Figure 8.5

sort of curve would correspond to that of the gambler who prefers one large pay-off to the financial equivalent of a number of smaller ones. This might be the utility curve of a compulsive gambler. It could, however, represent the utility curve of a perfectly rational decision-maker whose company was in such desperate straits that only a very large gain could save it from collapse.

8.4.3 Application of the Concept of Utility

Taking the example of Section 8.3.1, we remember that the option of drilling immediately gave a return of £31m with a probability of 0.4. On the other hand, there was a 0.6 probability of no return at all giving an overall 9m loss.

Using the concept of expected value the expected value of this investment is £16m − £9m = £7m. Supposing the utility of the Scottish-based company is as follows:

A gain of £31m; utility + 60,
A loss of £9m;   utility − 100.

Thus, the expected utility for this strategy is:

$$60 \times 0.4 - 100 \times 0.6,$$
$$= 24 - 60,$$
$$= -36.$$

Thus, the adoption of expected utility as a criterion has resulted in the rejection of this strategy.

8.4.4 Construction of Utility Curves

Clearly, one of the major problems associated with the construction of utility curves is the identification of the group concerned with making the decision. It is then possible to construct the utility curve by presenting the decision-maker with a series of options. For example, we could ask the decision-maker about a hypothetical project. Suppose there is a project which will pay off with $+£10,000$ or $-£10,000$; what probability of success would make him just indifferent about whether to undertake the project of not? Supposing the decision-maker replies he would require an 80% probability of success to make him indifferent about undertaking the project. Now in order to develop this method we need to attach a utility value to one pay-off. Supposing the utility of $+£10,000$ is $+10$, then it follows that:

$$+10 \times 0.80 + U(-10,000) \times 0.20 = 0,$$
$$8 + U(-10,000) \times 0.20 = 0,$$
$$\therefore \ U(-10,000) = -40.$$

Now we have three points on the utility curve,
$$U(+10,000) = +10,$$
$$U(0) = 0,$$
$$U(-10,000) = -40.$$

We can obtain further points on the utility curve by continuing to pose such questions to the decision-maker. The problem with this approach is that the situations presented to the decision-maker are rather artificial and hypothetical and it will be difficult for the decision-maker to present consistent and unambiguous conclusions. This procedure can be given more realism however by attempting to relate it to either past or current projects. Efforts which have been made in the past to chart the utility curve of decision-makers have often shown quite surprisingly risk-averse behaviour.

8.5   Economics of Information

No matter how well we have defined our available strategies and set up our framework for taking decisions we still have to take decisions in the face of considerable uncertainty, with the associated risk of an unfavourable outcome. Clearly, if we had better information we could reduce the risk of an unfavourable outcome, and if we had perfect information then we could eliminate this risk entirely. Such information, however, can usually only be obtained at additional cost and therefore the question arises as to how much this additional information is worth.

Let us take a practical example. In Exercise 8.1 we considered the problem of selling a car and we had the options of
(i) getting an M.O.T. certificate and attempting to sell the car,
(ii) putting the car on sale without an M.O.T. (iii) taking the car to the breakers.

This problem can be represented by a decision tree (Figure 8.6).

It will be recalled that the option of selling without an M.O.T. gave the highest expected value (£70) and this therefore would be the optimum decision. Now if, however, an investigation was carried out to establish unequivocally whether the market is strong, moderate or weak we could improve on this.

If the survey definitely established that the market was strong then we would adopt option (i) at a return of £140. If the survey established that the market was moderate we would adopt option (ii) with a return of £70; and if it showed that the market was weak then we would adopt option (iii) with a return of £50.

Now we know the probabilities of the different outcomes of the survey (i.e. strong = 0.3, moderate = 0.3, weak = 0.4). Hence, with the survey we would have expected out-turn of:

$$0.3 \times 140 + 0.3 \times 70 + 0.4 \times 50, \quad \text{(see Figure 8.7)}$$
$$= 42 + 21 + 20,$$
$$= £83.$$

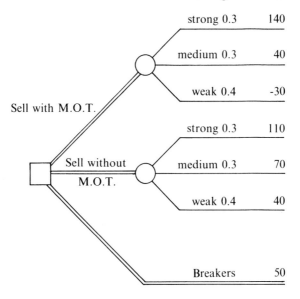

Figure 8.6

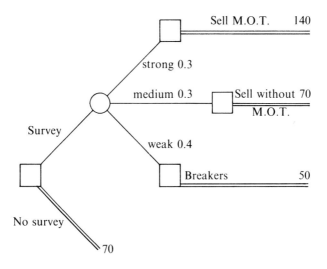

Figure 8.7

Thus, this information has increased the expected value of these decision processes from £70 to £83. Thus, we can say that the expected value of perfect information is £13 and it would, therefore, be worth paying up to this amount for the results of this investigation.

Exercise 8.4

Suppose in the example discussed above the probabilities of strong, weak and medium markets are 0.6, 0.2 and 0.2. In this case, what is it worth paying for a market survey which would give the definite strength of the market?

Exercise 8.5

Betabrek Ltd. (see Ex. 8.3) claim to have found a test market which would guarantee to correctly forecast whether their health food promotion would be successful. How much would it be worth to have such a test market available?

8.6 Modifying Probabilities Using Bayes' Theorem

In many situations, in the absence of clear historical evidence, we often have to make subjective judgements about the probability of future events occurring. We may then revise these probabilities in light of further evidence. This is done using *Bayes' Theorem*.

8.6.1 Bayes' Theorem

The theorem is a means of linking observed results with possible causes. Suppose TV repair tubes are made by manufacturers' M_1 and M_2, and suppose events E_1 and E_2 represent the production of defective or effective TV tubes.

It turns out that one TV tube selected at random is defective and we wish to work out the probability that it came from manufacturer M_1. This is known as the posterior probability and is given by $P(M_1|E_1)$. Bayes' theorem states that:

$$P(M_1|E_1) = \frac{P(E_1|M_1)P(M_1)}{P(E_1|M_1)P(M_1) + P(E_1|M_2)P(M_2)} .$$

$P(E_1|M_1)$ is the *prior* probability i.e. the probability of a defective tube given it is manufactured by manufacturer M_1. $P(M_1)$ is the probability that a tube chosen at random came from manufacturer M_1.

Suppose 40% of the tubes are produced by M_1 and 60% by M_2, and 1% and 2% respectively of the tubes produced by M_1 and M_2 turn out to be defective.

Then $P(M_1|E_1)$

$$= \frac{0.01 \times 0.40}{(0.01 \times 0.40) + (0.02 \times 0.60)}$$

$$= \frac{0.004}{0.004 + 0.012}$$

$$= 0.25$$

Exercise 8.6

Patients showing a given set of symptoms are thought to have a 0.70 probability of having contracted Blogg's disease. A further test for Blogg's disease has been discovered. It is found that 60% of patients with Blogg's disease give a positive response to this test. Unfortunately, 10% of patients who do not have Blogg's disease also give a positive test.

Supposing a patient who was showing the initial set of symptoms gives a positive result to the new test. What is the probability that he is suffering from Blogg's disease?

8.6.2 Relationship of Bayes' Theorem to Decision Theory

The above example helps us to see the way Bayes' theorem can aid decision-taking. For example, suppose a surgeon has to decide to operate or not. Then the information supplied by the application of Bayes' theorem should be very useful in this respect since it enables him to revise his initial judgement in the light of fresh information.

Let's take another example. Suppose the director of a company is interested in launching a new product. Supposing, he feels subjectively that there is a 0.60 probability that there will be a strong market for this product, a 0.20 probability of a moderate market and a 0.20 probability of low market. Suppose an initial market survey was carried out which gave a good response. Past experience has shown that there is a 0.5 probability of a good response if the market is strong, 0.3 if the market is moderate and 0.2 if the market is weak. We may want P(Market is strong | Good response) [s | GR]

Here, we can employ Bayes' theorem adopting the decision-maker's subjective judgement as prior probabilities.

$$P(s \mid GR) = \frac{P(GR \mid s)P(s)}{P(GR \mid s)P(s) + P(GR \mid m)P(m) + P(GR \mid w)P(w)}$$

where s, m, w = strong, moderate and weak markets.

Now, from above, $P(GR \mid s) = 0.5$, $P(GR \mid m) = 0.3$ and $P(GR \mid w) = 0.2$.

Prior probabilities are given by $P(s) = 0.6$, $P(m) = 0.2$, $P(w) = 0.2$.

Thus, from Bayes' theorem, we have:

$$P(s \mid GR) = \frac{0.5 \times 0.6}{0.5 \times 0.6 + 0.3 \times 0.2 + 0.2 \times 0.2}$$

$$= \frac{0.30}{0.30 + 0.06 + 0.04}$$

$$= 0.75$$

Thus, Bayes' theorem has enabled him to modify his subjective judgement in the light of the new information.

Exercise 8.7

In the above example, suppose there is a bad response to the initial survey. If previous experience teaches us that the probability of a bad response when the markets are strong, moderate and weak are 0.1, 0.4 and 0.5 respectively, what is the decision-makers' revised probability of the market being weak?

Exercise 8.8 Sparky Electronics

Sparky Electronics makes printed circuit boards for Plum microcomputer manufacturer. As part of the agreement Sparky pay a penalty clause of £20 each time they supply a defective board (which Plum themselves then correct and use). At present, some 20% of the boards supplied by Sparky incur this penalty. One of the engineers has found a novel method of fabricating the circuit boards. It is reckoned that this will reduce the defective proportion to 5%. It does, however, increase the direct cost of manufacturing the boards by £4 per board. A new testing device has also been developed. Unfortunately, it does not give 100% correct results. It has been applied to a number of known good and bad units with the following results: 80% of the known good components gave a positive test but 10% of the known defective ones gave positive tests also. The direct cost of each board is £10 and any board that does not register a positive test is scrapped. Carrying out the test costs £1 per time. Sparky receive £18 for every effective board delivered. Advise Sparky.

8.7 Decision Analysis in Practice

Few decision-makers will simply adopt the results of decision analysis without question. There may be other unquantifiable factors that the decision-maker wants to take into account.

Nevertheless, the formal analysis should provide an intellectual framework within which the decision can be considered and it should highlight the causes and effects sequence of the decision problem. Carrying out the analysis should help to reduce the possibility that likely strategies are overlooked. It is, of course, possible that, in a complex situation, different analysis will conceive different decision trees. This adds a further dimension of subjectivity to the problem.

9

Production Planning: Stock Control

9.1 Inventory Control – Introduction

Most organizations carry substantial stocks or inventories and in many cases these inventories may comprise a significant proportion of the assets of the organization. The function of inventories is to incorporate flexibility and to decouple the different parts of the production-distribution-consumption chain. Obviously, a factory could not operate efficiently if it did not hold stocks of raw materials and, unless each item is processed through the plant individually, there are bound to be stocks of partially finished goods in different parts of the production system. All retail outlets need to hold extensive stocks of product if they are to provide an adequate service to their customers.

Stock-holdings comprise a large investment both from the point of view of the individual company and the nation as a whole. It is therefore important that such investment is wisely controlled.

9.2 Stock Control

9.2.1 Types of Inventory

(i) Raw materials
The purpose of holding stocks of raw materials is to decouple the production process from the supply of these materials.

(ii) Work in progress
These are the stocks of partially finished product which build up in the various phases of a production process, whether or not they

have been specifically planned for. Such stocks decouple later stages of the production process from earlier stages. This is important since it is not possible to achieve perfect synchronization between all stages of the manufacturing process.

(iii) Finished goods
Stocks of finished goods provide a buffer between customer demands and production. Most manufacturers will hold stocks of finished goods so that orders from customers can be met from stock, although batches of non-standard products may be made when specific orders are received.

9.2.2 Costs Associated with Stock holding

We shall now consider the costs associated with stock holding systems.

(i) Cost of replenishing stock (set-up costs)
Each time an order is placed for a replenishment order certain costs are incurred, depending on whether the goods are obtained from within or outwith the organization. If goods are obtained from outwith the organization, costs associated with placing the order include the costs of issuing the order, postage, receiving, checking the goods and placing them into storage.

On the other hand, if goods are obtained from the company's own manufacturing facilities, the cost of placing the order will also involve the cost of changing over product lines. This may involve costs associated with tools and materials; moreover, production will be lost during the changeover period. The contribution that would have been obtained from such production (assuming that it would have been possible to sell it) should thus also be included in set-up cost.

(ii) Stock holding or carrying costs
Quite clearly, higher levels of inventory involve higher costs. The major cost is the opportunity cost of capital tied up in stock. If not invested in stock, this capital would be available for investment either in a bank or in other income-earning investment (perhaps additional investment in plant and materials). In addition, there are the costs associated with storage of goods (cost of providing and running premises, insurance, etc.). With certain products there may

also be risks of deterioration or even obsolescence.

Annual stock-holding costs are generally expressed as a percentage of the annual inventory value.

(iii) Stock-out costs

Costs of running out of stock include the profit on any sales that are lost as a consequence and also potential future losses through the possibility of a customer transferring his future business elsewhere.

There are many imponderables involved in assessing the exact magnitude of these costs, thus much work is centred on the concept of providing a specific 'service-level' (probability of running out of stock on a given stock cycle).

9.2.3 General Problems of Controlling Stocks

In most stock control situations we are faced with the problem of attempting to balance the costs described in the previous section. Clearly, severe damage to the profitability and liquidity of a company can be caused by holding excessive levels of stock. There may be many factors which contribute towards this. These may include a desire by the marketing function to give quick delivery, resulting in excessive stockpiling; excessive product variety; poor production scheduling and even private stockpiling of components by middle management.

Situations in which excessively low stocks are held are by no means uncommon, however, resulting in frequent costly set-ups and poor service to customers.

9.3 Stock control techniques

9.3.1 Pareto Analysis

We have now seen some of the basic stock handling problems that we may encounter. In a practical situation, however, it is possible to be overwhelmed by the sheer number of stock-lines that a company holds in its stores. By *stock-line* we mean the number of distinguishable products — thus a 2 centimetre length bolt is considered as a different product from a 2½ centimetre length bolt. It is not uncommon for a company to have several hundred or even many thousand stock-lines in its stores. This makes it difficult for the analyst to develop insight into the problem and to judge where the allocation of greatest effort might effect the greatest improvement in the operation of the system.

One approach to try to break down the problem into a more manageable form involves the use of a technique known as Pareto analysis. This approach involves ranking lines according to the cash value of turnover associated with that line. In practice, it is often found that a comparatively small proportion of lines account for a very substantial proportion of turnover. (It is not uncommon for the top 20% of lines to account for 80% or more of the total turnover). At the other end of the scale it is likely that a comparatively large proportion of the lines will only make up a few per cent of overall turnover. By classifying items in this way it may be possible to break the problem down to more manageable proportions.

It is usual to break the lines down into three broad categories.

Category A
High turnover items which may comprise only 10—20% of the number of lines but account for 70—85% of total turnover.

Category B
Middle value items comprising perhaps 20—30% of the number of lines but amounting to 10—25% of turnover.

Category C
Low turnover items — perhaps 60—70% of the total number of lines — but amounting to 5—15% of turnover only.

Obviously, the above procedure is not an exact analysis, the exact number of classes and choice of appropriate divisions between classes being to some extent arbitrary.

In the following example we show how to carry out a Pareto analysis on a restricted number of lines. Table 9.1 shows the turnover of twenty-five individual stock-lines which have been chosen at random.

Table 9.1 Figures from twenty-five stock-lines taken at random

Item	Annual Turnover (£)
A	261
B	8
C	524
D	22
E	618
F	64
G	10
H	4
I	2
J	3
K	2
L	27
M	4
N	4
O	125
P	219
Q	2
R	6
S	277
T	38
U	18
V	3
W	53
X	102
Y	4
TOTALS:	2400

Table 9.2 shows stock-lines in descending value of annual turn-over. We may decide that items E, C, S, A and P should constitute Category A (79% of turnover) and O, X, F, W and T (a further 16% of turnover) should make up Category B. The remaining items which constitute only 5% of turnover could be classified as Category C.

9.3.2 Use of the Pareto Analysis

Carrying out the Pareto analysis enables an organization to gain more insight into the stock problems it faces. It may also decide that it is more important to effect improvements in control of its Category A items, rather than B or C category and concentrate its resources accordingly. This could involve using different stock

Table 9.2   Stock-Line in Descending Order of Annual Turnover

% of Items	Item	Annual Turnover	Cumulative Annual Turnover	% of Total Annual Usage	Category
	E	618	618		
	C	524	1142		
	S	277	1419		A
	A	261	1680		
20%	P	219	1899	79%	
	O	125	2024		
	X	102	2126		
	F	64	2190		B
	W	53	2243		
40%	T	38	2281	95%	
	L	27	2308		
	D	22	2330		
	U	18	2348		C
	G	10	2358		
60%	B	8	2366	98.5%	
	R	6	2372		
	H	4	2376		
	M	4	2380		C
	N	4	2384		
80%	Y	4	2388	99.5%	
	V	3	2391		
	J	3	2394		
	I	2	2396		C
	Q	2	2398		
100%	K	2	2400	100%	

control systems for different categories; keeping more complete records of movements of category A items than others, or expending more effort in assessing future demand of category A items than other categories. It may, however, be necessary to modify our classification to take into account other important attributes. If, for example, a warehouse was cramped for space it may be desirable to reclassify a particularly bulky category B or C item as Category A.

Further difficulties may occur if the sales of a high-turnover item are dependent on the sales of a low-turnover one. This occurred in one instance where a paper company's sales of paper for books (high-value turnover item) depended on an adequate supply of paper for fly-leaves (low-value turnover item).

9.4 Stock Control Systems

Having gained some insight into the stock system through the use of Pareto analysis and possibly having broken the lines down into categories, it is necessary to devise suitable systems of stock control. The two major systems are the *re-order level* system and the *periodic review* system.

9.4.1 The Re-order Level System

In this system, a replenishment order (for a fixed quantity, Q — the *re-order quantity*) is placed when stock on hand falls below a fixed value M (the *re-order level*). By 'stock on hand' we mean current stock plus any replenishment orders still outstanding. There will almost invariably be some delay between placing the replenishment order and its subsequent receipt. This time period is called the *lead time, L*.

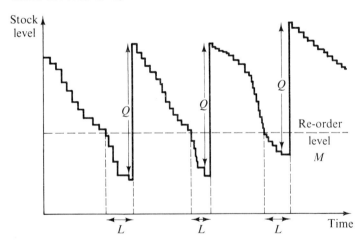

Figure 9.1   Operation of the re-order level system of stock control over time

Buffer stock or safety stock may be held to guard against fluctuations in demand during the lead time period. The amount of buffer stock held is the amount that the *re-order level* exceeds the expected demand during the lead time.

The re-order level system can be used in a very simplified form in the 'two bin' system. In this system, one bin contains a quantity exactly equal to the re-order level, and the second bin contains the remainder of the stock. Supplies are taken from the second bin and when this becomes empty we know we have reached the re-order level and hence a further order is generated. Such a system might be useful for low value components and obviates the necessity for keeping detailed records of stock movements.

9.4.2 The Periodic Review System

This system involves reviewing stock levels at *fixed intervals of time*, the *Review Period, R*, and placing replenishment orders at the end of each interval. The replenishment order is variable and corresponds to the amount of stock required to bring the stock ordered plus the stock on hand up to *target stock levels, S*. Figure 9.2 shows a typical operation of a periodic review system.

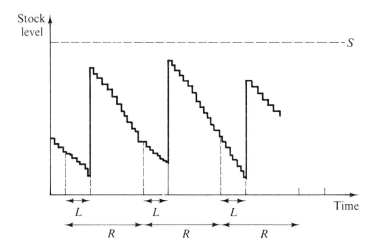

Figure 9.2   *Operation of the periodic review system of stock control*

9.4.3 Comparison of Systems

The *re-order level* system involves ordering fixed quantities of stock at different periods of time, whilst the *periodic review* system involves ordering variable quantities at fixed time intervals.

Re-order level systems require continuous surveillance to ascertain whether the stock level has fallen below the re-order levels. With periodic review systems it is only necessary to monitor stock levels at the time of the periodic review. Hence re-order level systems may require more administrative effort than periodic review ones, though this may not be a serious problem if the system is computerized.

Periodic review systems may enable orders for goods to be combined to obtain transport economies; to obtain discounts when the discount is based on the total value of the order; or to meet given production schedules. This is clearly not possible with re-order level systems, where orders are generated at unpredictable intervals. Generally, periodic review systems require higher average stock levels to maintain the same level of customer service. The reason for this is that in periodic review systems we receive information about current stock levels much less frequently and hence are at risk from demand fluctuations over a longer time period. Hence, on average, higher stock levels need to be held to maintain the same levels of service. This point will be illustrated quantitatively in forthcoming sections.

The most appropriate system to use in a given situation will depend on the context of the problem we are considering. A factory which produced bolts and set screws supplied customers' orders from stocks of finished products. Stock levels were under constant surveillance, owing to the fact that they were checked each time an order was received from a customer. There were, in addition, no particular advantages to be gained from adhering to particular sequences of producing different products. A re-order level system seemed to be most appropriate in this situation.

A small bicycle retailer sold a number of different models of bicycles produced by a limited number of suppliers. Lead times from suppliers were remarkably short (generally under a week). A re-order · level system would have involved the considerable administrative inconvenience of placing orders throughout the month and also checking their receipt. A periodic review system where orders for all models were placed once per month was easily the most sensible arrangement for this small business.

9.4.4 Other Systems

There are systems available which contain some aspects of the re-order level system and some elements of the periodic review system[1].

9.5 Re-order Level Systems: Calculation of Optimum Parameter Values

We have seen that a re-order level system is completely described by two parameters, the re-order quantity (Q) and the re-order level (M). In this section we shall try to determine what values of Q and M will enable the system to be run at minimum cost.

9.5.1 Re-order Quantity

Clearly, large order quantities will result in few set-ups and hence low set-up costs. On the other hand, small order quantities will enable stock-holding costs to be minimized. Minimizing total cost involves a trade-off between these two elements of costs.

Let Q represent order quantity,
Let A represent annual demand for the product,
Then number of replenishments per year $= \dfrac{A}{Q}$.

Now if the cost of placing an order is C_o, then annual ordering costs $= \dfrac{A}{Q} \cdot C_o$.

Average inventory cost
= Average stock levels $\times$ Unit cost per item $\times$ stock carrying cost.

Let C_m = unit cost per item
I = stock-holding cost (expressed as a fraction of stock value)

To calculate average stock levels we note that, in the average stock cycle, the stock falls from (Q + buffer stock) to buffer stock (see Figure 9.3).

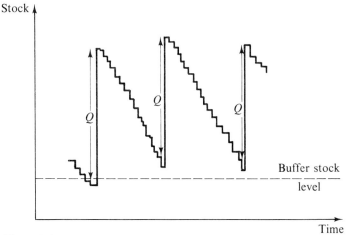

Stock

Buffer stock
level

Time

Figure 9.3

Hence, average stock = Buffer Stock (B) + ½ order quantity
$$= (B + \frac{Q}{2}).$$

∴ Annual stock holding costs = $(B + \frac{Q}{2}).\ C_m I.$

∴ Total annual cost of stock system,

$$C(Q) = \frac{A}{Q}.C_o + (B + \frac{Q}{2})\ C_m I$$

We can show these costs in Figure 9.4:

We can find the minimum cost of running the system by differentiating with respect to Q (assuming buffer stock is independent of Q). We get:

$$\frac{dC(Q)}{dQ} = \frac{IC_m}{2} - \frac{AC_o}{Q^2}$$

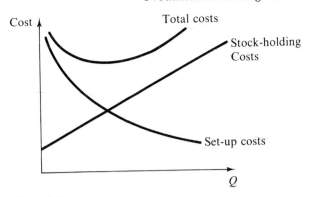

Figure 9.4

This will be minimized where $\dfrac{dC(Q)}{dQ} = 0$

i.e. where $Q^* = \sqrt{\dfrac{2AC_o}{IC_m}}$

This order quantity corresponding to minimum overall cost Q^* is known as the *economic batch quantity* (EBQ).

It will be noted that the above total cost curve is very flat in the region of the minimum. This means that, providing an order quantity in the neighbourhood of the economic batch quantity is chosen, the cost penalty of not being exactly at the optimum is likely to be quite small. This is important since a number of the elements in the above model are difficult to quantify precisely. For example, there are considerable difficulties in quantifying the exact cost of set-up and the figure used for demand will be a forecast and thus subject to possible error.

Example

Suppose the forecast demand for a particular item was 300 units per year. The cost of placing an order was £2 per order. The value of each item is £30 and the stock-holding cost is 10% per year.

Then $Q^* = \sqrt{\dfrac{2AC_o}{IC_m}}$

$$= \sqrt{\frac{2 \times 300 \times 2}{0.10 \times 30}}$$

$$= \sqrt{400}$$

$$= 20 \text{ units}$$

i.e. Economic Batch Quantity = 20 units.

Exercise 9.1

In the above example recalculate the economic quantity order (i) if the cost of placing an order rises to £3 per order (ii) if the stock-holding cost falls to $7\frac{1}{2}\%$. Comment on your results.

9.5.2 Re-order Levels

Re-order levels are set equal to average demand during the lead time plus buffer stock to cover against demand fluctuations in the lead time (see Figure 9.5).

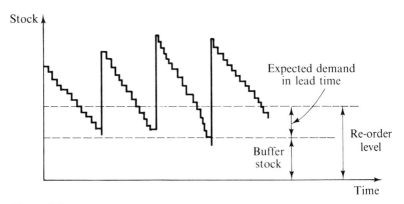

Figure 9.5

Re-order level (M) = expected demand during lead time + buffer stock (B)

If d is the average weekly demand and L weeks is the lead time, then

Re-order level, $M = d \times L + B$

The level of safety stock will depend to what extent we are
.prepared to risk a stock-out. Since it is difficult to quantify the
exact cost of a stock-out, this problem is approached by setting a
specific *service level*. This service level is the probability of not
running out of stock on any *stock cycle*.

Suppose, for example, that weekly demand is normally
distributed with mean demand d (as before) and standard deviation
σ_d; then demand during the lead time period of L weeks will also be
normally distributed with mean dL and standard deviation $\sigma_d\sqrt{L}$.
This follows from the Central Limit Theorem (see Chapter 4)

Thus re-order level, $M = dL + k\sigma_d\sqrt{L}$,

where k is the number of standard deviations required to give the
desired service level ($k = 2$ will give 97.7%, $k = 3.1$ will give
99.9%).

Example

Suppose we have an item whose demand is represented by a normal
distribution with mean 100 per week and standard deviation 10 per
week. Suppose lead time = 4 weeks. Then, if we consider demand
during the lead time we find that the mean demand is 400 units,
with standard deviation $\sigma_m = \sqrt{4} \times 10 = 20$.

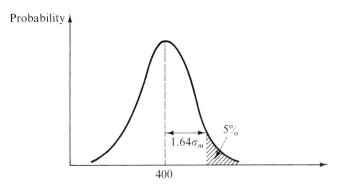

Probability

1.64σ_m

5%

400

Number of units demanded in lead time

Figure 9.6

Now, if we stocked exactly 400 units, we would on average run out of stock once every two stock cycles (our average demand is greater than the mean on 50% of occasions). This would give us a service level of 50%.

If we want a 95% service level, we see that demand will be less than $+1.64\sigma_m$ on 95% of all occasions. Hence for 95% service level,

$$M = 400 + 1.64 \times 20 = 433.$$

If we want a 97.5% service level then we need to consider 1.96 standard deviations from the mean, i.e.

$$M = 400 + 1.96 \times 20 = 439.$$

For a 99.9% service level,

$$M = 400 + 3.1 \times 20 = 462.$$

Thus, it can be seen that six additional units of safety stock were required to improve service level by 2.5% from 95% to 97.5%, while a further 23 were required to improve service level by 2.4%, from 97.5% to 99.9%.

Thus, each additional percentage improvement in service level requires a corresponding greater increment in safety stock. If one decides that one wishes to make practically certain of never running out of stock, this may involve carrying prohibitive amounts of safety stock.

9.5.3 Service Level and Proportion of Orders that can be Met from Stock

We should be careful not to confuse the concept of service level with the proportion of total demand that can be met from stock (a common mistake). Service level simply gives the probability of running out of stock in any given replenishment cycle. In general, the proportion of demand met from stock will be much greater than this.

On average there will be A/Q replenishment cycles per year. If P

is the probability of not running out of stock during the cycle (i.e. service level) then expected number of stock-outs per year is $(1-P)$ A/Q.

In our example, suppose that the economic batch quantity $= 500$ items, then there would be $5000/500 = 10$ set-ups per year (assuming a 50-week year).

If we were working to a 95% service level, this corresponds to a stock-out every two years and it is quite likely that we would only fail to supply demand for a comparatively small number of units when this stock-out occurred.

Hence, it is likely that only a small number of the 10 000 demand in the two-year period would not be met from stock (i.e. proportion of total goods ordered supplied from stock would be much greater than 95%).

Exercise 9.2

Calculate the economic order quantity for a batch of goods if the unit cost is £1.00, annual turnover is 3000 units, cost of placing a replenishment order is £10 and cost of holding an item in stock for a year is 15% of its value.

Exercise 9.3

(a) A company are operating a re-order level system for a given product with re-order quantity 300 units and re-order level 200 units.
If weekly demand is normally distributed with mean value 50 and standard deviation 20, what service level is offered if lead time is three weeks?
(b) If service level of 97.7% is required what re-order level should be chosen?

9.6 Re-order Level System: Quantity Discounts

Sometimes when we are ordering goods, we find that quantity discounts are available. Such discount corresponds to a reduction in unit costs providing the quantity ordered exceeds some minimum level. The availability of such discounts leads to discontinuities in the annual cost of operating the system. It is necessary to test out whether increasing an order quantity to the next price break point is worthwhile.

Taking a specific example; if we have an item A, whose annual demand $A = 600$ units, set-up cost $C_o = £10.00$ per unit, stockholding costs $= 20\%$.

Suppose cost
per unit was:
£6.00 for order quantities   1—199
£5.70 for order quantities   200—999 (i.e. 5% discount)
£5.40 for order quantities   1,000+ (i.e. 10% discount)

If we calculate economic batch quantities for each of these costs we find:

Price per unit	Economic batch quantity
£6.00	100 (feasible)
£5.70	103 (infeasible)
£5.40	105 (infeasible)

The economic batch quantity which corresponds to a unit cost of £5.70 (i.e. 103) is infeasible. This is because the price of £5.70 is only available if the order quantity exceeds 200. A similar argument applies to the £5.40 unit cost.

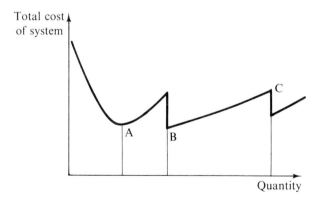

Figure 9.7

Essentially, therefore, the problem is reduced to comparing the cost of running the system at the economic batch quantity for £6.00 unit cost (point A in Figure 9.7) with the cost of running the system at the re-order quantities where quantity discounts just become available (points B and C).

Now, total cost of running the system

= purchase costs + re-ordering cost + stock-holding costs
(ignoring buffer stocks).

$$\text{Cost} = A \times C_m. + A\frac{C_o}{Q} + \frac{Q}{2}C_m I.$$

Using symbols already introduced (note that C_m is now a function of Q).

At Point A ($Q = 100$)

$$\text{Cost} = 600 \times £6.00 + \frac{600}{100} \times £10 + \frac{100}{2} \times £6 \times 0.2,$$
$$= £3,600 + 60 + 60$$
$$= £3,720.$$

At Point B ($Q = 200$)

$$\text{Cost} = 600 \times £5.70 + \frac{600}{200} \times £10 + \frac{200}{2} \times £5.7 \times 0.2,$$
$$= £3,420 + 30 + 114$$
$$= £3,564.$$

At Point C ($Q = 1000$)

$$\text{Cost} = 600 \times £5.40 + \frac{600}{1000} \times £10 + \frac{1000}{2} \times £5.4 \times 0.2,$$
$$= £3,240 + 6 + 540,$$
$$= £3,786.$$

Thus, point B where the order quantity is just sufficient to qualify for the 5% discount gives minimum system running cost.

Exercise 9.4

In the above example suppose the unit costs are now:

0—49	£6.00
50—99	£5.50
100—199	£5.25
200 +	£5.00

What is the optimal order quantity now?

Exercise 9.5

A car part has an annual demand of 120 units, ordering cost is £2 per order and annual inventory carrying cost is 25%. What order quantity would you recommend if the following discounts are available?

Order size	Discount	Unit Cost
0—49	0	£30
50—99	5%	£28.50
99 +	10%	£27.00

9.7 Periodic Review System: Calculation of Optimum Parameter Values

As was mentioned in an earlier section, this system is completely determined by the review period (R) and the target inventory level (S).

(i) Review period (R)
It is possible to find a review period that minimizes the annual cost of acquiring and holding stock, although in practice choice of review period is likely to be dominated by other considerations. Now the annual running cost of the system = average inventory held × stock-holding cost + cost of placing order.

Supposing there are r reviews per year, then average quantity ordered will be A/r.

Hence, average stock held will be $A/2r + B$, where B is the buffer stock.

Hence, stock-holding cost $= (\dfrac{A}{2r} + B)\, I\, C_m$

and set-up costs $= r \times C_o$ (no. of set-ups per year × cost of set-up).

Thus total cost per year $(TC) = (\dfrac{A}{2r} + B)IC_m + rC_o.$

Now if we make the approximation that the level of buffer stock is independent of the number of review periods, we can optimize the above function and obtain

$$\frac{d(TC)}{dr} = \frac{-AIC_m}{2r^2} + C_o = 0 \text{ at minimum cost point.}$$

Hence, cost of running the system is minimized for $r = \sqrt{\dfrac{AIC_m}{2C_o}}.$

In practice, however, the periodic review system is chosen so that orders for entire categories can be placed at the same time. Many of the advantages of this system such as administrative convenience, and possibilities of obtaining transport economies or adhering to particular production schedules derive from this. Applying the model for optimum review period above will obviously result in different lines having different review periods. Thus, in practice, the review period chosen is likely to be heavily influenced by some of the factors mentioned above, not simply obtained by uncritical use of the model.

(ii) Target inventory level (S)

As we have mentioned in an earlier section, at the end of each review period an order is placed so that the stock on hand plus the order placed reaches a target stock level, S. With the re-order level system we are only liable to a stock-out once the re-order level is reached (since the re-order level is a positive quantity). Hence, we are only at risk from a stock-out during the lead time period, and it is only necessary to carry buffer stock against demand fluctuations during this period.

In the periodic review system we are exposed to the risk of stock-out for a much longer period. Let us consider Figure 9.8 which shows the operation of a typical periodic review system. Suppose we are at the re-order point A. When we make an order at this point it is received at the expiry of the lead time at B. We do not have the opportunity to make any further orders until the point C, and goods ordered then are not received until the expiry of a lead time

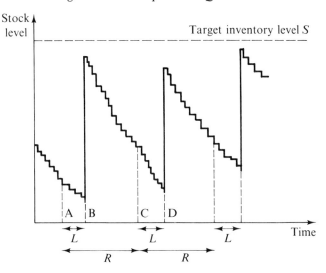

Figure 9.8   Operation of typical periodic review system

at point D. Thus, orders made at time A, together with stock on hand, will have to be sufficient to cover expected demand and fluctuations in demand until point D. This is an entire review period plus lead time away and we are at risk from a stock-out during the entire period.

Suppose demand is normally distributed with mean weekly demand d and standard deviation σ_d.

Then, expected demand during period $A - D = d(R + L)$. Buffer stock to be held during this period $= k\sigma_d\sqrt{(R + L)}$ where k is the number of standard deviations to give the required service level:

$$\therefore S = d(R + L) + k\sigma_d\sqrt{(R + L)}.$$

Example

Suppose the demand for an item was normally distributed with mean weekly demand, 100 units, standard deviation, 20 units, and lead time, 3 weeks. It was intended to run a periodic review system with review period, 5 weeks and service level, 97.5%.

Then $S = d(R+L) + k\sigma_d\sqrt{(R+L)}$

$$= 100(5+3) + 1.96 \times 20\sqrt{(5+3)}$$

$$= 800 + 1.96 \times 20\sqrt{8}$$

$$= 911.$$

Exercise 9.6

In the above example what should the target stock level be if we want a 99.9% service level? How many stock-outs per year would then be expected?

Exercise 9.7

Given that the customer demand is normally distributed with an average value of 5 units per week, and standard deviation of 2 units per week, what is the length of the economic review period (to the nearest week) if the ratio of unit annual cost of stock-holding to the cost of placing the replenishment order is 1:5?

If reviews are made in accordance with the economic review period, with what value of target stock level (S) should replenishment orders be placed if lead time is 3 weeks and if we wish to provide a 95% service level?

10

Planning and Control of Projects

10.1 Introduction

Before undertaking any project it is important to devise an adequate plan for controlling it. This has the advantage of causing us to think carefully about how we intend to undertake the project, possibly identifying snags and to discover alternative approaches to the project. More importantly, drawing up a plan will enable a programme to be established against which progress and performance can be measured. Since time and money are intimately related it is essential to control the progress of the project if the cost of it is to be kept in check.

10.2 Control Techniques

10.2.1 Desirable Features

It is desirable that the control technique adopted should have the following facilities.

(1) It should facilitate carrying out the various parts of the project in a logical sequence. For example, we would not wish an electrical wiring job to be carried out which later had to be re-wired in order to allow insulation to be installed.

(2) The progress of the project towards meeting the desired completion date (and also intermediate completion dates called 'milestones') can be monitored. Failure to meet a deadline may be very expensive in that it can involve the operation of penalty clauses in construction projects. In North Sea platform construction work

failure by only a short period to meet a weather-window can result in the project suffering months of delay.

(3) It should facilitate the control and scheduling of resources. This is clearly important because resources are expensive, and because, in some instances, the level of resources available is strictly limited. For example, the number of men available for work on a North Sea oil construction project is strictly limited by the availability of beds on the platform.

(4) The technique should help us to react to unexpected delays. In 1976 the Olympic Games were to be held in Montreal but, because of labour disputes and other problems, construction of the stadium was months behind schedule, with less than a year to go before the Games were to start. In this situation, it may be tempting to try to speed up all sections of a project in an attempt to make up for lost time. This will not be the most cost-effective way to proceed, however, since speeding up certain activities will have no effect on the overall completion date. It is desirable that our control technique should enable us to identify the most cost-effective programme of catching up.

10.2.2 Network Analysis

The techniques of network analysis have facilities which satisfy the above criterion.

Networks have been used in many practical situations. North Sea oil platform construction projects involving hundreds of millions of pounds have been controlled by such networks. Sometimes, a series of networks, each representing a different level of aggregation or detail are employed. Another major project application was the development of the Victoria underground line. In addition to such large-scale applications there have been many more mundane applications particularly in the construction industry.

10.3 Critical Path Methods

10.3.1 The Network

Critical path methods use networks for the planning and control of projects. The *network* consists of a diagrammatic representation of the sequential relationships between a number of separate jobs that go to make up a project. The project is divided up into a number of specified *jobs* or *activities*. Each activity involves the expenditure of time, effort, money and other resources. In a network an activity is represented by an arrow. By convention the arrows flow from left to right.

An *event* is that point in time at which preceeding activities are complete and succeeding activities not yet started. It is represented by a *node*.

It should be pointed out that the network is intended to represent only the sequential relationship of activities. Length of arrow and direction are not signficant.

In order to place an arrow in the appropriate point of a network it is necessary to answer the following questions.
1. Which other jobs must be complete before this one can start?
2. Which other jobs can be done at the same time?
3. Which other jobs cannot start until this one is finished?

Let us take a simple domestic example; making a cup of tea. Supposing this project is broken down into the following basic activities:

1. Get out cups, kettle, teapot, etc.
2. Boil water.
3. Make tea.
4. Add milk and sugar to cup.
5. Pour tea.
6. Stir tea.

Consider the start of this project. Quite clearly, no other activities can take place before activity 1 (getting out cups, kettle, teapot, etc). In addition, no other activities can be carried out simultaneously. Thus, this activity will be represented by the first arrow in our network and it must be complete before we can start on any other job. We then look to see which job can now start and find that activity 2 (Boil water) can now take place. Considering the second question, however, we realise that it is quite possible for activity 4, 'Add milk and sugar to cup' to proceed simultaneously.

Once the activity of making tea is completed, it is possible to pour the tea into the cup. There is no logical reason, however, why the activity of adding milk and sugar to the cup must be completed before this activity takes place. Finally, having poured the tea into the cup and having added milk and sugar it then becomes possible to stir the tea at which point the cup of tea is ready.

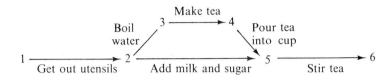

Figure 10.1

Although this can be regarded as a trivial example it does emphasize some of the most important features of networks. In particular, it illustrates that the network shows what is reasonably possible and exemplifies the strict logic of one job preceding another. In particular, it does not take into account any limitations in resources.

10.3.2 Events

As we have explained in the previous section, each point of intersection in the network is called a *node* or an *event*. This corresponds to the previous job having been completed but subsequent ones not yet having started. For reference purposes, it is necessary to number all events and this is generally done by starting at the beginning and numbering all subsequent events in ascending order. This has been done in Figure 10.1 and thus each activity is now characterized by the event numbers at either end of the activity. Thus, for example, the activity 'get out utensils' is characterized by event Nos. 1—2 and the activity 'add milk and sugar' is characterized by event Nos. 2—5. It is accepted practice to try to ensure that each activity has an event number at its head greater than that at its tail.

In some cases a *dummy* may be used to ensure that each activity has a unique specification. In the network below (Figure 10.2) both activities B and C start at event 2 and finish at event 3, hence both have activity number 2—3.

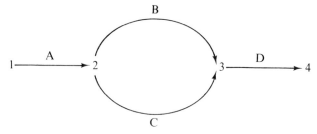

Figure 10.2

In this situation a dummy activity may be used to avoid confusion as follows:

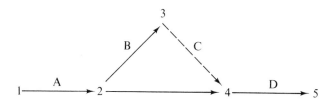

Figure 10.3

Such a dummy activity takes no time to carry out.

Exercise 10.1

A firm who were developing a new kind of radio decided that the project would be broken down into the following activties:
1. Carrying out market research.
2. Raising finance.
3. Developing product.
4. Advertising product.
5. Putting the product on the market.
   The market research must be completed before raising finance can commence. Developing product and advertising product can follow once finance is raised. The product can only be put on the market once all other activities have been completed.
   Draw the network diagram relating to this project.

10.4 Scheduling

The process of scheduling involves setting a timetable to the plan which we have already drawn up. This will enable us both to assess the overall duration of the project and also to be able to check actual progress against this schedule as the project takes place. It is necessary to establish the time required for each activity and this is called the *job duration*.

This job duration may be established on the basis of previous performance, or if there is inadequate information on this, simply on personal judgement. On a simple network it is usual to write the duration of each activity beside the corresponding arrow.

Having done this, it now becomes possible to calculate the *earliest event* times at which each event can occur. In other words the earliest event time is the earliest time by which all activities leading to the event can be completed.

Let us take the previous example of making a cup of tea, the network for this is reproduced below with appropriate activity times associated (in seconds).

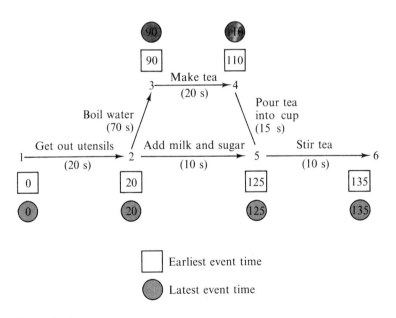

Figure 10.4

If we now work through the earliest event times for the individual events we get:

Event No.	Earliest Event Time (s)
1	0
2	20
3	20 + 70 = 90
4	90 + 20 = 110
5	Either 110 + 15 = 125*
	*This is the earliest event time.
	or 20 + 10 = 30
6	125 + 10 = 135

*125 is the earliest event time for event 5 because *all* preceeding activities must be complete.

The earliest time that event 6 can be arrived at is then the earliest time for completion of the entire project. By taking the event numbers in the correct sequence it is possible to avoid missing a path which might give a later time. The earliest event times are shown by a *square* box on the diagram.

The *Latest Event Time* is the latest time at which a particular event can occur without causing a delay to the project (i.e. the latest time by which all jobs leading to that event must be completed).

Now the earliest event time of the last event is the earliest completion date for the whole project. Thus, this time is also of necessity the latest event time for the final event, otherwise the entire project will be delayed.

Considering again the network used for the calculation of earliest event time, we can mark on the latest event times in a small *circle* starting with event number 6. Latest event times can then be calculated as follows:

Event No.		Latest Event Time (s)
6		135
5		135 − 10 = 125
4		125 − 15 = 110
3		110 − 20 = 90
2	either	125 − 10 = 115
	or	90 − 70 = 20 (Latest event time)
1		20 − 20 = 0

It can be seen that this process is simply the reverse of the procedure used to calculate earliest event times.

10.4.1 Activity Times

When we are managing a job, however, we are concerned with the scheduling of individual activities. Thus, it is important to identify earliest and latest activity times which are defined below.

The earliest start date (E.S.D.) which is the earliest date a job can start, is the earliest event time of the event at the start of that job plus one unit.

The earliest finish date (E.F.D.) which is the earliest date a job can finish, is the earliest event time of the event at the start of the job plus the duration of the job.

The latest start date (L.S.D.) is the latest date by which a job must start in order not to delay the project, and is calculated by deducting the job duration from the latest event time of the event at the finish of the job and adding one unit.

The latest finish date (L.F.D.) which is the latest date by which the job should be finished, is the latest event time of the event at the finish of the job.

The reason for adding one unit is to indicate that the job begins at the beginning of the next time period. Thus, if the earliest start date of a job is given by day 1, this means the beginning of day 1. There are thus 20 days between earliest start date 1 (i.e. beginning of day 1) and earliest finish date day 20 (i.e. end of day 20). Considering again our example in Figure 10.4 we have:

Job	Duration	Earliest E.S.D.	E.F.D.	Latest L.S.D.	L.F.D.
1—2	20	1	20	1	20
2—3	70	21	90	21	90
2—5	10	21	30	116	125
3—4	20	91	110	91	110
4—5	15	111	125	111	125
5—6	10	126	135	126	135

If we consider all these individual activities we can see that some of them have identical starting and finishing dates, i.e. they must be carried out in a fixed time period. It also follows that if any of these activities are delayed then this will lead to a delay in the overall project. Such jobs are said to be *CRITICAL* and they are said to lie on the *CRITICAL PATH*. It will be noted that job 2—5 has some freedom of movement; this flexibility is called *FLOAT*. Up to a point, delays on this activity will not affect the completion date of the project.

Further example

The small Scottish oil company described in Chapter 8 has decided to go ahead with exploration in its sector. It intends to carry out both a test drill and a seismic test. Broadly, this project consists of the following main activities:

Obtain finance for project	6 weeks
Obtain platform from yards	5 weeks
Recruit workforce	6 weeks
Fitting platform and towing to mooring in sea	8 weeks
Training men	3 weeks
Prepare seismic equipment	2 weeks
Carry out seismic tests	6 weeks
Carry out test drilling	9 weeks

Financing the project must precede all other activities. The platform must be obtained before fitting and towing out to sea. Recruitment of the workforce can be undertaken while the platform is being obtained and once this is done their training can be started. Drilling cannot take place until the men are fully trained.

Preparing seismic equipment and carrying out tests is done by a small number of scientists and does not depend on completion of training of the workforce, since unskilled workers are used in this part of the project. Seismic tests are carried out from a survey ship and hence do not depend on the platform being in position.

The network for this project is shown in Figure 10.5.

Calculation of Earliest Event Times

Event No.		Earliest Event Time
2		6
3		6 + 5 = 11
4		6 + 6 = 12
5	Either	11 + 8 = 19* This is earliest event time
	or	12 + 3 = 15
6		12 + 2 = 14
7	Either	14 + 6 = 20
	or	19 + 9 = 28* This is earliest event time.

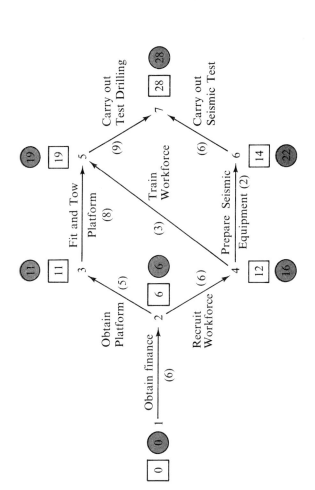

Figure 10.5

Calculation of Latest Event Times

Event No.		Latest Event Time (s)
7		28
6		28 − 6 = 22
5		28 − 9 = 19
4	Either	22 − 2 = 20
	or	19 − 3 = 16* This is latest event time
3		19 − 8 = 11
2	Either	11 − 5 = 6* This is latest event time
	or	16 − 6 = 10

Now looking job durations and earliest and latest start and finish dates we have the following:

Job	Duration	Earliest E.S.D.	E.F.D.	Latest L.S.D.	L.F.D.
1—2	6	1	6	1	6 *
2—3	5	7	11	7	11 *
2—4	6	7	12	11	16
3—5	8	12	19	12	19 *
4—5	3	13	15	17	19
4—6	2	13	14	21	22
5—7	9	20	28	20	28 *
6—7	6	15	20	23	28

We find that for the sequence of job 1—2, 2—3, 3—5 and 5—7 the earliest and latest start and finish dates coincide, these then are the *critical* activities.

Exercise 10.2

Supposing it is now found that the seismic tests can only take place once all the test drilling operations are completed. Modify your network and, assuming the same job durations as before, calculate earliest and latest start and finish dates for all activities. Which path is critical?

Exercise 10.3

A construction company wins a contract to build a motorway petrol station. The project consists of the following activities, which have the attached conditions.

Activity description	Activity name	Conditions	Activity duration (days)
Open up site	A	Starting activity	3
Basic civil engineering work	B	A must first be complete	15
Initial mechanical engineering work	C	A must first be complete	10
Complete mechanical engineering work	D	C must first be complete	4
Instrumentation	E	D must first be complete	4
Lay electrical circuits	F	C must first be complete	4
Complete civil engineering work	G	B,F,must first be complete	5
Landscape site	H	E,G,must first be complete	7
Stock up products	I	E,G,must first be complete	10
Check work and make final preparations for opening	J	H,I must first be complete; J is the final activity.	5

Draw a network for this project; calculate the earliest and latest start and finish dates for each activity. Where is the critical path?

10.5 Float

As we have seen *float* is the amount by which it is possible to change the position in time that a job is carried out without affecting the overall completion date of the project. It is also the amount by which it is possible to extend the duration of an activity without delaying overall completion. Any activity must be carried out between the earliest starting date of the activity and the latest finish date. Thus, the *total float* available must be the time between earliest start and latest finish dates minus the duration of the activity. Now, if we take the oil platform example and remember that the earliest start date indicates the beginning of the designated week and latest finish date indicates end of the week, we get the following:

Activity	Earliest Event Time at Start	Latest Event Time at Finish	Duration	Total Float
1—2	1	6	6	0
2—3	7	11	5	0
2—4	7	16	6	4
3—5	12	19	8	0
4—5	13	19	3	4
4—6	13	22	2	8
5—7	20	28	9	0
6—7	15	28	6	8

The following points are worthy of mention.

1. The critical activities all have zero float and form a continuous chain.

2. Jobs 2—4 and 4—5 which are continuous have the same float (4 weeks). Similarly, jobs 4—6 and 6—7 which are also continuous have also the same float (8 weeks). This is the *same* float not simply an identical figure.

If we look at the chain 2—4—5 we see that there is only a 4-week float on the whole chain. Thus, if this 4 week float is absorbed in job 2—4 it is not available in job 4—5. Similarly, the 8-week float on the sequence 4—6—7 is again the *same* float and can only be absorbed once in the sequence of jobs.

In view of this we introduce the concept of *free float* and this is defined as the amount of float which can be used without affecting subsequent activities. Free float is calculated by deducting the duration of the job from the difference between earliest event times at the start and earliest event times at the finish of the job. Hence, for the activities with float we get the following:

Activity	Earliest Event Time at Start	Earliest Event Time at Finish	Difference	Duration	Free Float
2—4	6	12	6	6	—
4—5	12	19	7	3	4
4—6	12	14	2	2	—
6—7	14	28	14	6	8

If we look at the sequence of jobs 2—4—5 there is a 4-week float available on the entire chain but if we take this on activity 2—4 it affects subsequent activities. On the other hand, if the float is still available when we come to job 4—6 it may be used without affecting any other activity.

Exercise 10.4

Calculate total float and free float for the activities in Exercise 10.2.

Exercise 10.5

Repeat the above exercise for the motorway service station example in Exercise 10.3.

10.5.1 Uses of Float

One of the primary uses of float is that it enables the user of the network to smooth out the rate of working without extending the overall project time. If every job were carried out at its earliest possible time this would lead to large fluctuations in work and hence fluctuations in labour and plant requirements. It is important, however, to stick to the strict logic of a project when drawing a network so that unnecessary restrictions are not built in. Once the network is complete and the critical path found, it is possible to examine all jobs with float to see if advantage can be gained by making some sequential.

Clearly, if it is intended to reduce the length of the overall project it is necessary to concentrate only on critical activities, up to the point where the length of the critical activities are reduced to the extent that some other activity becomes critical.

In the next section we shall examine how float can be used to smooth the use of resources in a project.

10.6 Resources

Resources in a project usually consist of manpower, machines, material and money. We have stressed in earlier sections that the initial network must be constructed purely on the logic of the situation and that no special consideration should be given to the availability of any resources. In this way we can avoid introducing sequential relationships which are logically incorrect.

Unfortunately, however, resources are generally limited (e.g. in a building project certain heavy items of equipment may be in limited supply as may also manpower for practical purposes).

One approach to the problem which may be suitable for simple networks is to draw the network to a time scale showing float and use float to adjust the timing of jobs requiring the restricted resource. Sometimes, it may be possible to carry this out entirely within float although on occasion it may prove necessary to prolong the entire project.

Consider the previous example of the small Scottish oil company. The bar chart (Figure 10.6) shows in full line the activities all starting off at their earliest starting date with a dotted line indicating float. Suppose a particular technologist is required for two weeks of activity 4—5 (training workforce) and for the entire two week duration of activity 4—6 (preparing seismic equipment). This can be easily achieved within the float available for the two jobs. Suppose, for instance, training the workforce takes place during weeks 13—15. The technologist could be employed during any two of these weeks in this activity. The two-week task of preparing the seismic equipment could be scheduled for any part of the periods weeks 16—22 without delaying the overall completion date of the entire project.

Supposing a certain piece of electronic equipment is required for the entire duration of jobs 5—7 (carrying out test drilling) and 6—7 (carrying out seismic testing). There is no way that the float available on job 6—7 can be utilized to allow the equipment to be used on both activities without causing delay. Even if event 6—7 starts at the earliest possible week there will inevitably be at least a one-week overlap, (i.e. job 6—7 takes place between beginning of week 15 and end of week 20). Thus, 5—7 cannot start until beginning of week 21; a one week delay. Thus, it will be necessary either to accept a one-week increase in project duration or to obtain a duplicate piece of equipment.

Exercise 10.6

Suppose the project is modified in the way described in Exercise 10.2. What implications does this have for scheduling the

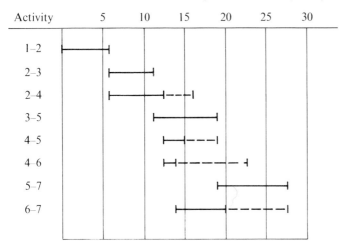

Figure 10.6

availability of the electronic equipment (required for carrying out test drilling and carrying out the seismic test)?

Exercise 10.7

A particular engineer is needed for the activities of fitting and towing the platform, training the workforce and carrying out the test drilling. What is the minimum delay that can be achieved?

Exercise 10.8

In the petrol station construction project (Exercise 10.3), a certain piece of equipment is required for the entire duration of activities D, F, G and H. Schedule your activities to minimize the delay caused to the overall project.

10.6.1 Resources in Large Networks

In practice, however, we may be dealing with projects involving several hundreds or even thousands of activities. This means the problems of resource utilization may be extremely complex with very large numbers of possible activities competing for the use of a given resource. It also means that we need to adopt priority rules for deciding which activities ought to go ahead, when resources are, in fact, constrained.

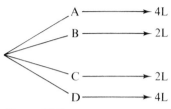

Figure 10.7

Consider the above diagram which represents four activities A,B,C,D all starting from one event. Supposing these activities all require continuously four, two, two and four labourers respectively. Supposing at the point in time when these activities are expected to start there are only eight labourers in the pool. There are then three possibilities:
1. A and D are started, B and C are delayed
2. A, B and C are started, D is delayed
3. B, C and D are started, A is delayed

Some sort of priority rule is clearly necessary to decide which of these three strategies ought to be chosen. Possibile priority rules could be:
1. Critical activities should take preference since these must be finished on time if the project is to be complete at its expected completion date.
2. Jobs with shortest duration could be done first so as to allow the situation to be re-assessed.
3. Jobs with earliest latest start (or finish) times could be done first as these are jobs on longest paths from their preceding (or succeeding) event to the end of the network.
4. Activities with most float should receive a lower priority.

10.7 Trade-off between Project Duration and Cost

The time estimates for activities given in our examples so far represent time taken involving 'normal' working methods. In general, such times will correspond to the minimum cost of carrying out these activities.

It is, however, usually possible to speed up a job by devoting additional resources to it. It may be possible, for instance, to persuade men to work overtime or to procure additional items of equipment. There will obviously, however, be a minimum duration below which it will be physically impossible to reduce the project. Speeding up a job in this manner will almost certainly involve higher total expenditure on that job.

If a project starts to run behind schedule there may be a tendency to rush round speeding up all jobs in an attempt to get back on schedule. This will not be at all a cost-effective way to proceed since many of the jobs speeded up may have plenty of float available and thus will not directly contribute to meeting our schedule. Speeding up critical activities, however, will have a corresponding direct benefit on overall project duration. Non-critical activities cannot be entirely ignored, however, because as we reduce the duration of critical activities we reduce the float on some of the non-critical sections of the network. If the reductions are continued then some of these non-critical sections will become critical.

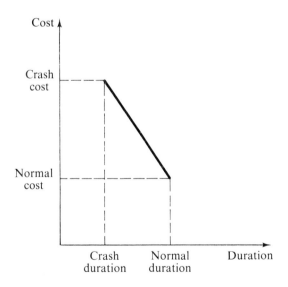

Figure 10.8

We can approach this problem as follows: for each job we will assume that there is a normal duration and an associated 'normal' cost and that there is also a 'crash' duration and associated crash cost. Now we can assume a linear relationship between these points as shown in Figure 10.8.

Thus, the cost per unit of time saved

$$= \frac{Crash\ Cost\ -\ Normal\ Cost.}{Normal\ Duration\ -\ Crash\ Duration}$$

Let us take the example of the small Scottish oil company discussed earlier in this chapter (Figure 10.9).

Supposing it is possible to crash certain activities as follows:

Activity	Normal Duration	Crash Duration	No. Weeks Saved	Normal Cost (000s)	Crash Cost (000s)	Total Cost (increase)	Cost per Week Saved
1—2 Obtain finance	6	5	1	500	600	100	*100*
2—3 Obtain platform	5	3	2	200	300	100	*50*
2—4 Recruit workforce	6	5	1	100	120	20	*20*
3—5 Fit and tow platform	8	5	3	2000	2600	600	*200*
4—5 Train workforce	3	2	1	200	260	60	*60*
4—6 Prepare seismic equipment	2	2	—	500	500	—	—
5—7 Carry out test drilling	9	9	—	250	250	—	—
6—7 Carry out seismic test	6	6	—	800	800	—	—

We should remember that the critical path falls on route 1—2—3—5—7.

Suppose we wish to *reduce the project by one week*. If we look at activities on the critical path, we see that the following alternatives are possible:

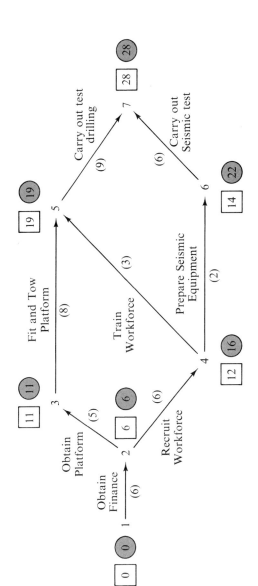

Figure 10.9

1. Save one week on activity 1—2 at cost of £100K.
2. Save one week on activity 2—3 at cost of £ 50K.
3. Save one week on activity 3—5 at cost of £200K.

It can be seen that the least-cost option is to reduce job 2—3 by a week at cost of £50K. It should be noted that the float on the section of network 2—4—5 has now been reduced from 4 to 3 weeks.

To reduce the *duration of project by two weeks* it is clearly optimal to reduce activity 2—3 by a further week which reduces it to its minimum duration. Total cost is now £100K.

We have the following options available if we wish to *reduce the project by a third week*. (Considering activities on the critical path which can be shortened).

1. Save one week on job 1—2 at a cost of £100K.
2. Save one week on job 3—5 at a cost of £200K.

Clearly, it is cheapest to save the week on job (1—2) at a cost of £100K (cumulative cost is £200K). This leaves job 3—5 as the only job on the critical path which is now susceptible to crashing. A *fourth* and *fifth* week can be saved at a cost of £200K per week. Thus, the overall project duration is reduced to 23 weeks at a cumulative cost of £600K.

The crashed network is shown below in Figure 10.10.

It will be noted that the float available on sector 2—4—5 is completely exhausted. Thus, both the sector 2—3—5 and the sector 2—4—5 are now critical. Thus, any attempt to speed up the project by reducing the duration of 2—3—5 will have to be balanced by a reduction of 2—4—5 by an equivalent amount. Thus to save a *sixth* week we have the following options:

    (i) 1 week on job 3—5 (£200K) + 1 week on job 2—4 (£20K), total £220K

    (ii) 1 week on job 3—5 (£200K) + 1 week on job 4—5 (£60K), total £260K.

Therefore the cheapest alternative is (i) and the cumulative cost of reducing the project by six weeks is £820K.

Although it is still feasible to reduce activity 4—5 by one week there is no economic benefit in doing so and six weeks is the

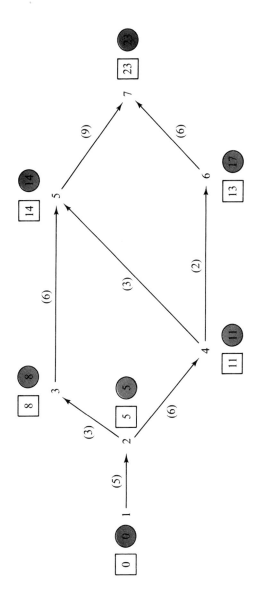

Figure 10.10

maximum reduction possible. This example does illustrate some of the main problems. Additional weeks saved result in increasing cost per week and non-critical sectors of the network eventually become critical.

Exercise 10.9

In the petrol station construction example (Exercise 10.3) it is possible to crash certain activities as below:

Activity	Normal Duration	Normal Cost	Crash Duration	Crash Costs
A	3	£1000	2	£1500
B	15	£5000	12	5900
C	10	£4000	9	4200
D	4	£3500	3	3750
E	4	£4800	3	5000
F	4	£3000	2	4200
G	5	£2000	3	3200
H	7	£8000	Crashing not possible	
I	10	£6000	6	8000
J	5	£2000	Crashing not possible	

(a) It is wished to reduce the duration of the project by four days. What is the most economical way of proceeding?

(b) What is the minimum possible project duration? How much would it cost to carry out the project in this minimum possible time?

10.8 Computing Applications

10.8.1 Use of Computers in Network Planning

It will be quite clear by now that using a network to control a project which consists of hundreds or even thousands of activities will involve heavy amounts of tedious calculations. In addition, any error in calculations will cause a knock-on effect which may extend through the rest of the network. Since many of the calculations are of a deterministic and routine nature, a computer can be employed to relieve this computational burden.

A number of standard program packages have been written for this purpose. Such packages will be available on most scientific computers. In addition, packages are becoming increasingly available on microcomputers and often the standard of output produced is very high.

Details of the network must be supplied to the computer in an unambiguous manner. One way of doing this is to quote the event number at the beginning and end of each activity together with activity duration. Alternatively, a list of activities, their duration and statement of immediately preceding activities can be used.

The computer program will identify obvious logical errors such as a loop (i.e. a series of arrows in a closed circuit) and will also detect a 'dangling' or 'open-ended' arrow. Obviously, however, the program can only check that the data is logically consistent and has no way of telling whether other information is incorrect (such as an incorrect activity duration). It is for this reason that considerable care should be taken in checking the accuracy of the input data.

10.8.2 Example of Use of Network Package

The example presented below is the motorway petrol station example (Exercise 10.3). This has been run using a package available on a microcomputer. The network for the project is shown in Figure 10.11.

10.9 Some Practical Problems in the Use of Networks

There are a number of practical points to be borne in mind when using a network to control a project. Firstly, the network should be drawn up with the closest possible collaboration with the individuals who are responsible for carrying out the project. Only in this way can we ensure that the network does, in fact, actually represent the project which is being controlled.

It is important to check the logic of the network very carefully since one simple error, or the omission of a single activity, can have disastrous consequences.

Once the network is constructed it is possible to assess the duration of activities and to calculate event times. This will enable us to schedule jobs in the light of resource limitations. If the overall completion date is unacceptable it may be possible to adjust this by attempting to speed up critical activities. Careful note should, however, be taken of activities just less than critical since reduction in duration of critical activities could result in them being brought into the critical path.

Once a workable schedule has been devised, the progress of the project can be measured against the time schedule. This is done by assessing progress at regular intervals and marking off jobs completed, jobs partly completed, and jobs not yet started. Remaining time to be spent on activities partly completed is estimated. A re-calculation of event times will show the current situation of the project indicating whether work is ahead or behind and to what extent. It will also indicate whether there has been any change in the route of the critical path.

Updating the network is, of course, a far less tedious process when computing facilities are available. In the construction industry a local site engineer may be left to update the network manually and in these circumstances it may be difficult to persuade him that this method of control is worthwhile. A Danish company have introduced a system whereby they keep in telex contact with their various sites around the world, feeding information backwards and forwards and updating their networks centrally.

There are also experiments being conducted in the UK where mini-computers are used on construction sites, providing local control over activities.

A further practical problem is the question of the appropriate level of detail to incorporate into the network. Really large-scale projects such as a nuclear power station, construction or missile system development, consist of a number of related projects.

These can be planned using a series of sub-networks which are cross-connected at certain key events into a master network. In this way each sub-contractor or department can produce a plan for its own work which may then be co-ordinated with the overall programme.

10.10 Project Cost Control

The planning network can be used as a basis for the analysis and control of costs by making each activity a budget element. Prior to commencing the project, estimates are made of the various types of costs which each activity will incur. This enables realistic cost estimates to be derived and also gives detailed breakdown of costs for control purposes.

Once the project is underway it is essential that there is a feedback of data against the activities for which the original estimates were made. Summaries can be prepared to show overall trends and detailed analyses may be employed to isolate causes of variations between planned and actual cost performance.

For further details on how this control can be actually carried out it is suggested that the reader refer to [1].

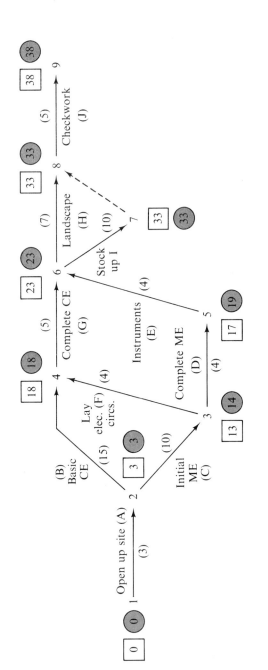

Figure 10.11

ACTIVITY NUMBER	DESCRIPTION	DURATION	TARGET START	TARGET FINISH	ACTUAL START °SCH DELS	ACTUAL FINISH °REM DURS	PRECEDING ACTIVITIES NUMBER	LINK	DELAY
100	OPEN SITE	0:3					100	0	0:0
200	BASIC CIV ENG	3:0					100	0	0:0
300	INIT MECH ENG	2:0					300	0	0:0
400	COMPLETE MECH ENG	0:4					400	0	0:0
500	INSTRUMENTATION	0:4					300	0	0:0
600	LAY ELECT CIRCUITS	0:4					200	0	0:0
700	COMPLETE CIVIL ENG.	1:0					600	0	0:0
800	LANDSCAPE SITE	1:2					500	0	0:0
							700	0	0:0
900	STOCK UP PRODUCTS	2:0					500	0	0:0
							700	0	0:0
1000	CHECK AND FINAL PREP	1:0					800	0	0:0
							900	0	0:0

Exhibit I shows the input data. This takes the form of a list of activities, their duration and immediately preceding activities. Durations should be given in weeks and days (assuming a 5-day week). A facility is available for updating the network by including actual start and finish dates.

REFERENCE : PETROL STATION COMPLETION PROJECT
PROJECT COMPLETION TIME :   7 WEEKS 3 DAYS
REAL RUN DATE   :   NOT APPLICABLE

ACTIVITY NUMBER	DESCRIPTION	DURATION	EARLY START	EARLY FINISH	LATE START	LATE FINISH	FLOAT	TARGET START	TARGET FINISH
100	OPEN SITE	0:3	0:1	0:3	0:1	0:3	CRITICAL		
200	BASIC CIV ENG	3:0	0:4	3:3	0:4	3:3	CRITICAL		
300	INIT MECH ENG	2:0	0:4	2:3	2:4	4:3	0:1		
400	COMPLETE MECH ENG	0:4	2:4	3:2	3:1	3:4	0:2		
500	INSTRUMENTATION	0:4	3:3	4:1	3:5	4:3	0:2		
600	LAY ELECT CIRCUITS	0:4	2:4	3:2	2:5	3:3	0:1		
700	COMPLETE CIVIL ENG.	1:0	3:4	4:3	3:4	4:3	CRITICAL		
800	LANDSCAPE SITE	1:2	4:4	5:5	5:2	6:3	0:3		
900	STOCK UP PRODUCTS	2:0	4:4	6:3	4:4	6:3	CRITICAL		
1000	CHECK AND FINAL PREP	1:0	6:4	7:3	6:4	7:3	CRITICAL		

Exhibit II indicates the activity scheduling. Project duration, earliest and latest start and finish date for each activity is provided together with float and an indication of whether or not an activity is on the critical path.

```
HORNET  DEMO  BAR CHART
JOB NAME  : PETROL STATION EX.
REFERENCE : PETROL STATION COMPLETION PROJECT
PROJECT COMPLETION TIME : 7 WEEKS 3 DAYS
REAL RUN DATE           : NOT APPLICABLE
```

ACTIVITY NUMBER	ACTIVITY DESCRIPTION	:0	:1	:2	:3	:4	:5	:6	:7	:8	:9	:10	:11	:12
									COMPLETED WEEKS					
100	OPEN SITE	CCC												
200	BASIC CIV ENG		CCCCCCCCCCCCC											
300	INIT MECH ENG		SSSSSSSSS—											
400	COMPLETE MECH ENG				SSS—									
500	INSTRUMENTATION				SSS—									
600	LAY ELECT CIRCUITS				SSS—									
700	COMPLETE CIVIL ENG.					CCCCC								
800	LANDSCAPE SITE						SSSSSSS—							
900	STOCK UP PRODUCTS						CCCCCCCCCC							
1000	CHECK AND FINAL PREP								CCCCC					

Exhibit III is basically a bar chart which can be used to aid scheduling of activities. Critical activities are represented by CCC, non-critical by SSS, and float by – – –

ACTIVITY NUMBER	DESCRIPTION	DURATION	RESOURCE NUMBER	RESOURCE DESCRIPTION	VALUE	ACTIVITY NUMBER
100	OPEN SITE	0:3				100
200	BASIC CIV ENG	3:0				200
300	INIT MECH ENG	2:0				300
400	COMPLETE MECH ENG	0:4	#1	EQUIPMENT	1	400
500	INSTRUMENTATION	0:4				500
600	LAY ELECT CIRCUITS	0:4	#1	EQUIPMENT	1	600
700	COMPLETE CIVIL ENG.	1:0	#1	EQUIPMENT	1	700
800	LANDSCAPE SITE	1:2	#1	EQUIPMENT	1	800
900	STOCK UP PRODUCTS	2:0				900
1000	CHECK AND FINAL PREP	1:0				1000

Exhibit IV indicates input data concerned with resource limitation. This allows us to indicate the nature and amounts of resources required. As an example we have stated here that activities, complete mech eng, lay electrical circuits, complete civil engineering and landscape site each require one unit of resource #1 equipment.

```
RESOURCE  #1          EQUIPMENT
LIMIT  1              DELAY  NONE        FACTOR  NONE
-------------------------------------------------------------------------------

WEEK  0  DAY  1  0     WEEK  1  DAY  1  0     WEEK  2  DAY  1  0
              2  0                  2  0                  2  0
              3  0                  3  0                  3  0
              4  0                  4  0                  4  2  *
              5  0                  5  0                  5  2  *

WEEK  3  DAY  1  2  *  WEEK  4  DAY  1  1     WEEK  5  DAY  1  1
              2  2  *              2  1                  2  1
              3  0                  3  1                  3  1
              4  1                  4  1                  4  1
              5  1                  5  1                  5  1

WEEK  6  DAY  1  0     WEEK  7  DAY  1  0     WEEK  8  DAY  1  0
              2  0                  2  0                  2  0
              3  0                  3  0                  3  0
              4  0                  4  0                  4  0
              5  0                  5  0                  5  0

WEEK  9  DAY  1  0     WEEK 10  DAY  1  0
              2  0                  2  0
              3  0                  3  0
              4  0                  4  0
              5  0                  5  0
```

Exhibit V allows resource limitations to be built in. In this case we have assumed that only one unit of resource equipment #1 is available. The program, however, simply schedules each activity at its earliest start time and indicates where an overload has occurred. No indication of how the resource load can be smoothed out is provided. Many packages have more sophisticated ways of handling this problem.

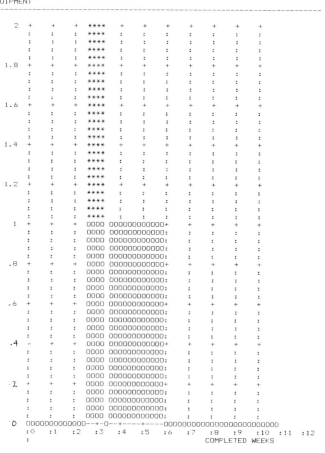

Exhibit VI presents in a pictorial form the information contained in Exhibit V.

11

Queues and Congestion Problems

11.1 Introduction

All of us are familiar with queues and congestion situations in everyday life. Typical examples include waiting for an operator to answer at a telephone switchboard, queuing to check in your bags at an airport and, later, one's plane being 'stacked' for landing, and queuing at the check-out of a supermarket. Industrial situations might include components waiting in line for machining by a machine tool and vehicle chassis passing along an assembly line.

Queues occur because the arrival of customers (either human beings or physical entities) for service does not match exactly with the provision of service facilities. It is inevitable that this must occur in very many cases, otherwise the level of provision of service facilities would be hopelessly uneconomic. Consider, for example, the level of investments in roads necessary to obviate constraint on traffic movements even at peak periods, or the number of check-outs at a supermarket necessary to provide immediate service to all customers. Provision of excess service facilities, as well as being uneconomic, results in the facilities being under-utilized and hence idle for long periods of time.

Given that congestion situations are inevitable it is important that we make an effort to try to understand them. There may be any number of questions we want to answer. For example, what number of check-out points in a supermarket provides a 'reasonable' level of service (perhaps 90% of customers receiving service within five minutes)? What is the effect of providing a cash-out only facility at a bank? What will be the effect of providing an additional machine tool on the production schedule of a machine shop, and so on? One approach to an understanding of these situations is to develop models of queuing systems.

11.2 Characteristics of Queuing Systems

Figure 11.1 represents the structure of a queuing system, the elements of which are as follows.

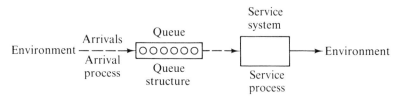

Figure 11.1

11.2.1 Arrival (or Input Process)

This is the process which generates customers for the service facility. In most queuing processes customers do not arrive in a perfectly regular manner; numbers arriving in given periods fluctuate over time. In these cases, it is necessary to attempt to derive the probability distribution of arrivals. This can be done either by trying to discover the probability distribution of the number of arrivals per unit time or the probability distribution of the inter-arrival time (i.e. the time between arrivals).

11.2.2 Service System

There are two aspects of the service system which we are interested in. These are the structure of the service mechanism provided, and the probability distribution of service times.

In connection with the structure of the queue we are interested in whether there is one server or more than one server (multiple servers); if there are multiple servers we want to know whether they all serve all customers or whether some are specialized (e.g. cash-out only tellers in a bank). If there are a number of servers providing the same service we call these service *channels*.

We are also interested in whether one server provides the total service to the user or whether users have to proceed from one service point to another for a complete service (e.g. cafeteria with separate service points for soup, main course, sweet, etc.). In this situation, each service point is called a *phase* and the output from the first phase becomes the input for the second phase and so on.

11.2.3 Structure of the Queue

(1) Firstly, we are interested in *queue discipline* (i.e. the criteria used for deciding which customer receives service next). There are a number of possible disciplines:

(a) First in—First Out (FIFO)
Customers are served in order of their arrival at the queue. This is a very common system for queues involving people; also items on a production line would generally be serviced in this fashion.

(b) Service in Random Order (SIRO)
In this form of queue discipline the next customer is chosen at random from those waiting for service and does not depend on the amount of time already spent in the queue. Service at a telephone switchboard, or entry to buses in certain Mediterranean countries may take place in this way.

(c) Last in—First out (LIFO)
This form of queue discipline involves customers reaching the queue last receiving service first. This may apply in the steel industry for steel ingots queuing for soaking-pit space; compulsory redundancies in a firm are often made on this basis although this is a queuing situation in which the customer may be happy to defer 'service' for as long as possible!

(d) Other queue disciplines
Other queue disciplines are associated with priority rules where customers belong to different classes and have different priorities, e.g. ability of private patients to obtain priority over National Health ones for certain types of operation.

(2) Do all the users wait in a single queue or are there multiple queues? In post offices there is usually a single queue from which customers are fed into the first available service channel. In banks, however, there is often a separate queue at each service channel.

(3) If there are multiple queues, how do users choose which queue to join (at random, or the shortest one)? Are they allowed to switch queues *(jockeying)*?

(4) Do all customers who arrive join the queue or may some leave immediately *(balking)*? Do some customers leave after spending a certain amount of time waiting for service *(reneging)*?

(5) Is there a limit to the size of the queue so that when it is full, all new arrivals are turned away?

11.3 Measures of Performance

Since we intend to construct models of queuing systems, it is useful to have available measures of the performance of the system. Suitable measures could be
  (i) Server utilization,
 (ii) Number of customers in queue (or system),
(iii) Time spent in queue (or system).

(i) Server utilization
This is defined as the fraction of time that a given service channel is busy. Clearly, if server utilization is very high with little idle time then a slight increase in the rate of arrivals may result in very significant lengthening of the queue.

(ii) Number of customers in system (queue)
By number of customers in the *system* we understand the number of customers in queue or waiting line plus customer (if any) undergoing service.

  We shall be interested in the mean number of customers in the system. This is important because potential customers may be deterred by the sight of a lengthy queue even if the expected queuing time is quite short.

(iii) Time spent by customers in system (queue)

Clearly, the mean time spent by customers in the queuing system is an important indicator of the effectiveness of service provided. From the customer's point of view, the shorter the period spent waiting for service, the better the facility provided.

Exercise 11.1

Describe two or three queues with which you are familiar. Describe the service system and queue structure for each queue.

11.4 Simple Queuing Models

11.4.1 General

Development of models of queuing situations are sometimes beset with mathematical difficulties. We shall start by analysing the simplest queue structure. This is a queue with a single service channel.

Figure 11.2

11.4.2 Arrival distribution

We shall assume that customers arrive in purely random fashion. In this situation, the probability of a customer arriving during a given unit of time is independent of what happened during the previous interval of time. We also assume that the number of customers in the queuing system is insignificant compared with the total number of potential arrivals. If the mean arrival rate is λ per unit time, then the expected number of arrivals in time, t, is λt.

Providing arrivals are random, the arrival of one customer does not affect the probability of future arrivals, then the Poisson distribution will be applicable. Hence, the probability of k arrivals in time t is given by:

$$P(k \text{ arrivals in time } t) = \frac{(\lambda t)^k e^{-\lambda t}}{k!}$$

Now if the mean arrival rate is λ, then the mean time between arrivals $= \dfrac{1}{\lambda}$.

It can also be shown that if the probability distribution of number of arrivals is given by the Poisson distribution, then the probability distribution of inter-arrival times is given by the *exponential* distribution below (see Chapter 3).

$$f(t) = \lambda e^{-\lambda t},$$

where $f(t)$ is the probability distribution of inter-arrival times.

In many real life situations, e.g. arrival of cars at a petrol filling station, telephone calls at a switchboard, the conditions for the Poisson distribution are fulfilled.

11.4.3 Distribution of Service Time

We shall also make the assumption that the probability distribution of the number of services which are completed in a given time is given by the Poisson distribution. This means that if there is a long line of customers, keeping the server continually busy, then serviced customers would depart from the service in a random fashion, and the fact that a service had finished in one time interval would not influence the probability of another service being completed in the next.

Thus if μ is the service rate then the probability of k service completions in time t is given by:

$$\frac{(\mu t)^k}{k!} e^{-\mu t} .$$

If μ is the rate of service completions then the mean service time $= \dfrac{1}{\mu}$ and the service times are exponentially distributed, i.e. $b(t) = \mu e^{-\mu t}$, where $b(t)$ is the probability distribution of service times.

An implication that follows from this, however, is that the probability of service being completed at any instant is quite independent of the time when service began. Although this might well hold for, say, telephone calls at a switchboard it may be less realistic in some other real life situations (e.g. cars receiving petrol at filling stations).

11.4.4 Time-Dependent Solutions

If we now attempt to derive from first principles, relationships for the queue parameters (e.g. length of queue) as a function of time, we run into severe mathematical difficulties and finally end up with a mathematical expression that is both extremely complex and cumbersome[1].

It is, unfortunately, generally true of queuing problems that mathematical expressions for time-dependent quantities are either unmanageable or unobtainable.

In practice, however, the number of queuing situations where we are interested in behaviour at start-up may be relatively limited. After a time a queue will normally reach a state of *statistical equilibrium* in which the value of the parameters of the queue will be independent of time since start-up (i.e. probability of there being a given number of customers in the system will be independent of time since the queue began).

It is these *steady-state* parameter values that we shall attempt to derive in the next section.

11.4.5 Derivation of Equilibrium State for Single-Server-Model, Poisson Arrivals, Exponentially Distributed Service Times

Let P_n *be the probability that there are n customers* in the queuing system. If there are n customers present in a given system then an

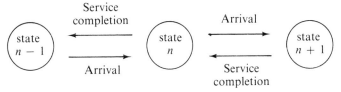

Figure 11.3

arrival changes the system to an $(n+1)$ system. Similarly, a *departure* changes an $n+1$ system back to an n system.

A departure changes an n system to an $n-1$ *system, whilst an arrival changes an $(n-1)$* system to an n system (see Figure 11.3).

Consider N identical queuing systems, then $P_n N$ of these systems will contain exactly n customers. Rate at which n systems change to non-n systems is given by:

$$\lambda P_n N + \mu P_n N = (\lambda + \mu)P_n N \qquad (11.1)$$

arrivals   departures

If however we are in a state of statistical equilibrium this must be balanced by the rate non-n systems become n. This is

arrival	departure
at $(n-1)$ system	from $(n+1)$ system
$\lambda P_{n-1}N$ +	$\mu P_{n+1}N.$

$$\qquad (11.2)$$

Hence, equating these two equations and eliminating N, we get

$$\lambda P_{n-1} + \mu P_{n+1} = (\lambda + \mu)P_n. \qquad (11.3)$$

If statistical equilibrium is to be maintained for $n=0$ system the rate of change of such systems to $n=1$ systems by arrivals must be balanced by rate of change of $n=1$ systems to $n=0$ systems by departures.

$$\mu P_1 = \lambda P_0 \qquad (11.4)$$

i.e. $P_1 = \dfrac{\lambda}{\mu} P_0$

For $n = 1, \lambda P_0 + \mu P_2 = (\lambda + \mu)P_1$ (from Equation 11.3) $\qquad (11.5)$

but, $P_0 = \dfrac{\mu}{\lambda} P_1,$

Hence, $\mu P_1 + \mu P_2 = (\lambda + \mu)P_1,$

$\therefore P_2 = \dfrac{\lambda}{\mu} P_1 = (\dfrac{\lambda}{\mu})^2 P_0.$

We can proceed in this way for P_3 etc. and we get

$$P_n = (\frac{\lambda}{\mu})^n P_0.$$

Since P_n is a discrete probability distribution $\sum\limits_{n=0}^{\infty} P_n = 1$

i.e. $\sum\limits_{n=0}^{\infty} (\frac{\lambda}{\mu})^n P_0 = 1$

$$P_0 \sum\limits_{n=0}^{\infty} (\frac{\lambda}{\mu})^n = 1$$

Now if $x < 1$, $\sum\limits_{n=0}^{\infty} x^n = \frac{1}{1-x}$

$$\therefore P_0 = (1 - \lambda/\mu)$$

Thus $P_n = (\frac{\lambda}{\mu})^n (1 - \frac{\lambda}{\mu})$

The value of $\frac{\lambda}{\mu}$ is denoted by ρ the *traffic* intensity

Hence, $P_n = \rho^n (1 - \rho)$.

The relationship $P_0 = 1 - \rho$ can be understood intuitively, since $(1 - P_0)$ is the proportion of time the server is idle it follows that the probability of zero customers in the section must be $1 - \rho$.

Example

Suppose we have a manual telephone switchboard with one operator. Calls arrive randomly at the rate of three per minute, i.e. $\lambda = 3$ per minute.
Service time is exponentially distributed and service rate $\mu = 4$ per minute.

Traffic intensity $\rho = \frac{\lambda}{\mu} = \frac{3}{4}$

Hence, probability of zero customers in the system

$$P_0 = 1 - \rho = 1 - \tfrac{3}{4} = \tfrac{1}{4}$$

Probability of one customer in the system:

$$P_1 = \rho\,(1-\rho) = \tfrac{3}{4} \times \tfrac{1}{4} = \frac{3}{16}.$$

Probability of two customers in the system:

$$P_2 = \rho^2(1-\rho)$$

$$= \frac{9}{16} \times \tfrac{1}{4} = \frac{9}{64}.$$

Exercise 11.2

Supposing in the above example that service rate is increased to five per minute, recalculate the probability of 0, 1 and 2 customers in the system. Discuss how your results differ from the above.

11.4.6 Mean Number of Customers in the System

The mean number of customers in the system is given by:

$$\bar{n} = \sum_{n=0}^{\infty} nP_n$$

$$= 1(1-\rho)\rho + 2(1-\rho)\rho^2 + 3(1-\rho)\rho^3 + \ \ldots$$

$$= (1-\rho)\rho(1 + 2\rho + 3\rho^2 + \ \ldots)$$

But, $1 + 2\rho + 3\rho^2 \ \ldots \ = \dfrac{1}{(1-\rho)^2}$ (if $\rho < 1$)

$$\bar{n} = \frac{\rho}{1-\rho}$$

The mean number of customers in the queue (rather than the system) is given by

$$\bar{n}_q = \frac{\rho^2}{1-\rho}$$

Hence, if we take our earlier example with $\lambda = 3$, $\mu = 4$ and $\rho = \frac{3}{4}$, we find that the average number in the system

$$\bar{n} = \frac{\rho}{1-\rho} = \frac{3}{4}/(1-\frac{3}{4}) = 3.$$

The average number in the queue

$$\bar{n}_q = \frac{\rho^2}{1-\rho} = (\frac{3}{4})^2/(1-\frac{3}{4}) = 2\frac{1}{4}.$$

Note that the difference between these two figures (3/4) equals the proportion of time there is someone receiving a service.

Exercise 11.3

As in Exercise 11.2 suppose the service rate is raised to five per minute. Recalculate average numbers of customers in the system and queue.

11.4.7 Waiting Time

By a similar analysis to that undertaken earlier it can also be shown that the mean time spent in the system is given by

$$T_s = \frac{1}{\mu} \times \frac{1}{1-\rho} ,$$

and that mean time in the queue

$$T_q = \frac{\lambda}{\mu(\mu-\lambda)} .$$

Thus, in the previous example with $\lambda = 3$, $\mu = 4$, $\rho = 3/4$ we have

$$T_s = \frac{1}{\mu} \times \frac{1}{1-\rho} = \frac{1}{4} \times 1/\frac{1}{4} = 1 \text{ minute}$$

$$T_q = \frac{\lambda}{\mu(\mu-\lambda)} = \frac{3}{4} \text{ minute}$$

(of course the difference between T_s and T_q is simply the mean service time which is ¼ of a minute).

Exercise 11.4

Again, assume mean service rate is sped up to five per minute (as in Exercise 11.2); calculate average waiting time and average time spent in system.

Exercise 11.5

A car breakdown service is provided by a single operator whose servicing times are exponentially distributed with a mean rate of eight jobs per day. Customers arrive completely randomly at a mean rate of five per day.
(1) What is the probability that there are two cars waiting for service at a given time?
(2) Calculate the mean number of cars waiting for service at any given time.
(3) Calculate the mean waiting time for each job.

11.5 Sensitivity Analysis of the Single Server Queue, Poisson Arrivals, Exponential Services

From the queuing models derived in the previous section it is possible to examine how queue length increases with traffic intensity.

Table 11.1

Traffic Intensity	Expected No. in System	Expected Length of Queue
0.1	0.11	0.01
0.3	0.43	0.13
0.5	1.00	0.50
0.7	2.33	1.63
0.8	4.00	3.20
0.9	9.00	8.10
0.95	19.00	18.05
0.99	99.00	98.01
0.999	999.00	998.00

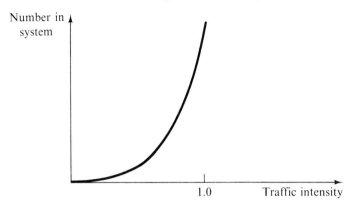

Figure 11.4

Suppose mean service rate is ten per hour ($\mu = 10$), thus mean service time is six minutes. The table below gives time spent in the system for different values of arrival rate (λ).

Table 11.2 Time Spent in System

Arrival Rate	Traffic Intensity	Time Spent in System (min) $(T_s = \dfrac{1}{\mu} \times \dfrac{1}{1-\rho})$	Time in Queue (min)
1	0.1	6.66	0.66
3	0.3	8.57	2.57
5	0.5	12	6
7	0.7	20	14
8	0.8	30	24
9	0.9	60	54
9.5	0.95	120	114
9.9	0.99	600	594
9.99	0.999	6000	5994

This sensitivity analysis shows that for light traffic intensities (say ρ less than 0.5) queue length and time spent in queue are low. For higher values of utilization, number in queue and queuing time increase very rapidly and beyond $\rho = $ about 0.8 a very small increase in arrival rate makes a considerable increase in queue length and queuing time. Thus, when a server is relatively busy a very small increase in arrival rate can cause a queue to expand enormously. Conversely, if a busy server can slightly increase his service rate this may play a major role in reducing queue length.

Of course, increasing queue length and waiting time are caused by inherent randomness in the arrival and service distributions. If services took constant times and if arrivals could be scheduled at fixed times then, providing arrival rate did not exceed service rate, there could be no waiting at all. This is the rationale behind appointment systems.

Exercise 11.6

A factory which operates for eight hours per day, for 240 days per year purchases a very large number of identical machines which they can service themselves, at a cost of £4.00 per hour for labour and parts by their single specialist. Alternatively they can have them serviced by the supplier at a cost of £8,000 per year, including labour and parts. The supplier's other terms are that a service man will be sent immediately when required but it is their policy never to have more than one service man in a factory at any one time.

The machine breakdowns occur at random every three days and the cost of lost production is £6 per hour whilst the machine is not operating.

Their own service times are exponentially distributed with a mean of two days per service, while the supplier's servicing times are exponentially distributed with a mean of 1.5 days per service

(1) Which method of servicing would you advise using?
(2) Can you think of any other ways of reducing the cost of time lost through breakdowns?

11.6 Multiple Service Channels

We are now going to consider a slightly more complex situation, that of the queue with multiple service channels.

Figure 11.5

Arriving customers join the single queue and feed into free service channels on a FIFO basis. It is assumed that arrivals are random and that the service times of the servers is exponentially distributed and that they all have the same mean service rate of μ per unit time.

If there are no more people in the system than the number of servers ($n \leq S$) no queue develops and there is no waiting time. If however, $n > S$ then S customers will be served and $n - S$ will wait in queue. The combined service rate of all the servers is $S\mu$. Clearly, $S\mu$ must be greater than λ if the queue is not to become unbounded.

It can be shown following a similar analysis to that of Section 11.3 that the following results hold.

Probability of n customers in the system

$$P_n = \frac{(\frac{\lambda}{\mu})^n P_0}{n!} \text{ (for } 0 \leq n \leq S),$$

$$P_n = \frac{(\frac{\lambda}{\mu})^n P_0}{S! S^{n-s}} \text{ (for } n \geq S),$$

and P_0, the probability of no customers in the system, is given by

$$P_0 = \frac{1}{\sum\limits_{n=0}^{S-1} \frac{\left(\frac{\lambda}{\mu}\right)^n}{n!} + \frac{\left(\frac{\lambda}{\mu}\right)^S}{S!} \frac{1}{\left(1 - \frac{\lambda}{S\mu}\right)}}.$$

Note for $S = 2$ this simplifies to $P_0 = \frac{2\mu - \lambda}{2\mu + \lambda}$

$$S = 3 \text{ to } P_0 = \frac{2\mu(3\mu - \lambda)}{6\mu^2 + 4\mu\lambda + \lambda^2}$$

Number of customers in System (queue)

If traffic intensity ρ now equals $\frac{\lambda}{\mu S}$,

$$\bar{n} = \frac{\left(\frac{\lambda}{\mu}\right)^S \rho}{S! (1 - \rho)^2} P_0 + \frac{\lambda}{\mu} ,$$

and $\bar{n}_q = \bar{n} - \dfrac{\lambda}{\mu}$

Time spent in System

$$T_s = \frac{\left(\dfrac{\lambda}{\mu}\right)^S \dfrac{1}{\mu S}}{S! \,(1 - \rho)^2} P_0 + \frac{1}{\mu}.$$

Time in Queue

$$T_q = T_s - \frac{1}{\mu}.$$

Now, although the above sets of equations may seem quite formidable, they are in fact quite straightforward to use in most situations. For example, take the example of the single server queue in Section 11.3.5 where $\lambda = 3$ and $\mu = 4$. Suppose an additional server whose service rate is also $\mu = 4$ is added making the queue a two-server queue.

$$\text{Then } P_0 = \frac{2\mu - \lambda}{2\mu + \lambda} = \frac{8 - 3}{8 + 3} = \frac{5}{11}$$

(this is the probability of zero customers in the system; note it was ¼ for the single server queue).

$$P_n = \frac{\left(\dfrac{\lambda}{\mu}\right)^n P_0}{n!} \quad (\text{for } 0 \leqslant n \leqslant S)$$

∴ Probability of *one* customer in system

$$P_1 = \tfrac{3}{4} \times \frac{5}{11} = \frac{15}{44} = 0.34.$$

$$P_n = \frac{\left(\dfrac{\lambda}{\mu}\right)^n}{S! \, S^{n-s}} P_0 \quad \text{for } n \geqslant S.$$

$$P_2 = \frac{\left(\frac{3}{4}\right)^2 \times \frac{5}{11}}{2! \, 2^0} = \frac{9}{16} \times \frac{5}{11} \times \frac{1}{2} = \frac{45}{352} = 0.13$$

(note $\frac{9}{64}$ for single server).

Thus, probability of zero in the system has increased while the probability of one or two is reduced. This is what would be expected since a better level of service is now being given than before.

Number of Customers in System (Queue)

$$\rho = \frac{\lambda}{\mu S} = \frac{3}{4} \times 2 = \frac{3}{8} \cdot$$

$$\bar{n} = \frac{\left(\frac{\lambda}{\mu}\right)^2 \rho}{S! \, (1 - \rho)^2} P_0 + \frac{\lambda}{\mu},$$

$$= \frac{\left(\frac{3}{4}\right)^2 \times \frac{3}{8}}{2! \left(\frac{5}{8}\right)^2} \times \frac{5}{11} + \frac{3}{4},$$

$$= \frac{9}{16} \times \frac{3}{8} \times \frac{5}{11} \times \frac{1}{2} \times \frac{64}{25} + \frac{3}{4},$$

$$= \frac{54}{440} + \frac{3}{4},$$

$$= 0.87. \text{ (note single server, } \bar{n} = 3).$$

$\bar{n}_q = 0.12$ (single server, 2.25).

Time spent in the System

$$T_s = \frac{\left(\dfrac{3}{4}\right)^2}{2!\left(\dfrac{5}{8}\right)^2} \times \frac{1}{8} \times \frac{5}{11} + \frac{1}{4}.$$

$$T_s = \frac{9}{16} \times \frac{1}{8} \times \frac{5}{11} \times \frac{1}{2} \times \frac{64}{25} + \frac{1}{4},$$

$$= \frac{36}{880} + \frac{1}{4},$$

$$= 0.04 + 0.25,$$

$$= 0.29 \text{ min (1 min for single server queue)}.$$

Time spent in queue $= 0.04$ min.

Numbers and time spent in the system are considerably less than for a single server queue. This is, of course, as expected since the level of service is now higher.

Exercise 11.7

Repeat Exercises 11.2, 11.3 and 11.4 for a two-channel queue, assuming arrival rates and service rate of each server are as before.

11.7 Economics of Queuing Systems

There are obviously important economic implications of queuing situations. For example, if the queues at a supermarket become excessively lengthy some potential customers may decide not to purchase anything, hence the supermarket will lose any profit that it might have made from this customer's purchases. In addition, memories of lengthy waits at the supermarket check-out might well inhibit a customer from returning to that store on a future occasion.

The other side of the coin is that the more check-outs provided by the manager, then the greater his costs become. Although costs of the waiting line are ill-defined he will be trying to trade off costs of waiting against cost of providing service (see Figure 11.6). This will also involve manning more of the check-outs during a busy period than during quiet periods.

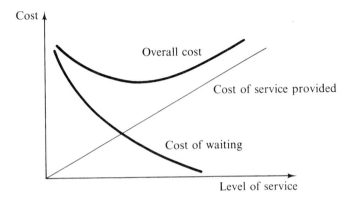

Figure 11.6

There may be other situations where the costing of waiting time can be more accurately quantified. For example, a garage has a large parts store. Mechanics arrive at the store at the rate of 10 per hour seeking a tool or part. These mechanics cost the company £6 an hour in all to employ. If the storeman is busy the mechanic has to wait until he is free. A single storeman can process 12 requests per hour and his service times are exponentially distributed. The manager of the store is considering whether to employ an additional storeman. A storeman earns £4 per hour.

For a single storeman average waiting time:

$$T_q = \frac{\lambda}{\mu(\mu - \lambda)},$$

Now $\lambda = 10$, $\mu = 12$

$$\therefore T_q = \frac{10}{12(12 - 10)} = \frac{10}{24} \text{ hours} = 25 \text{ minutes.}$$

For two storemen:

$$T_q = \frac{\left(\dfrac{\lambda}{\mu}\right)^S \dfrac{1}{\mu S} \cdot P_0}{S!\,(1 - \rho)^2}$$

Now $\rho = \dfrac{\lambda}{\mu S} = \dfrac{10}{24}$

$$P_0 = \frac{2\mu - \lambda}{2\mu + \lambda} = \frac{24 - 10}{24 + 10} = \frac{14}{34} = \frac{7}{17}.$$

Hence, $T_q = \dfrac{\left(\dfrac{5}{6}\right)^2 \times \dfrac{1}{24} \times \dfrac{7}{17}}{2! \left(1 - \dfrac{5}{12}\right)^2}$,

$$\frac{\dfrac{25}{36} \times \dfrac{1}{24} \times \dfrac{7}{17}}{2! \times \left(\dfrac{7}{12}\right)^2} ,$$

$= 0.018$ hr,

$= 1.1$ min.

This means waiting time is reduced to just over one minute. During an hour, on average 10 requests are processed and for each of these the additional server reduces waiting time by 24 minutes. $\therefore$ value of the time saved is £6 $\times$ 10 $\times \dfrac{24}{60} =$ £24.0.

Hence the employment of an additional storeman at £4 per hour saves the company £24.0 in terms of mechanics' time saved. This is therefore an investment that is very worthwhile making.

Exercise 11.8

'Air Chance' is a major airline with a large number of short-haul jets. At present, its maintenance base is considering making changes to its overhaul operations. The present situation is that only one jet can be repaired at a time and the expected repair time is 36 hours, whereas the expected time between arrivals is 48 hours. This has lead to frequent and prolonged delays in repairing incoming planes even though the base operates continuously. The average cost of an idle plane to the airline is £500 per hour. It is estimated that each plane goes into the maintenance shop six times per year. It is believed that the input process for the base is Poissonian and that the probability distribution of repair time is exponential.

Alternative A is to provide a duplicate maintenance shop so that the two planes can be repaired simultaneously. The cost depreciated over five years is £150,000 per plane per year.

Alternative B is to replace the present maintenance equipment by the most efficient (and expensive) equipment available, thereby reducing the expected repair time to 24 hours. The cost depreciated over a period of five years is £200,000 per plane, per year.

Comment on these alternatives.

11.8 Service Time Distribution

We have mentioned in Section 11.3 that in many practical situations the assumption of exponential service times (implying that probability of a service ending in a given instant is independent of the time since the service began) may not hold up in a good many real-life congestion situations.

It is possible, however, to derive models of queue parameters for arbitrary probability distributions providing mean service time $\frac{1}{\mu}$ and standard deviation σ of the service time distribution is known. For a single-server queue we have (assuming random arrivals):

Probability of n customers in system: $P_n = \rho^n(1-\rho)$.

Expected number in the system:
$$\bar{n} = \rho + \frac{\lambda^2\sigma^2 + \rho^2}{2(1-\rho)},$$
$$\bar{n}_q = \bar{n} - \rho.$$

Expected time in system:
$$T_s = \frac{\bar{n}}{\lambda}$$

We should note the following:
$$T_q = T_s - \frac{1}{\mu}.$$

(1) Expected times and numbers of customers now depend on the standard deviation of service times. The form of the equations however, are intuitively acceptable, the greater variation in service time corresponding to lengthier queues and longer queuing time.

(2) When the service time is exponential and so that $\sigma^2 = \dfrac{1}{\mu^2}$, as would be expected the basic single server model equations result.

(3) If service time is constant (equal to $\dfrac{1}{\mu}$) so that $\sigma^2 = 0$, then $\bar{n}_q = \dfrac{\rho^2}{2(1-\rho)}$. Thus, the number in the queue is exactly half the length in the model derived in Section 11.4.6. As mentioned earlier this is to be expected, since one of the sources of variation has been removed.

Exercise 11.9

Calculate the expected number in the queue and expected time spent in the queue for a single server queue with 6 arrivals per minute and 10 services per minute
 (i) if the service time is exponentially distributed;
(ii) if the service time is constant.
    (Arrivals are random)

11.9 Usefulness and Limitations of Queuing Theory

We have confined ourselves in this chapter to relatively straightforward queuing situations. A number of more complex situations, such as where a limit is placed on the maximum number of customers in the system and where the service mechanism consists of a number of phases, the output from one queue becoming the input from the next can, however, be handled. The reader is referred to more advanced treatises[1,2] for an analysis of these situations.

We have already mentioned, however, problems of handling transient situations. This makes it difficult to handle situations in which arrival rate and service rate are continually changing. One approach to this problem might be to divide up the time considered into intervals where, for practical purposes, arrival and service rates are not varying and derive the steady-state equations for each period. On the other hand, in certain situations, the rate of variation may be so great that the queue never settles down to steady-state behaviour.

Problems in which there is statistical dependence between arrival rates and service rates (i.e. server speeds up to cope with lengthening queue) and situations in which there are interactions between a number of queues may also cause considerable difficulties. For these reasons, a technique known as *simulation* which is described in the next chapter may be used to handle these situations.

Nevertheless, there are a good many practical situations where the basic conditions for applicability of a queuing model do, in fact, hold. We have also gained a number of useful insights into the behaviour of queuing situations e.g. the sensitivity of queuing time to small increases in arrival rate at high levels of traffic intensity.

12

Simulation

12.1 Introduction

All mathematical models used in management techniques can be divided into two categories (1) Analytical models and (2) Simulation models. So far, in earlier chapters of this book we have concentrated on *analytical* models.

Many analytical models are of the optimizing type (i.e. given particular objectives they will identify courses of action which will optimize the achievement of that objective. (For instance, a decision-tree model may be used to identify that sequence of decisions which will maximize the expected value of the decision-maker.)

The basic idea of simulation is rather different. The idea of simulation is to utilize some device to imitate a real life system in order to experiment with the device and observe its behaviour. The models employed may be physical (such as the testing of parts of aircraft in wind tunnels) or they may be electronic or hydraulic models of production processes (so-called 'analogue' models). The type of simulation models with which we shall concern ourselves in this chapter, however, will be mathematical models which consist of a series of mathematical or logical relationships.

A simulation model does not in itself automatically give the optimal operating policy. It simply explores the result of operation with particular combinations of inputs and operating policies. It is up to the user to experiment with different inputs or different operating policies in order to work to some sort of optimum. For example, later, we shall be considering a simulation model of a consultant's appointment system. It is up to the model user to design appointment systems that result in improved performance; the model is simply used to predict the consequences of using each system.

12.2 Practical Uses of Simulation Models

Simulation models have been successfully used in many practical situations. These include:

(1) Examination of bottlenecks which occur in production processes due to various operations in the process having capacity constraints which are out of phase with each other.

(2) Examination of the effect of different queuing regimes on speed of service at the Post Office.

(3) The simulation of aircraft arrivals at Heathrow in order to investigate the optimum design for passenger, baggage and cargo handling facilities.

(4) Exploring how different patterns of student entries and different resource allocation policies can influence university development.

(5) Computer manufacturers have used simulation techniques to enable them to design the various hardware and software components to reduce queuing for access to the various devices.

12.3 Types of Simulation Models

Simulations can be deterministic or probabilistic.

Deterministic simulations are often of large-scale systems and can be used to answer 'What if' type of questions. For instance, if such a model of a company is constructed it can be used to ascertain the financial effects of, say, a 10% drop in demand for a particular product. The basic assumption of deterministic models is that the distribution of any random variable can be represented by one value only (i.e. no probability distributions are involved).

Most models of the national economy are deterministic simulation models. They allow such questions as 'What will be the effect of devaluing sterling by 20% and maintaining other economic policies?' to be answered. Certain companies have large-scale models of their operations. This enables questions such as 'What is the effect of a 5% drop in sales, or a 10% rise in the price of energy?' to be answered.'

Probabilistic simulations incorporate random phenomena and this type of simulation is sometimes known as a *Monte Carlo Simulation*. These models include random variables which are represented by probability distributions. We shall limit our discussion to probabilistic simulations in this chapter.

12.3.1 Probabilistic Simulation: the Consultant's Appointment System

Our discussion of simulation will present fewer difficulties if it takes place in the context of a suitable practical example.

Consider a consultant who sees ten patients every Wednesday afternoon. (His surgery continues until all ten patients have been seen). The consultant wishes to devise a suitable appointment system. Clearly, one option would be to fix all the appointments for the beginning of the afternoon, although this option would have the disadvantage of incurring excessive patient queuing time. On the other hand, his consultation time is uncertain and if he spreads out the appointments over the afternoon then he is in danger of wasting his own time.

He has, however, kept records of the consultation times for his previous 100 patients. This is given in Table 12.1. We shall see in this chapter how a simulation model of this system could be used for trying out different appointment systems.

Table 12.1

Consultation Time (min)	No. of Patients	Consultation Time (min)	No. of Patients
4	1	12	7
5	4	13	5
6	7	14	5
7	11	15	3
8	14	16	3
9	15	17	2
10	11	18	2
11	9	19	1
		Total	100

12.3.2 Elements of a Simulation Model

A simulation is characterized by the presence or absence of discrete items, or as they are usually called in simulations *entities*. In the consultant's appointment system the relevant entities are the consultant himself and patients who are passing through his appointment system.

Each entity may have a number of *attributes* which may be either numerical or logical, fixed or variable. For instance, in the example relating to the consultant's appointment system the consultant may have the attribute busy (i.e. he is carrying out a consultation) or idle (he has completed one consultation and is awaiting another). This is a logical variable. He also has the numerical attribute service time associated with him. The entities 'patients' have logical attributes 'waiting', 'undergoing consultation', 'consultation complete'. Numerical attributes will be waiting time and service time.

12.3.3 Running the Model Through Time

In the above example, we are interested in the behaviour of the system over time. It is thus necessary for us to develop some mechanism for advancing the system through time. There are two ways of approaching this problem. The first is to use a time-advance technique in which one continually advances from one unit of time to the next. The disadvantage of this approach is that nothing may happen during many time intervals and that in consequence much effort may be wasted in this approach. For instance in the consultant's appointment system at the beginning of the period in question the first patient may enter the consulting room and the consultation then begins. The consultation may then continue during the next few minutes and nothing of significance may occur.

The second approach avoids this wastefulness by using an *event-advance* mechanism. An event denotes the beginning or end of some kind of activity. In the example, we are considering the following events take place: patient arrives at consulting rooms, consultation begins and consultation ends.

Note, however, that in certain circumstances where a large number of activities are involved time-advance procedures could be more efficient.

12.3.4 Probability Distributions in Simulations

All probabilistic simulation involves one or more probability distributions. We shall discuss the treatment of such distributions in this section. In the example of the consultant's appointment system it will be noted that the single probability distribution which relates to the consultant's appointment system is the distribution of consultation times. If we assume that the distribution of consultation times in the future correspond to those of the past we have the distribution given in Table 12.2.

The most convenient way of representing a distribution of this kind is by using random numbers. A random number has the property that it has the same probability of occurrence as any other number in the sequence. Thus, if we have two digit random numbers running from 00 to 99 the probability of any given number appearing at any point in the sequence will be 1/100.

Table 12.2

Consultation Time (min)	No. of Patients	P	Consultation Time (min)	No. of Patients	P
4	1	0.01	12	7	0.07
5	4	0.04	13	5	0.05
6	7	0.07	14	5	0.05
7	11	0.11	15	3	0.03
8	14	0.14	16	3	0.03
9	15	0.15	17	2	0.02
10	11	0.11	18	2	0.02
11	9	0.09	19	1	0.01

Thus, if we assign random numbers in proportion to the probability of particular outcomes we can represent the probability distribution realistically. For example the consultation time of 4 min (in Table 12.2) has an 0.01 probability of occurring. If we represent this outcome by random number 00 this will provide an accurate representation of this probability since there is a 0.01 probability of selection 00 from the two digit random number 00—99.

In this way, it is possible to associate all consultation times with appropriate random numbers as in Table 12.3.

Table 12.3

Consultation Time	P	Random No.	Consultation Time	P	Random No.
4	0.01	00	12	0.07	72 – 78
5	0.04	01 – 04	13	0.05	79 – 83
6	0.07	05 – 11	14	0.05	84 – 88
7	0.11	12 – 22	15	0.03	89 – 91
8	0.14	23 – 36	16	0.03	92 – 94
9	0.15	37 – 51	17	0.02	95 – 96
10	0.11	52 – 62	18	0.02	97 – 98
11	0.09	63 – 71	19	0.01	99 ·

12.3.5 Sources of Random Numbers

There are tables of random numbers in all good statistical tables. In addition, computers which have simulation software available all have means of generating random numbers. In the latter case, the random numbers are what is called *pseudo-random* numbers. These numbers are produced deterministically from certain recursive routines but they nevertheless fulfil the tests for random numbers discussed below. The advantage of using pseudo-random numbers (apart from the fact that it minimizes computer storage requirements) is that it is possible to repeat a particular stream of numbers at will.

There are a number of tests for checking that random numbers really are random. One obvious test is to count the number of times each digit from 0 to 9 occurs in the random number stream, and use the χ^2 test to check that no digit occurred with disproportionate frequency. Sequences such as 0123456789012345 etc, however, would pass this test but would, quite clearly, not be random. Consequently, there are various run tests which can be used to check this aspect of randomness. These tests for randomness are discussed in most books on simulation[1].

Example: Consultant's Waiting Room

The consultant decides first of all to try out the following appointment system:

> 2.00 p.m.—5 patients arrive,
> 2.30 p.m.—5 patients arrive.

In order to simplify matters in this initial simulation we shall assume patients arrive exactly on time. It will be sensible in this situation to adopt an event-based system for time advance. As we discussed earlier the following events are significant:

(i) Patient enters consulting room,
(ii) Consultation begins,
(iii) Consultation ends.

Consultation begins at 2 p.m., random number stream to be used 20, 74, 94, 22, 93, 45, 44, 16, 04, 32.

Probability distribution of consultation times is as shown in Table 12.3. We are interested in collection of the following features of the system (i) Consultant idle time; (ii) Patient waiting time.

Table 12.3

Time	Event	Consultant idle time	Patient waiting time (min)	
2.00	Patients 1—5 arrive			
2.00	Patient 1 begins consultation (Random no. 20→ 7 min consultation)	0	0	(Patient 1)
2.07	Patient 1 consultation ends *and* Patient 2 consultation begins (Random no. 74→ 12 min consultation)	0	7	(Patient 2)
2.19	Patient 2 consultation ends and Patient 3 consultation begins (Random no. 94→16 min consultation)	0	19	(Patient 3)
2.30	Patients 6—10 join queue			
2.35	Patient 4 consultation begins (Random no. 22→ 7 min consultation)	0	35	(Patient 4)
2.42	Patient 4 consultation ends and Patient 5 consultation begins (Random no. 93→ 16 min consultation)	0	42	(Patient 5)

Table 12.3 (cont.)

2.58	Patient 5 consultation ends and patient 6 consultation begins (Random no. 45→ 9 min consultation)	0	28	(Patient 6)
3.07	Patient 6 consultation ends and patient 7 consultation begins (Random no. 44→ 9 min consultation)	0	37	(Patient 7)
3.16	Patient 7 consultation ends and patient 8 consultation begins (Random no. 16→ 7 min consultation)	0	46	(Patient 8)
3.23	Patient 8 consultation ends and patient 9 consultation begins (Random no. 04→ 5 min consultation)	0	53	(Patient 9)
3.28	Patient 9 consultation ends and patient 10 consultation begins (Random no. 32→ 8 min consultation)	0	58	(Patient 10)
3.36	Patient 10 consultation ends and surgery finishes.			

The overall result shows that total consultant idle time is zero. Total patient waiting time is 325 mins. (in other words 32.5 min per patient on average).

12.4 Repeatability of Simulation: Example

The results obtained in the above simulation, however, are simply the results obtained with a given stream of random numbers. In other words, it gives only *one* out of a whole distribution of possible output values. This is a very important difference between analytical and simulation models and, in practice (using a computer), it is usual to run each simulation possibly more than 100 times.

Exercise 12.1

Repeat the previous simulation twice more using the following streams of random numbers
 (i) 03, 62, 61, 89, 01, 25, 38, 57, 93, 40,
(ii) 37, 57, 66, 37, 49, 42, 03, 57, 81, 96.

What are the consultant's idle time and patient waiting time for these cases? What are the averages taken over all three simulations?

   Although you have only been asked to carry out three runs of this simulation it should be clear that if you had more time or the services of a computer it would be possible to continue until you had achieved a realistic output distribution of idle and waiting times.

12.5 Experimentation with Other Systems

All we have achieved so far, however, is to explore the effects of operating with the appointment system under which five patients arrive at 2 p.m. and 5 at 2.30 p.m.

   We can, however, use our model to experiment with other possible appointment systems to see whether they give superior results. At this point we should emphasize again that it is up to the user of the model to suggest the alternative systems and try them out, there is no way that the model will directly suggest them.

Exercise 12.2

Using the three sets of random number streams previously given try out the following appointment system:

2.00 p.m.	4 patients arrive
2.30 p.m.	3 patients arrive
3.00 p.m.	3 patients arrive

Exercise 12.3

Can you suggest an appointment system which might offer equivalent or superior results to the one used above? Try out your system with the same three streams of random numbers to ascertain whether it is in fact an improvement.

12.6 Realism of Simulation Models

It might be argued that this simulation model is unrealistic in that it makes certain simplifying assumptions which distort the situation. Perhaps one of the most serious is that it assumes patients will arrive at the exact moment for which their appointment is scheduled. In practice, of course, patients will arrive earlier or later or possibly not show up at all. In a simulation model, it is generally possible to take such complications into account providing it is felt that the additional complexity of model is worth the extra accuracy provided. This is not, however, generally the case for analytical models; there are numerous instances where if some simplifying assumption does not hold, then it is not possible to use the model.

Supposing we have collected past data on the arrival of patients at the consultant's waiting room and that it is given by the following probability distribution:

Table 12.4

Time	Probability	Random nos.
5 min early	0.10	00—09
3 min early	0.10	10—19
1 min early	0.10	20—29
On time	0.30	30—59
1 min late	0.10	60—69
3 min late	0.05	70—74
5 min late	0.15	75—89
No show	0.10	90—99

It is possible to assign random numbers to these outcomes in exactly the same way as before.

Exercise 12.4

Repeat the very first simulation (Section 12.3.5) using the following stream of random numbers for patient arrivals
    80, 39, 51, 84, 04, 21, 71, 78, 22, 21

Exercise 12.5

Repeat the previous example when the appointment system in Exercise 12.2 is used (i.e. 2.00 — 4 patients arrive; 2.30 — 3 patients arrive; 3.00 — 3 patients arrive).

Example: Oil rig project

In the oil-rig example in Chapter 10 we assumed that the precise duration of activities such as fitting out and towing out the platform to sea, preparing drilling equipment, etc., was known.

In practice, however, the duration of many of these activities will be subject to chance elements such as the weather, tidal conditions, etc. If we had previous years' weather records we could use them to construct a probability distribution of weather types and hence build possible delays through weather conditions into the model. Similarly, uncertainty in support schedules including helicopters ferrying the men on to the rig could be included. Providing the company has experience of this kind of work, the possibility of technical snags causing delay in the seismic or test drilling operations can also be incorporated.

In this way, the model of project duration can be modified to build in uncertainty due to delays of various kinds. Such a simulation model can be used to give a probability distribution of total project times. This could be particularly valuable if, for example, there was some penalty associated with the operation exceeding a given period of time.

Exercise 12.6

Suppose we have a section of a network as follows:

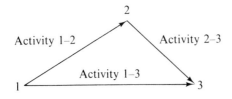

Figure 12.1

Supposing the time for completing each activity is probabilistic with distribution as follows:

| Activity 1 – 2 | | Activity 2 – 3 | | Activity 1 – 3 | |
Completion time	P	Completion time	P	Completion time	P
7	0.20	8	0.3	16	0.4
8	0.50	9	0.4	17	0.2
9	0.30	10	0.3	18	0.4

Use simulation techniques to derive a probability distribution of project completion times. What is the probability of the different paths being critical (all activity durations in weeks)?

12.7 Flowcharts and the Use of Computers for Simulation

Whether it is intended to carry out a simulation manually or by computer it is useful to draw a flowchart of the simulation model. This is particularly important for a complex situation in ensuring that all significant aspects of the problem are incorporated into the model.

The flowchart provides an orderly representation of the process under study and indicates which activities are under consideration and the interrelationships between them. It indicates the logical sequence in which activities are carried out and what happens when the sequence depends on the outcome of some kind of test. The level of detail provided in the flowchart will depend on the situation that we are considering.

Simulation programs can be written in general purpose scientific languages such as ALGOL and FORTRAN or BASIC. On a number of machines there are special facilities provided for simulation, however. These include the SIMON system and other languages such as GPSS.

There are difficulties in using microcomputers to carry out simulations because of the data storage requirements. Some developments in providing simulation facilities on microcomputers have recently been made, however.

In a flowchart any processing operation is indicated by a

Any decision process is indicated by a

Reading in or printing out information can be represented by a

12.8 Sensitivity Analysis and Risk Analysis

Simulation techniques are valuable in allowing a sophisticated form of sensitivity analysis, called risk analysis, to be carried out.

12.8.1 Sensitivity Analysis

Sensitivity in its conventional form involves investigating the effect of varying one parameter over a given range whilst keeping the value of the other parameters constant. Thus, this analysis shows how sensitive the result is to fluctuations in the value of this variable. For instance, if we were comparing two different schemes for building a bridge we might be interested to see the effect of a change in the price of concrete on the comparative costs of the two projects.

Such an analysis can be very valuable, particularly if we are uncertain about the value of the parameter in question. If the results of our sensitivity analysis shows that our results are not seriously affected by change in this parameter, then we don't need to expend too much effort on determining this parameter more closely. On the other hand, should this analysis show that the cost of the schemes are seriously affected by this parameter, then it may well be worth our while to expend considerable effort in attempting to define it more accurately.

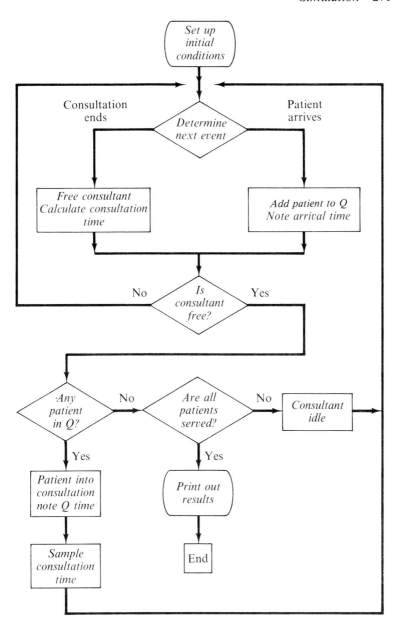

Figure 12.2 Flow chart for consultant's appointment system

12.8.2 Risk Analysis

As explained above, sensitivity analysis is valuable for investigating the effect of changing any one parameter on the total return of the project. In practice, if we are considering a financial analysis then most of the parameters which make up the investment may be uncertain and the overall outcome of the project is influenced by all those parameters fluctuating simultaneously. Thus, the outcome of the investment is likely to be a probability distribution.

For example, the cost of a water supply scheme for a developing country may depend on a number of factors; cost of dam construction, life of pipelines, treatment works, etc. The risk analysis is carried out by identifying all the probability distributions which contribute to the scheme and sampling from them, in turn, thus simulating the total cost of the scheme. If a large number of such simulations are carried out we can obtain a probability distribution for the total cost of the scheme, as in Figure 12.3.

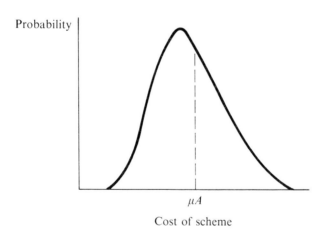

Cost of scheme

Figure 12.3

The mean cost of the scheme is μA and this is the value obtained by the conventional investment analysis which assumes that each variable can be represented simply by its mean.

Suppose there was an alternative Scheme B for the water supply.

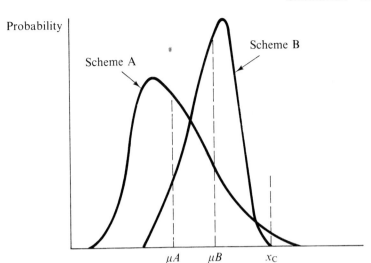

Figure 12.4

It may turn out that if we carry out the risk analysis for this scheme we get the result shown in Figure 12.4.

It may well turn out that the mean cost of scheme B (μB) is higher than that of scheme A (μA). This would be identified by conventional financial analysis and might well result in scheme A being adopted. However, risk analysis has identified the fact that scheme B has a much lower variance and in fact; there is a much smaller chance of the cost of scheme B exceeding some high value X_c than for scheme A. Thus, if it was particularly important to us that the cost of the project did not exceed X_c (supposing the capital was borrowed from an international agency and it was difficult to obtain supplementary monies) we might decide to choose project B in spite of its higher mean cost.

Example: Risk Analysis

In practice, a risk analysis will generally involve a number of probability distributions and will be undertaken on the computer.

To give a simplified hand simulation we will tackle a problem involving only two probability distributions. Supposing a business man is thinking of taking over an electrical business. Based on past information and his knowledge of the business he reckons that the probability distribution of monthly costs is given by:

Cost (pounds)	Probability (P)	Random Numbers
1300	0.10	00—09
1400	0.10	10—19
1500	0.40	20—59
1600	0.20	60—79
1700	0.20	80—99

Random numbers are ascribed to this distribution on the same basis as was discussed earlier in this chapter.

Suppose a further analysis of projected revenue yields the following distribution:

Revenue	Probability (P)	Random Numbers
1500	0.10	00—09
1600	0.10	10—19
1700	0.20	20—39
1800	0.40	40—79
1900	0.15	80—94
2000	0.05	95—99

Let's now carry out a risk analysis of this business over 20 months. This will require two streams of random numbers
82, 36, 92, 10, 03, 83, 63, 92, 26, 27, 29, 63, 91, 73
10, 10, 39, 28, 84, 82
&   29, 71, 83, 72, 92, 01, 94, 72, 39, 49, 59, 92, 72, 19, 00
09, 18, 38, 72, 39.
Now monthly net profit = Revenue − Cost.
Thus, we can carry out our risk analysis for the 20 months in question.

Month No.	Random No. for Cost	Simulated Cost	Random No. for Sales	Simulated Sales	Revenue = Sales – Cost
1	82	1700	29	1700	0
2	36	1500	71	1800	300
3	92	1700	83	1900	200
4	10	1400	72	1800	400
5	03	1300	92	1900	600
6	83	1700	01	1500	– 200
7	63	1600	94	1900	300
8	92	1700	72	1800	100
9	26	1500	39	1700	200
10	27	1500	49	1800	300
11	29	1500	59	1800	300
12	63	1600	92	1900	300
13	91	1700	72	1800	100
14	73	1600	19	1600	0
15	10	1400	00	1500	100
16	10	1400	09	1500	100
17	39	1500	18	1600	100
18	28	1500	38	1700	200
19	84	1700	72	1800	100
20	82	1700	39	1700	0

Monthly Net Revenue	Frequency	Probability
– 200	1	.05
0	3	.15
100	6	.30
200	3	.15
300	5	.25
400	1	.05
600	1	.05

Thus, the above table gives us a probability distribution for the net monthly return for this investment.

Exercise 12.7

Repeat the above risk analysis using the following random number streams.

78, 40, 29, 92, 21, 20, 63, 46, 16, 45, 41, 44, 66, 87, 26, 78

36, 57, 03, 28 and
80, 62, 74, 64, 26, 23, 57, 99, 84, 51, 29, 41, 11, 66, 30
41, 40, 97, 15, 72.

Exercise 12.8

The Howgate project consists of 3 phases, Phase I, Phase II and
Phase III. The probability distribution for the cost outcome of each
of these phases is given below, in £'000. The cost outcome for each
phase is independent.

Phase I	Outcome	Probability
	100—120	0.3
	120—140	0.3
	140—160	0.4

Phase II	Outcome	Probability
	200—250	0.2
	250—300	0.2
	300—350	0.3
	350—400	0.2
	400—450	0.1

Phase III	Outcome	Probability
	200—220	0.1
	220—240	0.3
	240—260	0.2
	260—280	0.2
	280—300	0.1
	300—320	0.1

(i) Construct a probability distribution for the total cost of this
capital project.

(ii) What is the probability of completing the entire project for (i)
less than £600,000 and (ii) less than £750,000?

(iii) Your company is given the opportunity to make a fixed price
bid for this contract. Discuss what strategy you might adopt.

References and Bibliography

Chapter 1

References

1. Beishon, J. and Peters, G. *Systems Behaviour* (Harper and Row: London, 1976).

Other Reading

Ackoff, R. L. *Scientific Method: Optimising Applied Research Decisions.* (John Wiley and Sons Inc.: London and New York, 1962).

Turban, E. and Meredith, R. *Fundamentals of Management Science* (Business Publications Inc.: 1981).

Waddington, G. H. *O.R. in World War II. Operational Research Against the U Boat.* (Paul Elek: London, 1975).

Walsh, E. *Understanding Computers* (John Wiley and Sons Inc.: New York, 1981).

Chapter 2

References

1. Huff, D. *How to Lie with Statistics* (Gollanz: London and New York, 1954).

Other Reading (Also for Chapters 3 and 4)

Anderson, D., Sweeney, D., Williams, T. *Introduction to Statistics* (West Publishing Co.: 1981).

Croft, D. *Applied Statistics for Management Studies* (MacDonald and Evans: London, 1979).

Freund, J. and Williams, F. *Elementary Business Statistics.* (Prentice/Hall International: New York, 1977).

Levin, R. *Statistics for Management* (Prentice/Hall International: New York, 1981)

Marston, P. *Applied Business Statistics* (Holt, Rinehart and Winston Ltd.: London, 1982).

(John Wiley and Sons Inc.: London and New York, 1962).

Turban, E. and Meredith, *op. cit.*

Chapter 3

References

1. Levin, R. *Op. cit.*
2. Kmietowicz, Z., and Yannoulis, Y. *Mathematical, Statistical and Financial Tables for the Social Sciences* (Longman: London, 1976).

Other Reading (cf. Chapter 2)

Chapter 4

Other Reading (cf. Chapter 2)

Chapter 5

References

1. Ayre, R. *Technological Forecasting* (McGraw-Hill: New York, 1969).
2. Firth, N. *Forecasting Methods in Business and Management* (Edward Arnold: London, 1977).
3. Coyle, R. *Mathematics for Business Decisions*, p.169 (Nelson: London, 1971).

Other Reading

Chisholm, R. and Whittaker, G. *Forecasting Methods* (Irwin: London, 1971).

Chapter 6

References

1. Anderson, D., Sweeney, D., Williams, T. *Introduction to Management Science* (West Publishing Co., 1979).

Other Reading

Coyle, R. Mathematics for Business Decisions (Nelson: London, 1971).
Loomba, N. *Management: A Quantitative Perspective* (MacMillan: London, 1978).

Chapter 7

General References for Chapter 7—12 inclusive.

Cook, J. and Russell, R. *Introduction to Management Science* (Prentice-Hall International: New York, 1981).
Gordon, G. and Pressman, I. *Quantitative Decision-Making for Business* (Prentice-Hall International: New York, 1978).
Turban, E. and Meredith, J. *Op. cit.*

Specific Reading for Chapter 7

Haley, K. *Mathematical Programming for Business and Industry* (MacMillan: London, 1967).

Stockton, R. *Introduction to Linear Programming* (Irwin: Homewood, Illinois, 1971).

Chapter 8

References

1. Bunn, D., Hampton, J., Moore, P. and Thomas, H. *Case Studies in Decision Analysis* (Penguin: London, 1976).

Other Reading

Coyle, R. *Decision Analysis* (Nelson: London, 1972).

Moore, P. and Thomas, H. *The Anatomy of Decisions* (Penguin: London, 1979).

Chapter 9

1. Lewis, C. *Scientific Inventory Control* (Butterworths: London, 1970).

Other Reading

Wild, R. *The Techniques of Production Management* (Holt, Rinehart and Wilson: London, 1971).

Chapter 10

References

1. Woodgate, H. *Planning by Networks* (Business Publications: London 1967).

Other Reading

Battersby, A. *Network Analysis* (MacMillan: London, 1979).

Spinner, M. *Elements of Project Management* (Prentice-Hall International: New York, 1981).

Chapter 11

References

1. Lee, A. *Applied Queuing Theory,* (MacMillan: London, 1966).

2. Mitchell, J. *Operational Research* (English Universities Press: London, 1972).

Other Reading

Cox, D. and Smith, W. *Queues* (Methuen: London, 1971).

Chapter 12

References
1. Tocher, K. *The Art of Simulation* (English Universities Press: London, 1963).

Other Reading
Meier, R., Newell, W. and Pazer, H. *Simulation in Business and Economics* (Prentice/Hall International: New York, 1969).

Answers to Exercises

Ex. 1.1   (a) 111,111
           (b) 90,909

Ex. 2.5   146.8 lb
           146
           135

Ex. 2.6   Range £4000
           mean deviation 980
           variance 1610
           sandard deviation 40.1

Ex. 2.7   Base weight 157
           Current weight 115

Ex. 3.2   (a) 1/16
           (b) 1/8
           (c) 1/17
           (d) 4/13

Ex. 3.3   (a) 0.06
           (b) 0.56
           (c) 0.94

Ex. 3.4   1/6, 5/36

Ex. 3.5   1st arr. breakdown prob. = 0.143
           2nd arr. breakdown prob. = 0.064

Ex. 3.6 $x = 2$ prob $= 1/36$, $x = 3$ prob $= 2/36$, $x = 4$
           prob $= 3/36$
           $x = 5$ prob $= 4/36$, $x = 6$ prob $= 5/36$, $x = 7$
           prob $= 6/36$
           $x = 8$ prob $= 5/36$, $x = 9$ prob $= 4/36$, $x = 10$
           prob $= 3/36$

$x = 11$ prob $= 2/36$, $x = 12$ prob $= 1/36$

Ex. 3.7 0.3273

Ex. 3.8 0.9776

Ex. 3.9 Approx. 6

Ex. 3.10 0.3370

Ex. 3.11 (a) 0.9185

(b) 0.7373

(c) 0.1875

Ex. 3.12 0.0839

Ex. 3.13 11.46%

Ex. 3.14 (a) 0.599

(b) 0.011

Ex. 3.15 159.84Ωs

Ex 4.1 0.1320

146.7 gm

Ex. 4.2 95% interval 291.8 to 308.2 hours

99% interval 287.1 to 312.9 hours

Ex. 4.3 21.61 to 22.39Ω

Ex. 4.4 Type II error

Ex. 4.5 (a) H_0: $\mu = 500$ h

H_1: $\mu \neq 500$

(b) 0.01

(c) $\bar{x} = 1908.8$ h

and $\bar{x} = 2091.2$ h

(d) 0.999

Ex. 4.7 sig at 5% level

Ex. 4.8 Consistent ($\chi^2 = 1.84$)

Ex. 4.9 Consistent ($\chi^2 = 2.25$)

Ex. 5.1 (a) 62, 65, 67, 72, 70, 67

(b) 60, 61, 63, 66, 65, 65

Ex. 5.2 1040

Ex. 5.3 (b) $Y = 2.11 + 844$ X

(c) £56.97 m

Ex. 5.4 $r^2 = 9.775$

$r = 0.9887$

Ex. 6.1 $Z = -1.3p^2 + 265p - 10,000$

Ex. 6.3 $S = 200 + 5N$

slope $= 5$

Ex. 6.4 From 3–4 slope -36.67

From 11–12 slope 1.22

Ex. 6.5	(1) $6X + 2$
	(2) $6X - 4/X^3$
	(3) $30X (2X + 1)$
	(4) $-(4X + 6)/5X^3$
Ex. 6.6	3 lbs
Ex. 6.7	101.9
Ex. 6.8	49.77, £41.22
Ex. 7.1	standard = 3,000
	delux = 6,000
Ex. 7.2	$F_1 = 24$ oz
	$F_2 = 4/3$ oz
Ex. 7.4	0.5., 0, 1.5
Ex. 7.8	Divisions 1 and 2 zero
	Division 3 at 200 units
	Division 4 at 150 untis
	No additional purchase

		Strong	Moderate	Weak
Ex. 8.1	(a) 1. Sell with MOT	140	40	-30
	2. Sell without MOT	110	70	40
	3. Breakers	50	50	50

       (b) (i) Breakers
          (ii) Sell with MOT
          (iii) Sell without MOT
       (c) Sell with MOT ($EV = £70$)

Ex. 8.2	(2) Proceed; if unsuccessful extend $EV = 12.5$
Ex. 8.3	Proceed; test in Poleteria; if successful, launch; otherwise stop. $EV = £150,000$
Ex. 8.4	£20
Ex. 8.5	£250,000
Ex. 8.6	0.93
Ex. 8.7	0.42
Ex. 8.8	Continue; contribution = £0.40 per board ordered
	New fabrication; contribution = £2.10 per board ordered
	Testing device; contribution = £2.45 per board ordered
Ex. 9.1	(i) 25
	(ii) 23
Ex. 9.2	632
Ex. 9.3	(a) 92.5%

(b) 219

Ex. 9.4	200 (cost = £3,130)
Ex. 9.5	50 (cost = £3,609.2)
Ex. 9.6	975.4
Ex. 9.7	10 weeks, 77
Ex. 10.2	Critical path — obtain finance - obtain platform - fit and tow platform - test drill - seismic test

Ex. 10.3

Activity	ESD	EFD	LSD	LFD
A	1	3	1	3
B	4	18	4	18
C	4	13	5	14
D	14	17	16	19
E	18	21	20	23
F	14	17	15	18
G	19	23	19	23
H	24	30	27	33
I	24	30	24	33
J	34	38	34	38

Critical path A-B-G-I-J

Ex. 10.4

Activity	Total Float	Free Float
Recruit workforce	4	—
Train workforce	4	4
Prepare seismic equipment	14	14

(elswhere float = 0)

Ex. 10.5

Activity	Total Float	Free Float
C	1	—
D	2	—
F	2	2
E	1	1
H	3	3

elsewhere float = 0

Ex. 10.6	No delay
Ex. 10.7	(modified project) — 3 weeks
Ex. 10.8	min. delay — 3 days
Ex. 10.9	(a) take 1 day from B

take 3 further days from following option:
   1 day from A
   3 days from I
   1 further day from B plus one from C
Cost = £1,800

	(b) 29 days, cost = £5,350
Ex. 11.2	3/5, 6/25, 18/125
Ex. 11.3	1½, 9/10
Ex. 11.4	3/10 min, ½ min
Ex. 11.5	(1) 0.146
	(2) 25/24
	(3) 5/24 days
Ex. 11.6	Supplier (£19,520 per annum)
	Own service (28,160 per annum)
Ex 11.7	0.54, 0.32, 0.10
	system 0.659; queue 0.059
	queue 0.019 min; system 0.219 min
Ex. 11.8	*Costs*
	present system = £432,000 per plane per year
	Alternative 'A' = £276,000 per plane per year
	Alternative 'B' = £344,000 per plane per year
Ex. 11.9	(i) 0.9, 0.150 min
	(ii) 0.45, 0.005 min
Ex. 12.1	(i) consultant idle time = 0
	patient waiting time = 255 min
	(ii) consultant idle time = 0
	patient waiting time = 271 min
Ex. 12.2	consultant idle time = 0 patient waiting time = 205
	= 0 patient waiting time = 135
	= 0 patient waiting time = 151
Ex. 12.4	consultant idle time = 0 patient waiting time = 315 min
Ex. 12.5	consultant idle time = 0 patient waiting time = 195 min
Ex. 12.7	*Net revenue frequency probability*

Net revenue	frequency	probability
0	1	0.05
100	3	0.15
200	6	0.30
300	7	0.35
400	—	0.00
500	3	0.15

Index